THE NEW FOURTH BRANCH

Twenty-first-century constitutions now typically include a new "fourth branch" of government a group of institutions charged with protecting constitutional democracy – prominently including electoral management bodies, anti-corruption agencies, and ombuds offices. This book offers the first general theory of the fourth branch, explaining that it is needed because in a world where governance is exercised through political parties, we cannot be confident that the traditional three branches are enough to preserve constitutional democracy. By concentrating within themselves distinctive forms of expertise, the fourth-branch institutions can deploy that expertise more effectively than when it is dispersed among the traditional branches. Several case studies of anti-corruption efforts, electoral management bodies, and audit bureaus show that the fourth-branch institutions do not always do a good job of protecting constitutional democracy, and indeed sometimes undermine it. The book concludes with some cautionary notes about placing too much hope in these – or, indeed, in any – institutions as the guarantors of constitutional democracy.

Mark Tushnet is William Nelson Cromwell Professor of Law emeritus at Harvard Law School. He clerked for Justice Thurgood Marshall before beginning his teaching career. He has written more than a dozen books, including *Weak Courts, Strong Rights: Judicial Review and Social Welfare Rights in Comparative Constitutional Law* and *Advanced Introduction to Comparative Constitutional Law*. He was president of the Association of American Law Schools in 2003, and in 2002 was elected a fellow of the American Academy of Arts and Sciences.

COMPARATIVE CONSTITUTIONAL LAW AND POLICY

Series Editors

Tom Ginsburg *University of Chicago*
Zachary Elkins *University of Texas at Austin*
Ran Hirschl *University of Toronto*

Comparative constitutional law is an intellectually vibrant field that encompasses an increasingly broad array of approaches and methodologies. This series collects analytically innovative and empirically grounded work from scholars of comparative constitutionalism across academic disciplines. Books in the series include theoretically informed studies of single constitutional jurisdictions, comparative studies of constitutional law and institutions, and edited collections of original essays that respond to challenging theoretical and empirical questions in the field.

Books in the Series

The New Fourth Branch: Institutions for Protecting Constitutional Democracy Mark Tushnet

The Veil of Participation: Citizens and Political Parties in Constitution-Making Processes Alexander Hudson

Towering Judges: A Comparative Study of Constitutional Judges Edited by Rehan Abeyratne and Iddo Porat

The Constitution of Arbitration Victor Ferreres Comella

Redrafting Constitutions in Democratic Orders: Theoretical and Comparative Perspectives Edited by Gabriel L. Negretto

From Parchment to Practice: Implementing New Constitutions Edited by Tom Ginsburg and Aziz Z. Huq

The Failure of Popular Constitution Making in Turkey: Regressing Towards Constitutional Autocracy Edited by Felix Petersen and Zeynep Yanaşmayan

A Qualified Hope: The Indian Supreme Court and Progressive Social Change Edited by Gerald N. Rosenberg, Sudhir Krishnaswamy, and Shishir Bail

Constitutions in Times of Financial Crisis Edited by Tom Ginsburg, Mark D. Rosen, and Georg Vanberg

Reconstructing Rights: Courts, Parties, and Equality Rights in India, South Africa, and the United States Stephan Stohler

Constitution-Making and Transnational Legal Order Edited by Tom Ginsburg, Terence C. Halliday, and Gregory Shaffer

Hybrid Constitutionalism: The Politics of Constitutional Review in the Chinese Special Administrative Regions Eric C. Ip

The Invisible Constitution in Comparative Perspective Edited by Rosalind Dixon and Adrienne Stone

The Politico-Legal Dynamics of Judicial Review: A Comparative Analysis Theunis Roux

The New Fourth Branch

INSTITUTIONS FOR PROTECTING CONSTITUTIONAL
DEMOCRACY

MARK TUSHNET

Harvard Law School

CAMBRIDGE
UNIVERSITY PRESS

CAMBRIDGE
UNIVERSITY PRESS

University Printing House, Cambridge CB2 8BS, United Kingdom

One Liberty Plaza, 20th Floor, New York, NY 10006, USA

477 Williamstown Road, Port Melbourne, VIC 3207, Australia

314–321, 3rd Floor, Plot 3, Splendor Forum, Jasola District Centre, New Delhi – 110025, India

103 Penang Road, #05–06/07, Visioncrest Commercial, Singapore 238467

Cambridge University Press is part of the University of Cambridge.

It furthers the University's mission by disseminating knowledge in the pursuit of education, learning, and research at the highest international levels of excellence.

www.cambridge.org
Information on this title: www.cambridge.org/9781316517833
DOI: 10.1017/9781009047609

© Mark Tushnet 2021

First published 2021

A catalogue record for this publication is available from the British Library.

Library of Congress Cataloging-in-Publication Data
NAMES: Tushnet, Mark V., 1945– author.
TITLE: The new fourth branch : institutions for protecting constitutional democracy / Mark Tushnet, Harvard Law School, Massachusetts.
DESCRIPTION: Cambridge, United Kingdom ; New York, NY : Cambridge University Press, 2021. | Series: Comparative constitutional law and policy | Includes bibliographical references and index.
IDENTIFIERS: LCCN 2021025423 (print) | LCCN 2021025424 (ebook) | ISBN 9781316517833 (hardback) | ISBN 9781009048491 (paperback) | ISBN 9781009047609 (epub)
SUBJECTS: LCSH: Constitutional law. | Independent regulatory commissions. | Separation of powers.
CLASSIFICATION: LCC K3289 .T848 2021 (print) | LCC K3289 (ebook) | DDC 342/.04—dc23
LC record available at https://lccn.loc.gov/2021025423
LC ebook record available at https://lccn.loc.gov/2021025424

ISBN 978-1-316-51783-3 Hardback
ISBN 978-1-009-04849-1 Paperback

Contents

Acknowledgments

This work has been long in development, delayed in part by interruptions in research caused by the global pandemic. For comments on the work, I thank Or Bassok, Vicki C. Jackson, David Law, and Orin Tamir, as well as participants at faculty workshops at Texas A&M University, Vanderbilt University, University of Minnesota, and the University of Chile Law Schools and participants in four online works-in-progress conferences, one organized by Micaela Heilbroner and others, another by Richard Albert, the third by Rosalind Dixon, and the fourth by the Board of Academic Advisors of the American Constitution Society. I also thank Externado University Law School, Bogota, Colombia, for giving me the chance to teach a course in which I developed many of the ideas presented here. Sebastian Spitz provided valuable research assistance in the project's late stages when work was impeded by the 2020 pandemic. The pandemic has also made it difficult for me to provide citations to specific pages in a few of the works cited and to confirm that a few quotations have been transcribed accurately.

1

Introduction

Chapter Nine of South Africa's Constitution is titled, "State Institutions Protecting Constitutional Democracy." Its list of institutions that "strengthen constitutional democracy" includes the public prosecutor, the Human Rights Commission, the auditor-general, and the Electoral Commission.[1] Seen in the context of the Constitution's written text, these institutions form a branch on a par with Parliament and the president.

Textual placement may not be important in itself. The authors of the South African Constitution were on to something important, though. They saw that the traditional Montesquieian enumeration of three and only three branches of government no longer identified the complete set of desiderata for institutional design.

Dissatisfaction with the Montesquieian enumeration was apparent as well in Roberto Mangabeira Unger's *False Necessity*, published in 1987. That enumeration, Unger wrote, was "dangerous" because it "generates a stifling and perverse institutional logic." The solution for Unger lay in multiplying the number of branches. He offered several examples: a branch "especially charged with enlarging access to the means of communication, information, and expertise," and a branch – labeled the "destabilization branch" – designed "to give every transformative practice a chance."[2]

In 2000, Bruce Ackerman described a "new separation of powers" that hinted at institutional proliferation as well, though, as Ackerman acknowledged, much more modestly. He sketched a new "integrity branch" devoted to rooting out bureaucratic corruption, which he described mostly as something that occurred

---

[1] Constitution of South Africa, Art. 181 (1). The other institutions listed are the Commission for the Promotion and Protection of the Rights of Cultural, Religious, and Linguistic Communities, and the Commission for Gender Equality.

[2] ROBERT MANGABEIRA UNGER, FALSE NECESSITY 449–51 (Cambridge University Press, 1987).

in citizens' daily interactions with their government – street-level corruption rather than apex corruption.[3] Ackerman sketched some design principles – "very high salaries," restrictions on post-service employment, and a guaranteed budget. Ackerman mentioned the British Audit Commission and anti-corruption efforts in Hong Kong and Singapore.[4]

Martin Laughlin's study of the "foundations of public law" concludes with a discussion of the modern administrative state and what he calls "the rise of the ephorate."[5] Loughlin draws the term from the Greeks via nineteenth-century German political theorist J. G. Fichte. The ephors "constantly observe how state business is conducted" and "have the right to make inquiries wherever they can." Crucially for Loughlin, the ephorate "must claim an original, rather than delegated authority," which is the basis for treating it as a "new branch of government."[6]

Referring to public administration scholar Frank Vibert's book on "the new separation of powers" and "the rise of the unelected,"[7] Loughlin includes within the ephorate many institutions of the modern administrative state, many more than those modern constitutions designate as institutions for protecting democracy (hereafter IPDs). I believe the reason lies in Loughlin's interest in offering a general account of the modern state rather than in providing a granular account of its specific component institutions.[8] He and Vibert build on accounts of the rise of the modern administrative state familiar to U.S. scholars of administrative law, emphasizing rapid technological change and urbanization. When initially offered, those accounts yielded prescriptions about removing party-political

---

[3] Bruce Ackerman, *The New Separation of Powers*, 113 Harv. L. Rev. 633, 694 (2000) ("If payoffs are a routine part of life, ordinary people will despair of the very idea that they . . . can control their destinies through the democratic rule of law."). *See also* John McMillan, *Re-Thinking the Separation of Powers*, 38 Fed. L. Rev. 423, 438–41 (2010) (describing the "national integrity system" in Australia and a "fourth branch" conceptualization of that system).

[4] Ackerman also advocated for the express acknowledgement of the existence of a "regulatory branch." For a similarly brief discussion of accountability institutions, this one focusing on ombuds offices, see Tom Ginsburg & Aziz Z. Huq, How to Save a Constitutional Democracy 194–97 (University of Chicago Press, 2019).

[5] Martin Loughlin, Foundations of Public Law 448 (Oxford University Press, 2010).

[6] *Id.* at 450, 454, 451.

[7] Frank Vibert, The Rise of the Unelected: Democracy and the New Separation of Powers (Cambridge University Press, 2007).

[8] Loughlin's formulations resonate with those of Niklas Luhmann. Loughlin also refers to Edward Rubin, Beyond Camelot: Rethinking Politics and Law for the Modern State (Princeton University Press, 2005), which offers the metaphor of the "network" as a replacement for the metaphor of branches. I hope to provide an account of IPDs that does not require readers to accept such sweeping general accounts about the modern state (even though those accounts might be correct in some sense, and might shed light on aspects of IPDs that my more narrow focus leaves out of view).

influence from decision-making – which, as Chapter 2 argues, is at the heart of the conceptual account of IPDs – and about enhancing the technical expertise of the modern bureaucracy, which is a component, though a subordinate one, in designing IPDs.[9]

There is now a significant scholarly literature on treating anti-corruption efforts as an integrity branch.[10] That literature, though, does not situate the integrity branch within the larger conceptual framework suggested by the title of the South African Constitution's Chapter Nine. My aim here is to do just that – or, more accurately, to identify first the conceptual logic (Chapter 2) and functional logic (Chapter 3) underpinning IPDs. Briefly: the conceptual underpinning is that the Montesquieian tradition cannot provide sufficient guarantees for constitutional democracy in a political world where political parties play central roles; the functional underpinning is that that difficulty is created by conflicts or convergences of interests in such a world.

South Africa's Chapter Nine finds parallels in other constitutions whose designers have concluded that the Montesquieian division requires supplementation. Here is an incomplete catalog of the ways in which modern constitutions group these new institutions, some more coherently organized than others: "Of Good Governance" (Morocco 2011, more fully specified as "The Institutions and Instances of Protection of Rights and Freedoms of Good Governance of Human and Lasting Development and of Participative Democracy");[11] "Independent Constitutional Bodies" that "act in support of democracy" (Tunisia 2011);[12] "Essential Justice Institutions" (Angola 2010);[13] "Transparency and Social Control Function" (Ecuador 2008);[14] "Other State

---

9   Loughlin refers in passing to the "epistemic communities" to which the ephorate orients itself. LOUGHLIN, *supra* note 5, at 451. Those communities play an important part in designing and justifying IPDs (see Chapter 4).

10 For two recent reviews by a leading scholar in the field, see ROBERT I. ROTBERG, THE CORRUPTION CURE: HOW CITIZENS AND LEADERS CAN COMBAT CORRUPTION (Princeton University Press, 2017) (with an extensive bibliography); ROBERT I. ROTBERG, ANTI-CORRUPTION (MIT Press, 2020).

11 The specific institutions are a broadcasting authority, a competition authority, an anti-corruption body, and councils on education, the family, and youth.

12 The specific institutions are the Elections Commission, the Human Rights Commission, the Audio-visual Communications Commission, the commission for sustainable development, and an anti-corruption commission.

13 The provisions deal with the ombuds office and with lawyers and access to justice.

14 The institutions are the Council for Public Participation and Social Control, the Office of the Comptroller General, and the Office of the Human Rights Ombudsman. A referendum in 2018 approved an amendment creating a Transition Council of Citizen Participation. The Council was empowered to evaluate and replace state institutions. The list of institutions subject to the Council's powers includes the ombuds office, the National Electoral Council, the Electoral Disputes Tribunal, and the Constitutional Court.

Organs" (Rwanda 2015).[15] Other constitutions scatter the IPDs throughout the constitution but, as I argue in Chapter 3, the textual placement should neither obscure nor limit our treatment of IPDs as a separate "branch" of government.

Those underpinnings in turn suggest some general principles for designing such institutions, principles that address issues of independence, accountability, and expertise (Chapter 4). Chapter 5 surveys contemporary constitutions to identify how if at all they actually deal with the conceptual and functional concerns through institutional design. The book concludes with case studies, of anti-corruption efforts in Brazil and South Africa, of electoral commissions and courts in the United States, India, and South Korea, and of audit bodies in Canada and India.

A note on the scope and nature of the inquiry: many things, including many institutions, can help protect constitutional democracy. Sometimes the military can intervene to do so.[16] According to some accounts, federalism can do so as well. So can the permanent civil service ("the bureaucracy" or, in a non-pejorative sense, the "deep state"). And, at the most general level, civil society, including the press, nongovernmental organizations, and what Professor Vicki Jackson calls "knowledge institutions,"[17] can help preserve constitutional democracies.

The inquiry would be both unwieldy and unilluminating were it to take up every institution that under some circumstances can protect constitutional democracies. Focusing on institutions whose *core tasks* are to do so seems better. So, for example, the military's core task is national defense, federalism's the satisfaction of locally varying preferences, and nongovernmental organizations the subject matters they take as their charge. These institutions might have the resources to incidentally protect constitutional democracy, or that protection might be an intended or unintended by-product of the performance of their core tasks.[18] In contrast, the core tasks of anti-corruption agencies

---

[15] The institutions are the National Commission for Human Rights, the National Unity and Reconciliation Commission; the National Commission for the Fight against Genocide; the National Electoral Commission; the National Public Service Commission; the Office of the Ombudsman; the Office of the Auditor General of State Finances; the Gender Monitoring Office; the Chancellery for Heroes, National Orders and Decorations of Honour; the Rwanda Academy of Language and Culture; the National Women Council; the National Youth Council; and the National Council of Persons with Disabilities.

[16] *See* Ozan Varol, The Democratic Coup D'État (Oxford University Press, 2017).

[17] Vicki C. Jackson, *Knowledge Institutions in Constitutional Democracies: Preliminary Reflections*, 6 Can. J. Compar. & Contemp. L. (forthcoming).

[18] Even the press's role in preserving democracy is an incidental by-product of its core task of providing information on a wide range of subjects (and, for an important segment of the press, making a profit thereby).

and electoral courts and commissions implicate constitutional democracy relatively directly.[19]

Some other criteria might be added: the IPDs examined here are all *public* institutions with some degree of responsibility, usually indirect, to the electorate.[20] That is not true, almost by definition, of civil-society organizations, although one could include them within the scope of the study by focusing on the legal arrangements – freedom of the press and freedom of association – that are used to preserve their ability to protect constitutional democracy. Yet, serious study of those institutions understood as IPDs would require examination of the ways in which and the degree to which actors within them are socialized to take preserving constitutional democracy as one of their goals. A third criterion is straightforwardly positivist: IPDs are identified as such in a significant number of constitutions, and, as I argue in Chapter 3, we can extract some functional principles associated with party politics and conflicts of interest that explain why these institutions – but not others – are properly grouped together.[21]

My aim here is primarily to map out some analytic issues associated with IPDs, to identify some general features of their design, not to advocate for adoption of any particular IPD or to describe "best practices" in design. The study brings together under one heading a group of institutions each of which has received extensive examination on its own terms. I believe that the approach taken here highlights more clearly than do institution-by-institution studies the conceptual, functional, and political logic driving the creation of IPDs. At the same time, though, the study is clearly preliminary, and I am confident that others will introduce qualifications and corrections to the arguments I make.

Much of the existing literature on IPDs generally or on specific IPDs is affected by the all-too-common tendency to romanticize the institutions scholars study. They present constitutional courts in their best light, explaining

---

[19] As we will see, some constitutions give constitutionally protected status to some institutions whose central missions are not closely related to the protection of democracy, although perhaps more closely related to that goal than the military's central mission. See Chapter 5. We will also consider whether central banks should be considered institutions protecting constitutional democracy; their core tasks involve economic management but they are given independence from political control for roughly the same functional reasons associated with electoral commissions and anti-corruption agencies. See Chapter 3.

[20] The permanent civil service and the military and other national security agencies, which can sometimes serve to protect constitutional democracy, do satisfy the criterion of indirect electoral responsibility.

[21] Here too the permanent civil service is an exception, and might properly be included in this study. The principle that guides civil servants is the impartial administration of the matters within its jurisdiction, and impartiality means (among other things) acting without regard to party politics. For that reason, I address some aspects of the permanent civil service in Chapter 4 on design principles.

failures or "abusive constitutional review" as mistaken choices by individuals staffing those courts, rather than as one of the many features, both good and bad, of such courts. Similarly with IPDs. Normatively committed to protecting democracy, scholars look for successes and treat them either as examples of a general tendency or as replicable.

Though equally committed to protecting (or extending) democracy – or so I hope – I take what I think is a more balanced approach, discussing successes and failures and directing attention to the underside of even successful IPDs.[22] IPDs can actually promote democracy, they can make no difference to a democracy's performance, and they can impede or undermine democracy, sometimes by weakening the already weak incentives party-guided legislatures have to combat corruption and ensure electoral fairness.[23] Here as in so many areas, attention to constitutional design can get us only so far. Pushing democracy across the line requires more than institutions alone.

Nor do I assume that well-designed IPDs succeed unless deliberately undermined by anti-democrats. Indeed, one conclusion of the inquiry is that the specifics of design may well be irrelevant. If IPDs do indeed end up functioning to support democracy (and they do not always do so), it may result from their mere existence: the proliferation of IPDs increases the chance that one such institution out of many might be available, almost at random, to do the democracy-preserving work that happens to be needed at the moment. Sometimes a constitutional court, sometimes an ombuds office, sometimes an electoral commission – but no single institution will reliably do that work.[24] And, unfortunately, the possibility of a random good performance might be offset by the possibility of an equally random bad performance – an

---

[22] I focus on reasonably well-designed institutions used in principle to *protect* constitutional democracy even when they sometimes weaken it. Sometimes political leaders use these institutions to undermine constitutional democracy: an electoral court under the thumb of an authoritarian leader denies a place on the ballot to a leading opposition candidate. That such cases exist is clear, but whether examining them contributes to understanding of either constitutional design or democratic stability is less so.

[23] We might analogize this to what I have described as the "democratic debilitation" that constitutional review can induce in legislatures: knowing that courts will address constitutional questions, legislators may decline to do so. Mark Tushnet, *Policy Distortion and Democratic Debilitation: Comparative Illumination of the Countermajoritarian Difficulty*, 94 MICH. L. REV. 245 (1995).

[24] This conclusion is to some extent in tension with the argument in SAMUEL ISSACHAROFF, FRAGILE DEMOCRACIES: CONTESTED POWER IN THE ERA OF CONSTITUTIONAL COURTS (Cambridge University Press, 2015), which argues for the general reliability of constitutional courts as democracy-preserving institutions. Stated broadly, my critique of Issacharoff's argument is that he identifies a possibility and offers many case studies in which those possibilities go unrealized.

intervention by an IPD that makes democracy a great deal worse. One way of summarizing the overall argument is this: suitably adapted, all the arguments made in favor of and against well-known forms of constitutional review are applicable to every other IPD.

In sum, a systematic examination of IPDs may best be understood as a contribution to scholarship on constitutional design. If it contributes to clearer thinking about how to protect democracy, all to the good, but we should not hold out too great hopes that such a collateral benefit will accrue.

2

Why a *Fourth* Branch?

The Structural Logic

Constitutional theory dating to Montesquieu identified three branches of government, each with a specific function: the legislature enacted general rules, the executive enforced the rules, and the judiciary resolved disputes about the rules' meaning and application. Every government had to have these branches in some form; that is, the branches were *necessary* elements in a governance structure. In addition, the branches were *exhaustive*; that is, taken together they did everything a government could do.[1]

One desirable feature of a governance structure is that it be reasonably stable. In ordinary times, the structure must grind out policies, execute them, and deal with ensuing problems in a routine way.[2] Modest shocks – a smallish war or some moderate economic disruptions or nagging failures of governance in limited domains – might lead to departures from the ordinary course, but after the shock dissipates or the failures are remedied, the structure should return to something like its prior state, perhaps modified a bit because people have learned that some adaptations should be built into the structure to be available as needed.[3]

Further, well-designed governments require some mechanisms for adapting to changes in the policy problems the world throws up, changes in the preferences of the nation's people (sometimes the result of changes in the

---

[1] John Locke identified an additional branch, which he called the federative. It is associated with international affairs and it has not figured substantially in modern constitutional theory.

[2] Large-scale failures of governance indicate that radical changes might be necessary – or, in present terms, that the existing system *should* be destabilized by the adoption of large-scale constitutional changes.

[3] Carl Schmitt's idea of the commissarial dictatorship has some resonances with this thought, though Schmitt's perception that governance structures had to be able to survive *extreme* shocks led to his well-known views about the impossibility of defining the contours of states of exception by binding law.

very composition of that people), and changes in the available technologies of governance.

What, though, ensures that a constitutional system achieves an appropriate combination of reasonable stability with adaptability? Or, put another way, what can we do to ensure as best we can that a governance structure can sustain itself over time? Classical constitutional theory identified two possibilities: "civic virtue" and "structures."

The republican tradition emphasized the role of civic virtue in promoting a governance structure's reproduction: citizens devoted to the regime would be alert to threats from within – "corruption," in republicans' terms – and would act against those who would undermine the system either by throwing the rascals out of office or, in the extreme, by armed resistance. Jürgen Habermas's ideas about constitutional patriotism are a modern version of this tradition, as are – perhaps unfortunately – some versions of ethnonationalist populism.

The difficulty with civic virtue as a guarantor of regime stability is obvious enough: constitutional and political theorists have not been able to come up with institutions (mechanisms) that have any substantial chance of reliably reproducing civic virtue in the citizenry. Sometimes they gesture in the direction of the family or the education system, but in doing so, they rely mostly on exhortations and hopes rather than mechanisms. At other times, they gesture in the direction of a resilient constitutional culture built up over time. Here, too, they offer no real explanations of how resilience arises and is sustained.

More promising are accounts according to which civic virtue is the natural precipitate of widespread participation in the world of commerce.[4] Repeated interactions among commercial traders, for example, might generate an understanding of the importance of trust in sustaining the market – and that can generalize to an understanding of how trust is essential to stabilize governance structures. Yet, the modern capitalist system does not provide these or other kinds of opportunities to cultivate civic virtue in commercial settings. Lacking institutions or mechanisms to support it, civic virtue has been difficult to work into contemporary constitutional theory.[5]

The idea that structures of governance could do a decent job of ensuring their own reproduction and adaptability goes back almost as far as the civic

---

[4] *See*, e.g., STEVEN ELKIN, RECONSTRUCTING THE AMERICAN REPUBLIC: CONSTITUTIONAL DESIGN AFTER MADISON (University of Chicago Press, 2006); ALBERT O. HIRSCHMAN, THE PASSIONS AND THE INTERESTS: POLITICAL ARGUMENTS FOR CAPITALISM BEFORE ITS TRIUMPH (Princeton University Press, 1977).

[5] I make some attempts to describe "civic virtue"-oriented institutions in Chapter 9.

republican tradition. For present purposes, we can associate it with James Madison. Madison saw threats to constitutional stability from two directions. Members of each branch would seek to aggrandize themselves at the expense of the others, and the government as a whole might infringe upon individual rights. And those who drafted constitutions in the United States and France at the end of the eighteenth century had an inchoate understanding of how structures might promote adaptability as well.

Begin with adaptability. An orderly mechanism for amending the constitution allows the system to adapt to changes in the technologies of governance. The fourth-branch institutions that are my primary concern in this book often provide good examples of how the amendment mechanism works. They can be understood as novel technologies of governance added to constitutions through amendments (or, sometimes, through constitutional replacements). And, absent special considerations, the ordinary process of policy-adoption through legislation and executive decision-making is sufficient to ensure adaptation to changes in preferences and the array of policy problems the nation faces.[6]

Now turn to the threats to stability. Consider first the threat posed by self-aggrandizement: Legislators would seek to enforce the law themselves, for example, by imposing sanctions on identified individuals. Executives would seek to legislate by decree and use their resources to force individuals to comply. And courts, though the weakest branch, might aggressively expand their jurisdiction and "interpret" laws in ways that effectively transformed those laws.

Constitution designers could write provisions purporting to prohibit these attempted incursions, either specifically – as in a constitutional ban on bills of attainder – or generally, as in the famous formulation in the Massachusetts Constitution.[7] But, Madison feared, these provisions would be mere "parchment barriers."[8] He argued that competition among the branches was a better

---

[6] Among the special considerations are problems of legislative gridlock and ossification, terms familiar in the literature of the modern U.S. administrative state. A well-designed constitution's provision for amendment might be sufficient to deal with these problems – or, put another way, their persistence might be an indication that the amendment mechanism is not well-designed.

[7] "In the government of this commonwealth, the legislative department shall never exercise the executive and judicial powers, or either of them: the executive shall never exercise the legislative and judicial powers, or either of them: the judicial shall never exercise the legislative and executive powers, or either of them: to the end it may be a government of laws and not of men." Const. of Massachusetts, art. XXX.

[8] THE FEDERALIST NO. 48 (James Madison) (Ian Shapiro ed., Yale University Press, 2009) (originally published 1788).

mechanism for guaranteeing that each branch did only what it was designed to do. As Madison put it, "Ambition must be made to counteract ambition. The interest of the man must be connected with the constitutional rights of the place."[9] Executive officials would have the resources (mostly military) to resist legislative attempts to enforce the law, and legislators would have the resources (mostly financial) to resist executive efforts to legislate. And, because the interests of the occupants of government position were connected to the rights of the position, executive officials and legislators would have incentives to use those resources.

As to rights violations, Madison offered a skeletal version of modern interest-group pluralism in arguing that the government as a whole would be unable to systematically violate rights. He contrasted small republics, in which rights-violations could indeed occur, with the extended republic the United States would be upon its creation. Small republics were, he argued, rather homogeneous. Members of the majority could find it in their interests to enact laws that violated individual rights, and the victims lacked sufficient voting power to defeat these proposals. An extended republic, in contrast, would have so many diverse groups spread throughout the nation that those who might be victimized by a local majority could call upon allies from around the country to aid their resistance.

More formally, the extended republic would have the constitutional *power* to displace local rights-threatening legislation. A local minority can locate allies elsewhere and offer to support their general political agenda – dealing with matters other than the rights-threatening legislation – in exchange for enacting a statute overturning locally oppressive statutes. For Madison, pluralism made this a generally available remedy. Further, on the national level, in an extended republic every interest group would be able to trade its votes to block proposals that threatened the group's rights.[10]

The mechanisms Madison identified to ensure regime stability were quite ingenious, and perhaps could work in principle. Reality defeated them, though. Consider first pluralism as the mechanism for rights protection.

---

[9] THE FEDERALIST NO. 51 (James Madison).

[10] A note on the scope of the theory is outlined in this chapter: It applies to nations after what Hannah Arendt called the political revolution, the transformation of subjects into citizens. But not to all such nations, because not all (perhaps none) have undergone what she called the social revolution, after which, having gained adequate material resources, all citizens would be able to participate in roughly equal ways in the nation's political life. *See* HANNAH ARENDT, ON REVOLUTION (Viking Press, 1963).

Some nations might be so small that homogeneity overcomes pluralism.[11] Perhaps more important, the pluralist mechanism requires that the threatened group be able to organize itself to act as a unified bargainer in political negotiations. Some groups might lack the resources to do so, and some might be divided internally over the priority to give defeat of rights-threatening laws as against other matters on the political agenda. Such groups might be unable to engage in the kind of hard bargaining required by the pluralist mechanism.

The argument about competition among the branches was defeated by the rise of political parties organized on a national scale. As a prominent article puts it, the United States now has a system of separation of parties, not separation of powers.[12] And this is true more or less everywhere, though the nature of party systems varies among nations, with different systems having different implications for the separation of powers.

We can see the difficulty most easily in parliamentary systems.[13] Where the party system is reasonably well-organized – with a handful of parties contesting each election with an eye to forming either a majority or a coalition government – the executive and legislature will collaborate rather than compete. The majority party or the governing coalition will decide whether acting through legislation or by executive decree best advances the government's program, without regard to Montesquiean formalities. So-called separation-of-powers systems, in which separate elections are conducted for the chief executive and the legislature, *can* use the Madisonian mechanism in a world of political parties, but only when government is divided, that is, when the chief executive is from one party and the legislature is controlled by other parties.

What if the party system is chaotic rather than well-organized? Then another principle comes into play: Alexander Hamilton's insistence on energy

---

[11] As we will see, Carl Schmitt can be read to hold that real social homogeneity lies as the foundation of every constitutional order. His student Ernst-Wolfgang Böckenförde argued that only "relative" homogeneity was required, implying that at least in some circumstances pluralism would be sufficient to resist rights-incursions by a "merely" relatively homogeneous majority. See Ernst-Wolfgang Böckenförde, "The Concept of the Political: A Key to Understanding Carl Schmitt's Constitutional Theory," in Constitutional and Political Theory: Selected Writings (Mirjam Künkler & Tine Stein eds., Oxford University Press, 2017).

[12] Daryl J. Levinson & Richard H. Pildes, *Separation of Parties, Not Powers*, 119 Harv. L. Rev. 2311 (2006).

[13] For a powerful discussion of the phenomenon described in the text, *see* The Guardian of the Constitution: Hans Kelsen and Carl Schmitt on the Limits of Constitutional Law (Lars Vinx trans. and intro., Cambridge University Press, 2015), at 125–50 (reprinting an essay by Carl Schmitt discussing "the development of parliament into the arena of a pluralistic system" [hereafter cited as Guardian of the Constitution]).

in the executive.[14] Executives will be elected on a party basis, but their parties might be personalistic. Even if they emerge from long-standing parties, executives will act on the incentives they have to aggrandize power. And, in a chaotic party system, the legislature will find it difficult to organize resistance – because "chaos" means precisely that the parties are unable to coordinate action among themselves on any single agenda.

Recent experience in Peru provides an instructive case study, the interpretation of which is likely to be quite contested. In the 2010s, Peru's parties were largely personalistic, with one large party organized around the family of Alberto Fujimori.[15] Anti-corruption allegations about politicians who received bribes from the construction company Odebrecht led the Fujimorista party to bring an impeachment proceeding against then President Pedro Pablo Kuczynski.[16] The impeachment failed because Kuczynski was able to exploit factional divisions within the Fujimoristas, but the political maneuvers Kuczynski engaged in weakened him politically. Keiko Fujimori, leading her party, renewed the impeachment effort by attacking her brother Kenji for negotiating with Kuczynski to get public works contracts in exchange for Kenji's political support. By this time, Kuczynski's support had basically disappeared, and he resigned.

One might see this as the successful working of Madisonian mechanisms even in a personalistic and rather chaotic party system. Yet, we should note as well that essentially every high-level Peruvian politician – including all three Fujimoris – has been charged with corruption, and all the allegations are entirely credible. It is not clear that Madison would have found acceptable a system in which political competition led to throwing one set of rascals out only to replace them with another set of rascals.

The story gets more complicated. Martin Vizcarra replaced Kuczynski as president. He created a "public integrity office" within the executive branch, which appears to have been effective in prosecuting corruption. Vizcarra became quite popular and was himself able to resist an effort to remove him from office (through a seemingly irregular proceeding). Public demonstrations broke out when the Fujimorista attorney general tried to fire the chief prosecutor, and the attorney general resigned. At this point in a story that continues to unfold, as of early 2020, one might have offered the following interpretation: the Madisonian mechanisms initially worked to destabilize the

---

[14] THE FEDERALIST NO. 70 (Alexander Hamilton).

[15] I draw here on excellent research assistance provided by Sebastian Spitz, Harvard Law School '21.

[16] For the larger context of the Odebrecht investigation, see Chapter 6.

political system, but eventually appear to have produced a new equilibrium in which some of the most evident forms of corruption have been successfully attacked. We cannot know, of course, how politics in Peru will develop over the next several years, and a succession crisis recurred in late 2020. The bottom line here is that the Peruvian experience over the past few years does not confirm the efficacy of Madisonian mechanisms for preserving *constitutional* stability.[17]

Writing against the background of German parliamentary development, Hans Kelsen saw that the Madisonian mechanism of competition among the branches could not ensure regime stability. He argued that guaranteeing stability was a fourth function of governance structures.[18] Its existence had perhaps been obscured by the Madisonian argument, which took the function to be performed as a by-product of the creation of branches whose primary purposes were the Montesquiean ones. The Madisonian argument did not require that politicians be committed in principle to preserving the constitution. Put another way, they did not have to make credible commitments to doing so, because institutional competition would do the job. Where that competition fails – that is, in a party-political world – we are forced to fall back on the politicians' commitment to preserving the constitution.[19] But, in such a world, politicians are committed only to advancing their party programs and cannot credibly promise that their commitments to the constitution will prevail over their programmatic goals.[20] We need some other institution, and for Kelsen that institution was to be the "guardian of the constitution."[21]

---

[17] As with all narratives that focus on institutional responses to corruption, this one does not address the question of whether corruption has roots that anti-corruption prosecutions leave in place, ready to regrow when circumstances change.

[18] *See also* BÖCKENFÖRDE, *supra* note 11, at 191 (describing the function of "regulat[ing] and stabiliz[ing] the political process"), 73 (describing the function as "enabl[ing], preserv[ing], and support[ing] the state as the condition of political order and unity"). Böckenförde, a student of Carl Schmitt's, is perhaps the most significant modern German scholar who attempts to meld the thought of Kelsen and Schmitt.

[19] PAUL TUCKER, UNELECTED POWER: THE QUEST FOR LEGITIMACY IN CENTRAL BANKING AND THE REGULATORY STATE (Princeton University Press, 2018), frames his inquiry into the proper domain of bodies (mostly for Tucker administrative agencies) independent of the traditional three branches almost entirely in terms of the limits on the ability of actors in those branches to give credible commitments to maintaining a stable course with respect to specific policies, of which Kelsen would have said preserving the constitution was one.

[20] I should note here that my exposition from this point on is not an effort at the exegesis of the specific writings of Kelsen and Carl Schmitt. It is instead my effort to construct an account of the fourth branch that is roughly consistent with their ideas but might be inconsistent with some of their specific points. Put another way, it is my effort to construct a constitutional theory inspired by but not bound to what Kelsen and Schmitt wrote.

[21] If Kelsen was correct in identifying a "new" function that would ensure regime stability, that function should exist in *any* governance order that claims to settle things (for more than a short

As is well known, Kelsen thought that an institution he called the constitutional court could serve as that guardian.[22] Its function was to preserve the constitution in conditions of party government, and that function dictated many of its characteristics. First, it was to be removed from the party system. Kelsen believed that only something like a court could possibly satisfy that requirement. Second, the guardian's task was to determine whether the Montesquiean branches (primarily the legislature and the executive) reflected the constitution's allocation of authority among them. That allocation was done through law, the constitution itself. And so, the guardian of the constitution would be interpreting and applying law.

Third, the law the constitutional court interpreted inevitably had substantial political content, not in the sense that it embodied party-political positions but in the sense that it reflected (or expressed or identified) deep judgments about what allocations of authority best promoted fundamental goals of the political order. What those goals are was contentious. Some would take the order's goals to be promoting the interests of the nation's people, others advancing their values, others ensuring that their preferences be reflected in law, yet others taking the common good as the goal.

This implied that the constitutional court's members could not be "mere" lawyers or ordinary judges. Working in civil law jurisdictions, Kelsen saw ordinary judges as skilled legal technicians who advanced through their careers deploying what he understood to be a relatively "pure" form of law that almost never implicated deep judgments about the political order's fundamentals. Such judges, in Kelsen's view, would not have the training, the experience, or the capacity to execute the constitutional court's functions well.[23]

---

period). So, for example, we should be able to identify a "guardian of the theocratic constitution" or a "guardian of the one-party constitution" in nations with such constitution. And indeed, we do: the Guardian Council in Iran, the Central Committee of the Communist Party in the People's Republic of China. In the remainder of this chapter (and book), I consider only fourth-branch institutions in regimes roughly qualifying as constitutional democracies, though with a rather expansive definition of that category. For a review of modern uses of the phrase "guardian of the constitution" in written constitutions and court decisions, *see* BRIAN CHRISTOPHER JONES, CONSTITUTIONAL IDOLATRY, at ch. 7 (Edward Elgar, 2020).

[22] I note, and discuss in an Appendix to this chapter, an alternative account of the creation of constitutional courts. According to that account, political parties act in their own long-term self-interest by creating a constitutional court that can protect their short-term political gains against undoing as soon as they are thrown out of office. This alternative account is compatible with Kelsen's, though it rests upon different premises. I develop in the Appendix reasons to question the adequacy of the alternative account.

[23] Kelsen discussed the position of the U.S. Supreme Court, seemingly anomalous from his point of view, and concluded that it was able to perform the role of guardian of the constitution

How could the guardians of the constitution be appointed? Clearly not through the ordinary bureaucratic methods of appointing ordinary judges in civilian systems. Every other appointment mechanism, though, threatened to recreate in the constitutional court the party-political problems that made a constitutional court necessary.

The contours of a solution emerged as constitution designers worked with Kelsen's scheme. First, there should be either formal or informal constraints on eligibility for the court. Roughly, at least some of the court's members should have some familiarity with the party-political system so they would know something about how the constitution allocated power according to its fundamental goals. To avoid injecting immediate party-political goals into the court's decisions, though, its members should not have held important positions within political parties.[24]

Second, at least in part to provide some support in the party-political system for the constitutional court's ongoing role, the Montesquiean branches should have a role in the selection process. Constitution designers appear to have concluded that judicial nomination commissions are an important feature of good design. Details vary, of course, but such commissions typically include members of the legislature, including members of the majority party or coalition and members of the opposition, some judges either of the ordinary courts or of the constitutional court, and some representatives of civil society. And again typically, none of these components has a majority on the commission. The commission identifies a relatively small number of potential appointees to the constitutional court, and the executive must choose from the commission's list.[25]

Much more could be said about the design of the Kelsenian constitutional court, but I move on because this book's goal is to analyze fourth-branch institutions generally, not only constitutional courts.

The conservative (and later Nazi) German legal theorist Carl Schmitt was Kelsen's great interlocutor. Like Kelsen, Schmitt understood the need for a

---

because it operated "in a jurisdictional state that subjects all public life to the control of the ordinary courts" through a common-law system that incorporated "the basic rights implicit in a liberal-bourgeois understanding of the rule of law...." GUARDIAN OF THE CONSTITUTION, *supra* note 13, at 82.

[24] Notably, former presidents of France are guaranteed seats on the French Constitutional Council. A norm against the presidents' active participation existed for several years but apparently has been abandoned. We can see in this provision something like an attempt to blend Kelsen's understanding of who the guardian of the constitution should be, with Schmitt's, discussed at text accompanying notes 26–33.

[25] Again, I elide many details and variations here. A particularly important detail involves the path to be taken if the executive refuses to choose an appointee from the list.

guardian of the constitution. But, Schmitt argued, Kelsen's focus on problems created by the party-political system led him to design the guardian badly. Schmitt leveled two arguments against Kelsen. The first went to the foundation of the guardian's function, the second to the inability of a court – and indeed law – to serve as the guardian.

Schmitt's position rested on his understanding of the constitution the guardian was to protect. For him, the constitution was not merely (or even) the words allocating power and defining rights in some foundational document. Rather, the constitution was a nation's self-identity, sometimes inferred from constitutional provisions but sometimes residing in other sources. The constitution's guardian would speak for the nation's people as a whole against efforts by party politicians to undermine or transform the people's identity. For Schmitt, only someone above politics could do that; in this he agreed with Kelsen. But neither the parliament nor a constitutional court could speak for the nation. Parliaments were divided along party lines, and constitutional courts spoke in law's register, not the people's.[26] For Schmitt, only someone chosen by the people – but outside of party politics – could speak for the people.[27] Schmitt believed that the German president under the Weimar Constitution was precisely such a person.

Schmitt's position required that the president, or equivalent figure, stand above party politics.[28] That was almost certainly not true in Weimar Germany and is true almost nowhere today.[29] The best cases for a Schmittian president

---

[26] For a particularly pointed formulation of Schmitt's concerns, *see* GUARDIAN OF THE CONSTITUTION, *supra* note 13, at 142–43 (asserting, inter alia, that the "parliamentary, democratic, party state is . . . an unstable coalition party state").

[27] Theorists have sometimes suggested that a monarch who ordinarily abstains from intervention in party-political disputes might speak for the nation under extraordinary circumstances. Kelsen discussed this account of a monarchs' role, describing it as "a fiction of remarkable boldness" (at least in modern circumstances). GUARDIAN OF THE CONSTITUTION, *supra* note 13, at 177.

[28] *See* GUARDIAN OF THE CONSTITUTION, *supra* note 13, at 150 (reprinting a discussion of "the president of the *Reich* as guardian of the constitution"), 171 (asserting that "The president of the *Reich* stands in the centre of a whole system of party-political neutrality and independence that is built on a plebiscitary basis" with an "immediate connection with the whole of the state").

[29] *See* GUARDIAN OF THE CONSTITUTION, *supra* note 13, at 14 (noting Kelsen's view that Schmitt's description of the President's position was "plainly false"). *See also* BÖCKENFÖRDE, *supra* note 11, at 188 ("That authority is no longer transferrable to a head of state like the president of the US or the presidents of Latin and South American states, who are elected to their office as the advocates of a particular political current"). Governors general in countries in the British Commonwealth might be good candidates, but in both Australia and Canada, governors general have used their powers in highly charged partisan circumstances with the effect of favoring one party over another. In 1975, the Australian governor general dismissed the Labour Party Prime Minister Gough Whitlam rather than acceding to Whitlam's request that he call an election for the Senate that promised to break a budget deadlock. In 2008, the Canadian

as guardian of the constitution come from nations where the president is a figurehead trotted out for civic ceremonies and, occasionally, for moralistic discourses about the nation's well-being. Yet, forceful interventions by figurehead presidents to preserve the constitution – by anything more than finger-wagging – would cause a constitutional crisis larger than the one that provokes the intervention. And, presidents with real power almost always *lead* one of the nation's major political parties: they can cause constitutional crises by ignoring the constitution, but they cannot resolve them by standing above politics.

Schmitt's second concern about the constitutional court as guardian flowed from his ideas about law. He approached the issue here from two directions. First, constitutional terms – those defining the jurisdiction of states and nation, those allocating power between legislature and executive, and those guaranteeing rights – were inevitably quite general.[30] Resolving controversies over their meaning in specific contexts would require the constitutional court to infuse those terms with controversial – which is to say, party-political – content. That, though, was inconsistent with what Schmitt took to be the very reason we have *courts*: to resolve disputes impartially. Constitutional interpretation was, for Schmitt, party-political, and so not impartial, at the core.[31]

Coming at the issue from a slightly different direction, Schmitt also saw law as *definitionally* apolitical, a self-contained body of doctrine and reasoning that constituted a formal system closed to input from policy concerns associated with party-political positions.[32] So, for example, courts interpreting contracts could rely only on doctrines shaped by a concern to develop an internally coherent whole; they could not consider assertions that one rule for

---

governor general agreed to prorogue Parliament so that the Conservative Prime Minister Stephen Harper could avoid an immediate vote of no confidence. Harper used the opportunity to rebuild his political fences and when Parliament reconvened the threat of the no-confidence vote had disappeared.

[30] *See* GUARDIAN OF THE CONSTITUTION, note 13, at 101 (referring to "the necessary incompleteness and vagueness of every written constitution," which makes decisions about their meaning "something other than a judge's decision, i.e., something other than adjudication").

[31] Notably, Kelsen agreed with Schmitt on the abstractness of rights provisions, and excluded them from the jurisdiction of the constitutional court he designed. He appears to have conceded, at least in passing, that this exclusion was not "a conceptual question asking for the essential characteristics of adjudication, but rather ... a pragmatic question that concerns the most useful way of organizing the function of adjudication."). GUARDIAN OF THE CONSTITUTION, *supra* note 13, at 193. Later constitution designers appear to have agreed with the conceptual point and have come to a different pragmatic judgment form Kelsen's.

[32] *See* GUARDIAN OF THE CONSTITUTION, *supra* note 13, at 108 ("The special position of the judge in the rule-of-law state ... rests only on the fact that ... his decision is derived, in a measurable and calculable way, from the content of another decision that is already contained in the statute.").

interpreting employment contracts would systematically favor employers, another employees. Schmitt did not reject the proposition that law could incorporate attention to policy considerations, a proposition rattling around in German legal theory when Schmitt wrote (and a proposition that, independent of its role in the intellectual history of law, is now widely accepted). But, on Schmitt's account, the only policies that law could incorporate were those with nearly universal support (and therefore policies set apart from party-political controversy).[33]

For Schmitt, it followed that whatever Kelsen's constitutional court would be doing, it would not be doing *law*. The separation-of-powers disputes on which Kelsen focused were always party-political; indeed, that was precisely why the Madisonian account of a self-guaranteeing constitution failed. The constitutional court would be infusing "law" – the scare-quotes are important – with party-political content however it resolved disputes because the only grounds available for such a resolution were party-political.

Kelsen responded by rejecting Schmitt's general account of law.[34] For Kelsen, ordinary law was infused with policy content, and it was foolish to deny that across wide ranges of ordinary law that policy content corresponded to (or was correlated with) party-political positions. Again, the law of employment contracts provides a good example: whether employment contracts with no provisions dealing with the length of the contract term were to be interpreted to create employment-at-will or a guarantee of employment unless the employer had cause to discharge the worker could be answered only by considering issues such as labor mobility, employer flexibility, and the like – all of which were associated with party-political positions.[35]

So, for Kelsen, constitutional courts were indistinguishable along the dimension of *law* from ordinary courts. Schmitt had a response. Again focusing on constitutional law's party-political content, Schmitt argued that party-political choices were legally unconstrained even if they could be

---

[33] For present purposes, I put to one side the possibility – in my view, the reality – that there are no such policies.

[34] *See* GUARDIAN OF THE CONSTITUTION, *supra* note 13, at 185–91 (criticizing Schmitt's account of ordinary adjudication as involving "the subsumption of a matter of fact under a legal rule"). Böckenförde offers a less rigid formulation, compatible in my view with current notions of adjudication: the constitutional court "is bound to a rationally verifiable, methodically secured context of argumentation." BÖCKENFÖRDE, *supra* note 11, at 191. (I note, though, that much here depends upon the meaning one gives to the phrase "context of argumentation.").

[35] Schmitt discussed, critically, the actions of German courts "in the area of labour disputes that have led to a clear distinction between the judge and the mediator," GUARDIAN OF THE CONSTITUTION, *supra* note 13, at 165, without noting the tension between his jurisprudential position and the actions actually taken by courts (acting as mediators).

incorporated into law once they were made. For Schmitt, though, the proper institutional location for unconstrained choices was pure politics. This is the (modest) implication of his famous formulation, "Sovereign is he who declares the exception." The power to make (and make effective) unconstrained choices is the hallmark of sovereignty. So, on Schmitt's account, Kelsen's view about *ordinary* law raised the prospect that we would have to regard as sovereigns the judges who made that law by incorporating unconstrained party-political policies into it.

That prospect was not realized with respect to ordinary law, though, because it was revisable by ordinary party-political processes – by legislation, in short. It *was* realized in constitutional law, though. The judges on Kelsen's constitutional courts would be sovereigns making unconstrained choices that were at their foundation party-political no matter how hard they tried to disguise their decisions in the language of a law above party-politics.[36]

So what? Kelsen's guardian of the constitution was designed to address the problem of ensuring constitutional stability in a party-political state. The constitutional-court-as-sovereign is a fully political body once we understand the foundations of constitutional law properly. A political body, yes, but perhaps it could still be a body above party politics. At this point questions of institutional design arise. Is it possible to design mechanisms for selecting and removing judges on constitutional courts that insulate them from the threats to the constitutional order created by party politics?

We can ask the same question within the framework of rational-choice accounts of politics and constitutional design. As we have seen, Madisonian mechanisms in a party-political world are unable to generate credible commitments to constitutional stability. Institutions that could do so must be able to assure parties with sharply conflicting programs that they will preserve the constitution rather than advance the goals of one or another party. That assurance is provided by designs that combine independence to ensure that the institution isn't captured by one party with accountability to ensure that the institution doesn't become a force independent of the political parties.[37]

---

[36] This is consistent with Schmitt's "decisionist" account of constitutional fundamentals, according to which the most basic choices in structuring a constitution are "mere" decisions, completely discretionary choices. Schmitt himself associated decisionism with the choices made by the nation's leader, but in theory – and on this account of a Schmittian understanding of the constitutional court – decisionism can be associated with such a court. *See also* BÖCKENFÖRDE, *supra* note 11, at 195 (describing the constitutional courts as "'political' to some degree").

[37] The mechanisms of independence can be ex ante through appointment systems that prevent capture, and ex post through the subjection of the institution's practices to criticism based upon

The short answer to the question about whether institutional design can solve the problems created by party politics is, No. The longer answer is this: we can design such mechanisms that will indeed insulate the constitutional court from those threats, but the mechanisms will do so effectively only under conditions that make it unnecessary to have a constitutional court as a guardian of the constitution. Here is the underlying argument. Consider a selection system that involves some participation by legislatures and executives. The Madisonian system of competition among parties can produce constitutional court judges who are in the aggregate above politics.[38] But (of course) where the Madisonian system works with respect to selection of constitutional court judges, it is likely to work as well (or nearly as well) with respect to legislative and executive protection of the constitution. And, where the Madisonian system does not work well with respect to the constitution itself – in a world of divided party government or chaotic legislatures, for example – it is unlikely to work well with respect to selecting judges for the constitutional court.[39]

Where does this leave us? The problems associated with a party-political legislative and executive system are not precisely the same as those associated with a party-political constitutional court. Perhaps such a court can do something – not as much as Kelsen appears to have thought, but something – to protect the constitution. Similarly, perhaps a party-political legislature can do something – not much, but something – in addition.

Another possibility animates the remainder of this book. Kelsen may have been right in seeing party politics as a threat to the constitution, and in seeing the need to create something to serve as a guardian of the constitution. He may have been wrong, though, in thinking that a single such institution, the constitutional court, would be sufficient. Perhaps we should take seriously the plural in the title of the South African Constitution's Chapter Nine: "Institutions Supporting Constitutional Democracy." In doing so, we might move the Madisonian argument to a higher level: not competition among institutions above party politics, but competition among institutions implicated in party politics but each in a slightly different way. A constitutional court might fail to protect the constitution against a specific threat, but perhaps the nation's ombudsperson will do so – or the nation's auditor

---

nonpolitical standards. Similarly, the mechanisms of accountability can be ex ante through appointment processes and ex post through removal processes.

[38] The clearest cases involve constitutional court judges with limited terms, allowing for regularly timed replacements, and chosen by legislative supermajorities.

[39] The argument about mechanisms for judicial removal takes the same form.

general, or its public prosecutor. A nation with enough institutions supporting constitutional democracy might be able to protect against specific threats as they arise. Not in any systematic way, though: It is not that the constitutional court is systematically going to a better job of protecting rights than an ombuds office, or a public prosecutor a better job at attacking corruption than a court, or …. Rather, the hope is that with respect to any specific threat to the constitution, at least one of the many institutions available to support the constitution will manage to do a good job, perhaps (often) for quite idiosyncratic and unreproducible reasons. That at least is the proposition that this book examines.

APPENDIX

Matt Stephenson, Tom Ginsburg, and Ran Hirschl explain the creation and to some degree the maintenance of constitutional courts with reference to the interests of political parties.[40] For Stephenson and Ginsburg, constitutional courts serve as "insurance" for political parties who foresee the possibility that they will lose office. These parties want to ensure as best they can that the substantive policies they have advanced are preserved even after the (former) opposition takes control of the political branches.

Hirschl's argument is similar but narrower: constitutional courts are created when a formerly hegemonic political party (for Hirschl, often one representing a dominant cultural, economic, or social elite) sees its ability to control the political branches coming to an end. They create a constitutional court charged with upholding the formerly hegemonic party's programs against alteration.

Like Kelsen's, then, these accounts link the constitutional court to the existence of a party-political order. Their focus, though, is different from Kelsen's. Kelsen's account deals with the preservation of the overall constitutional structure; substantive policies are irrelevant. The various insurance-like accounts, in contrast, deal almost exclusively with substantive policy (and with structural issues only to the extent that contending political parties have differing views about what sort of structure will best allow them to enact and preserve their substantive policies.)

---

[40] Matthew Stephenson, *"When the Devil Turns …": The Political Foundations of Independent Judicial Review*, 32 J. Legal Stud. 59 (2003); Tom Ginsburg, Judicial Review in New Democracies: Constitutional Courts in Asian Cases (Cambridge University Press, 2003); Ran Hirschl, Towards Juristocracy: The Origins and Consequences of the New Constitutionalism (Harvard University Press, 2004).

I believe that one serious problem with the alternative accounts is *temporal*. Assume that members of the constitutional court are appointed in a manner that has some connection to the political branches.[41] Consider first Hirschl's "hegemonic self-preservation" argument: Anticipating their loss of control of the political branches, hegemonic parties take shelter in the constitutional court. But, because they are no longer hegemonic, eventually these parties will lose control of that court too. Delaying their complete expulsion from political power is something, of course, but it does not explain why the former opposition continues to maintain a constitutional court.

The explanation for that is reasonably clear: having gained control of the constitutional court, the former opposition can now use it as a tool to advance *its* political program. Now, though, the hegemonic party's calculation becomes quite complex: its leaders must ask, "Are the (interim) benefits we get from sustaining our power until we lose control of the constitutional court large enough to offset the (perhaps permanent) political defeats the constitutional court will give us after that?" Hirschl's case studies suggest that they answered, "Yes," although the case studies basically end before the hegemonic parties lose control of the court.

Stephenson's and Ginsburg's accounts have a related problem. Their versions anticipate a rotation in office: one coalition holds power, then loses it, then regains it. The constitutional court can protect the coalition's programs against reversal during the period when it is out of power. A version of the temporal problem recurs here, though in a less acute form. The constitutional court serves as insurance for the initial coalition until the former opposition gains control of the court. But, one might think, perhaps the latter can occur only over a relatively long time period and the initial coalition's leaders expect to be back in power before it does.

Fair enough. But now consider applying the Madisonian argument about institutions counterbalancing each other in a party-political world where political contention focuses on substantive policies. The U.S. experience suggests that ordinary political contention guarantees a combination of reasonable stability in substantive policy and real possibilities of substantial policy change (including elaboration and repudiation of prior policies) over

---

[41] That assumption is consistent with appointment processes in nearly every nation with a constitutional court (India and Italy being exceptions), and is consistent with a normative account of why constitutional courts are compatible with the requirements of democratic self-governance. I note though that a constitutional court that conceives of and implements its role in a quite specific substantive way – roughly, in an Ely-like way – can be compatible with democratic self-governance no matter how its members are appointed.

extended periods.[42] If that is so – and the U.S. experience has to be treated with caution here because one component of the system is itself a constitutional court – it may be unclear why political leaders would want to create and sustain a constitutional court instead of relying upon political contention to achieve their goals.

---

[42] I refer here to "regime"-focused accounts of U.S. political history associated with the subfield of political science known as American political development.

3

Why a Fourth *Branch?*

The Functional Logic

As we have seen, Kelsen identified a fourth function of government, preservation of the constitution, and assigned it to a new institution, the constitutional court. The reason was that in a party-political world neither the legislature nor the executive could be trusted to perform the function except under specific, and probably unusual, conditions. Absent those conditions, legislatures controlled by one party would not investigate threats to the constitution posed by an executive of their own party, and would exaggerate the threats posed by an executive of the opposition party – and conversely, with executive oversight of threats posed by the legislature. Call this a problem of *conflict or convergence of interest.*

Kelsen's exchange with Schmitt established that there were risks associated with assigning the guardianship function to the ordinary judiciary. Although Schmitt was wrong to think that the way the ordinary courts applied the law necessarily precluded them from taking considerations of high politics into account in adjudicating cases, he and Kelsen agreed that the frequent association of high politics with party politics posed a threat to the independence of the judiciary that constitutionalism required. They might have agreed as well that it was desirable that the ordinary courts have a generally legalistic cast of mind, and that such a general cast of mind might impair their ability to arrive at constitutionally appropriate resolutions of constitutional conflicts. Call these problems of *independence* and *expertise.*

These problems emerge from a consideration of the reasons for requiring a fourth branch of government. Once they are brought into the open, though, we can see that other tasks within a constitutional system have similar characteristics. The most obvious are supervision of electoral fairness and rooting out high-level corruption.[1]

---

[1]   It is a standard view that high-level corruption is a threat to the constitutional order because of its effects on public support for that order. *See,* e.g., Aziz Huq, *Legal or Political Checks on Apex Criminality: An Essay on Constitutional Design,* 65 UCLA L. Rev. 1506 (2018).

As to elections, consider the U.S. constitutional provision that "each House shall be the Judge of the Elections, Returns, and Qualifications of its own Members." In a party-political world, the conflict-of-interest problems associated with that rule are obvious – and have been realized, as a survey of how each house has in fact resolved election disputes reveals.[2] Here party politics operates within each house of Congress. Practice in the states with respect to presidential elections typically has been assigned to party-political actors such as elected secretaries of state.[3] And as to high-level corruption, the problems are structurally identical to those Kelsen identified: bad incentives for party-political actors to investigate "their own" or "the other side's" wrongdoing.[4]

The problems of conflict of interest, independence, and expertise suggest the possibility that Kelsen had a too-limited vision of the tasks the constitutional court – or some other guardian of the constitution – might take on. After discussing in more detail the tasks that might be affected by those problems, I turn to the question of whether constitutional designers should consider expanding the constitutional court's remit to include the larger set of tasks, including supervision of electoral fairness and oversight of anti-corruption efforts – or whether, and if so why, designers should consider creation of a multi-institutional fourth branch of government.

A preliminary point is this: Why worry about whether the institutions to be discussed should be lumped together as a fourth branch?[5] Why not treat them simply as a congeries of institutions sharing certain characteristics? One answer is purely nominalist: as the survey of design choices in Chapter 5 indicates, at least some recent constitution designers have concluded that it makes sense to group institutions under a separate constitutional heading, and it is worth thinking about what the basis might be for such a choice.[6]

Another answer is that posing the "fourth branch" question sharpens thinking in constitutional systems that have (a) the traditional three branches and

---

[2] *See* Jeffrey A. Jenkins, *Partisanship and Contested Election Cases in the House of Representatives, 1789–2002*, 18 STUD. IN AM. POL. DEVELOPMENT 112, 135 (2004) (concluding that "partisanship has been a significant factor in contested election outcomes generally across time").

[3] *See* Richard Schragger, *Reclaiming the Canvassing Board: Bush v. Gore and the Political Currency of Local Government*, 50 BUFFALO L. REV. 393 (2002). For further discussion, see Chapter 7.

[4] I defer discussion of the ways in which the problem of expertise affects these and other tasks associated with preserving the constitution.

[5] I discuss Tarun Khaitan's argument on this question later in this Chapter.

[6] Not every institution now treated as part of a fourth branch is a modern innovation. The leading examples are the audit office, which under various names has a long history, and the ombuds office, which dates to 1713 or 1809 in Sweden and to 1920 in Finland (its first appearance outside of Scandinavia was in New Zealand in 1962). For sketches of these histories, see ROBERT I. ROTBERG, ANTICORRUPTION 131–39 (MIT Press, 2020).

nothing else, (b) a relatively difficult amendment rule, and (c) an interpretive tradition in which constitutional formalism, at least as to structures, is reasonably strong.[7] Consider, for example, *Morrison v. Olson*, in which the U.S. Supreme Court considered the constitutionality of a statute targeting high-level criminality and corruption.[8] It had to fit the statute into the three-branch framework. The problem in these systems is of course more general: whenever an independent guardian institution is devised to deal with corruption or with election fairness or something else and is enacted by statute because constitutional amendment is difficult, the institution has to be fit into that framework. Seeing the functions fourth-branch institutions perform provides at least some intellectual resources for explaining the majority's pragmatic or balancing opinion upholding the statute's constitutionality and might provide some resources for explaining why the statute was not inconsistent with that degree of constitutional formalism to which the system is committed.[9]

Now to an analysis of conflicts and convergences of interest. We must be careful in spelling out what amounts to a troubling conflict or convergence of interest. Consider substantive programs that provide benefits to constituents who might then be drawn to affiliate themselves with the party whose platforms include preserving or extending those programs. The Workers' Party in Brazil, for example, enacted a generous family allowance program, financed from the then substantial revenues from resource extraction, which cemented the affiliation of poor families to the Party – and had a nontrivial effect on reducing economic inequality within Brazil.[10] These programs aim at entrenching the party in power, or, put another way, they reflect the governing party's self-interest in staying in power.

---

[7] Australia and the United States are the primary examples. For Australia, see especially A. J. Brown, "The Integrity Branch: A 'System,' an 'Industry,' or a Sensible Emerging Fourth Arm of the Government?," in MODERN ADMINISTRATIVE LAW IN AUSTRALIA: CONCEPTS AND CONTEXT (M. Groves ed., Cambridge University Press, 2014), at 313–15. Brown's focus is on integrating Australia's statutory fourth-branch institutions into the existing Australian constitution. His primary point is that those institutions cannot be assimilated to ordinary administrative bodies, which Australian constitutionalism has accepted, because their independence from executive supervision is by statute significantly greater than that of ordinary administrative bodies.

[8] *Morrison v. Olson*, 487 U.S. 654 (1988).

[9] A further more speculative answer is that members of the traditional branches see themselves as colleagues of all other members of the same branch: "We're all legislators or judges, no matter what other differences there are." Perhaps – though I doubt that any of this could be verified empirically – members of fourth-branch institutions see themselves similarly: "We're all tasked with protecting constitutional democracy whether we're anti-corruption prosecutors, auditors, or election managers."

[10] The PiS party in Poland adopted a similar program, financed in part from general funding given the government by the European Union.

This sort of self-interest cannot be enough to take the policy out of the hands of ordinary party politics, though. Political parties' programs consist of promises that, if fulfilled, will enhance the parties' electoral support. Sometimes family allowance–type programs are enhanced shortly before elections, providing one-time benefits that, the government hopes, will remind voters on which side their bread is buttered. If the benefits really are benefits (and do not make the family-support program economically unsustainable in the long run), this is just ordinary politics at work.

As political scientist E. E. Schattschneider put it long ago, "New policies create a new politics."[11] Or, put another way, *all* political platforms aim at securing a party's self-entrenchment.[12] To treat self-entrenchment as problematic in itself would be to remove all policies from the domain of democratic control. What we need to do is identify political domains where conflicts or convergences of interests occur *no matter what the array of political power is.* The Madisonian mechanisms can work in other domains, but not in these.

Consider the family allowance example. One policy argument against that policy is that it is unsustainable.[13] And, as economists say, if something cannot go on forever it will stop.[14] We might describe an unsustainable family-allowance program as self-limiting: its political advantages have a "natural" lifetime, after which the opposition can take power. Most policy domains deal with policies like this – ones that might give the party-in-power some temporary political advantages, but those advantages are not sustainable. And if they are good on the merits *and* sustainable, we should not regard them as a problem to which constitutions should direct themselves.[15]

---

[11] E. E. SCHATTSCHNEIDER, POLITICS, PRESSURES, AND THE TARIFF 288 (Prentice-Hall, 1935).

[12] Some platforms might aim at *long-term* entrenchment, supported by political actors who concede that the platforms cannot be enacted in the short run (and advocacy thereof might contribute to short-run defeats). Here we should think of "fringe" or seemingly "minor" parties that aim for long-term influence.

[13] The Workers Party was able to enact the program because Brazil benefited from high prices for commodities such as oil that fueled the Brazilian economy. When commodity prices fell the family-allowance program became a drag on the economy. The Polish program might be vulnerable to reduction of EU financial support.

[14] The statement was made by economic adviser Herbert Stein in congressional testimony in 1976.

[15] Supporters of family-allowance programs counter the charge of unsustainability by invoking human capital theory: the family allowances enable recipients to build human capital that will make them more productive, thereby generating resources that will fund the program. For example, recipients might use the family allowances to attend school rather than work at low-level jobs, or the allowance might relieve psychological anxiety in ways that make recipients more productive immediately.

Sometimes, though, policies can have a permanent self-entrenching effect. Manipulation of election rules, including gerrymandering, can do so, for example, and so might corruption. These practices can erect impenetrable walls around the party-in-power. Here the conflict-of-interest explanation of why some sort of constitutional guardianship is necessary seems apt.

The convergence-of-interest explanation also has some bite in these domains as well, though the mechanism comes in two variants. The general description is that opposition parties do not challenge what the party-in-power does in these domains. The more obvious mechanism is that opposition parties don't want to oppose manipulation of election rules (or corruption) because they hope to take power and then manipulate those rules themselves (or benefit from corruption). Here the mechanism is this: Parties-in-power *try* to manipulate election rules to entrench themselves permanently, but their efforts are not always entirely successful. They might miscalculate and leave room for the opposition to "sneak in," or they might adopt election rules that would be permanently entrenching under ordinary circumstances but extra-ordinary events might intervene.[16] A second mechanism is that opposition parties accept permanent minority status in exchange for payoffs from the party-in-power – salaries and other financial benefits flowing directly from holding office, for example.

I think it helpful to divide the policy domains of interest into two categories: where the conflicts or convergences of interest are *intra*temporal and where they are *inter*temporal. The problems caused by self-entrenching election rules and corruption are intratemporal in the sense that they occur immediately upon the adoption of the rules.

In contrast, the problems caused by intertemporal conflicts of interest come to pass well after policies are adopted. The classic examples involve fiscal and environmental policies. In both domains, politicians have an interest in adopting policies that provide immediate benefits to constituents in the here and now and that impose costs on people not yet able to vote (perhaps not even born).

As to fiscal policy: today's politicians have an interest in adopting spending programs that benefit people today – the family allowance – without imposing taxes to pay for the programs. At some point, though, the programs have to be paid for, either by future increases in taxes or in excessive inflation. Today's politicians don't worry enough about how people in the future will pay for today's spending – and today's opposition politicians who do worry about that

---

[16] For example, see Chapter 7 (dealing with electoral commissions and courts).

will face voters who find the current benefits valuable and don't see themselves as bearing the costs in the future (perhaps because they will be dead when taxes are raised or inflation skyrockets).[17]

The similar problems with environmental policy are evident. Climate change might impose massive costs twenty or thirty years from now, but averting those costs today requires that voters forgo buying things they want today (through higher prices for goods produced in ways that will reduce future environmental risks or through taxes to pay for programs that will do so).

As the survey of constitutional provisions in Chapter 5 shows, many though not all constitutions today do provide special protection for central banks charged with supervising fiscal policy to avoid excessive inflation by disciplining governments that adopt too many debt-financed policies and may provide for environmental protection agencies. These constitutions acknowledge the existence of intertemporal conflicts of interests similar in character to intratemporal ones.

According to some accounts, important substantive provisions of constitutional law address intertemporal conflicts as well. Examining those accounts exposes some of the problems associated with building them into constitutional law, whether substantive or structural. The idea is captured in the idea that entrenching some provisions against change by a simple majority allows for an appeal from Peter drunk to Peter sober.[18] What a majority currently says it wants may not be in its long-term best interest. It is currently "drunk," but when it sobers up it will regret what it has done but will somehow be unable to undo the damage or, more troublingly, will never be able to sober up because this specific decision will lead it to imbibe over and over.

The idiom is appealing, but the problems with it are well-known. First, in the usual context of constitutional review, it assumes that the courts are currently sober, or at least more sober than the majority. Why that should be so is unclear, though, because we have no blood-alcohol tests that allow us to compare the relative sobriety of the people and the courts. Second, and more important, experience has shown that we can gin up arguments that pretty much any controversial legislation results from a failure to take long-term interests into account. Most dramatically, standard public-choice and economic-theory arguments can be produced to show that any economic

---

[17] The argument of course depends upon the proposition that today's voters discount future costs excessively – effectively to zero when they imagine that they will be dead by the time the costs have to be borne.

[18] Jamal Greene, *Pathetic Argument in Constitutional Law*, 113 COLUM. L. REV. 1389, 1455 (2013), quotes Stephen Holmes's use of the phrase. (Sometimes the name "Philip" is substituted.).

regulation favors a current group – often a small one – at the expense of long-term economic growth that benefits the society as a whole. With respect to substantive constitutional law, that is, if we take intertemporal conflicts as the basis for constitutional entrenchment, we run the risk of dramatically narrowing the range of policies on which a current majority can have its way.

The same is true in the domain of structures. As with substantive provisions, outside observers can rather readily identify intertemporal problems associated with a wide range of policies. Why limit the protection against debt-financed policies to the indirect role of central banks, rather than creating an independent institution – that is, something other than the legislature – that is required to adopt only "pay-as-you-go" policies about spending on social welfare programs?[19]

At a lower level of generality, even the core cases of committing environmental and fiscal regulation to independent institutions might cause problems. The intertemporal conflict of interest arises because today's decision-makers have no incentives to respond adequately to the effects of their decisions across time. Put another way, they are indifferent to the intertemporal distributional effects of their decisions. But what of the incentives of the central bank or environmental protection agency? Their professional concerns – what I have labeled expertise – makes them attuned to intertemporal distributional effects. It does not, though, make them sensitive to the *contemporary* distributional effects of their decisions.[20] For example, steps taken to achieve price stability can affect employment rates.[21]

Consider the fairly well-known example of relatively poor nations with exploitable natural resources. An independent environmental protection agency might – indeed, is likely to – overvalue environmental protection relative to the benefits of using the exploitation of natural resources to provide social-welfare payments that reduce poverty. The peace process in Colombia required the government to commit itself to substantial investments in rural areas to promote economic development and reduce the perceived causes of

---

[19] Constitutions that place limits on deficit spending use the constitutional court as the independent institution to enforce a pay-as-you-go policy. *See*, e.g., Constitutional Amendment no. 95 (Dec. 2016) (Brazil); Treaty on Stability, Coordination and Governance in the Economic and Monetary Union, title III (European Union).

[20] This is an important theme one can find in Paul Tucker, Unelected Power: The Quest for Legitimacy in Central Banking and the Regulatory State (Princeton University Press, 2018). *See also* Annelise Riles, Financial Citizenship – Experts, Publics, and the Politics of Central Banking 57–60 (Cornell University Press, 2018) (discussing distributive effects of central bank policies).

[21] For additional discussion, see Chapter 4.

violent rebellion, but the investments were large enough to generate concern about fiscal responsibility; a central bank with the power to constrain these "investments for peace" might make things worse over the long run.[22]

My current thinking is that constitution designers probably cannot reliably set out moderately general rules that sort inter- and intratemporal conflicts of interest into those that functionally justify the creation of a fourth-branch institution and that that should be left to ordinary politics. As we will see, the constitutional court is likely to take on (or be given) the task of reviewing decisions by ordinary legislatures and the other fourth-branch institutions. Its standard of review should take into account the possibilities (a) that the ordinary legislature's action in an area where it can discern potential conflicts of interest, whether inter- or intratemporal, might be overly affected by such conflicts, and (b) that the fourth-branch institution's action might be overly responsive to potential conflicts of interest.

There is a final large topic to deal with. Kelsen's argument led to the creation of constitutional courts. Why are other fourth-branch institutions needed? Again, as we will see in Chapter 4, many constitutions expressly assign responsibility for supervising elections to the constitutional court and implicitly assign anti-corruption responsibility to that court (usually through its power to supervise ordinary criminal investigations).[23] Sometimes constitution designers make that choice because of concern that the nation lacks enough trained professionals with sufficient stature to staff more than one guardian institution. Sometimes, though, the choice appears to be driven by design concerns rather than personnel ones.

The functional logic underlying the fourth branch does suggest reasons for creating several fourth-branch institutions. For, in addition to concerns about conflicts and convergences of interest, constitution designers need to attend to questions of expertise. Some fourth-branch institutions might require forms of expertise not readily available to the constitutional court, and some fourth-branch tasks might place undesirable burdens on that court.

The latter concern is most obvious in connection with using the constitutional court to supervise elections by determining who qualifies for the

---

[22] For a discussion of "peace investments" called for by the agreement, see Francisco Serrano, "The Economics of the Colombia-FARC Peace Accord," FOREIGN AFFAIRS, Aug. 30, 2017, https://www.foreignaffairs.com/articles/americas/2017-08-30/economics-colombia-farc-peace-accord, archived at https://perma.cc/U266-ZFAJ.

[23] The Brazilian Constitution requires that the constitutional court conduct the trials of legislators accused of crime, including corruption. Constitution of Brazil, art. 53. With about one-third of the legislature facing such charges, this provision has effectively paralyzed anti-corruption inquiries into criminality by sitting legislators.

ballot, counting votes, and the like – a subset of what Ran Hirschl calls "megapolitics."[24] As we saw in Chapter 2, the core of the constitutional court's work requires that it navigate through domains that combine law and high politics. In doing so, the constitutional courts always run the risk of coming to be seen as directly implicated in party politics. Supervision of elections exacerbates that risk: supporters of a major presidential candidate who is plausibly subject to disqualification under the constitution (but who has plausible arguments against disqualification) and is in fact disqualified by the constitutional court might well see the court's decision as party-political.[25] Similarly with excluding parties from the ballot and with drawing constituency boundaries.[26]

There are other risks associated with making megapolitical decisions. They might induce an overly strategic cast of mind in the judges, which might affect them even in their core work: no matter how hard they try, judges might find it quite difficult to exclude from their thinking the worry (or hope) that interpreting the constitution to require a major candidate's disqualification will have significant political effects.[27] Or, in the other direction, the judges might be *overly* legalistic, discounting political consequences too much.[28]

---

[24] Ran Hirschl, *The Judicialization of Mega-Politics and the Rise of Political Courts*, 11 ANN. REV. POLITICAL SCI. 93 (2008). Hirschl uses the term to encompass judicial consideration of questions going to fundamental matters of national identity as well.

[25] For an example from Brazil, see Chapter 6 (on the legal basis for disqualifying Lula from the 2018 presidential election).

[26] I emphasize that these are *risks*, and that the risks are not always realized. For a discussion of several instances where African high courts canceled or were thought likely to intervene in presidential elections, in which backlash sometimes occurred and sometimes did not, see James T. Gathii & Olabisi D. Akinkugbe, "Judicial Nullification of Presidential Elections in Africa: Peter Mutharika v Lazarus Chakera and Saulos Chilima in Context," July 29, 2020, https://papers.ssrn.com/sol3/papers.cfm?abstract_id=3642709, archived at https://perma.cc/ E2N5-RV8G.

[27] Compare here the suggestion that the constitutional courts in Israel and Germany have been careful to exclude from the ballot only parties with quite small followings, and that the German constitutional court's most recent decisions on these questions explicitly attend to the political significance of excluding a party that has significant support. For citations, see Chapter 4, at note 61.

[28] A detail from the Brazilian case study is instructive here. There has been significant concern in Brazil about the difficulties of administering a constitutional system without a serious doctrine of precedent. In the decision that had the effect of disqualifying Lula from the ballot, the deciding vote was cast by a judge who predicated her position on the binding role of precedent. In other circumstances, that might have been a useful incremental move toward developing a doctrine of precedent. In the circumstances, though, the judge's action seems at best overly legalistic (and, of course, at worst driven by politics). For details, see Chapter 6.

These effects might be especially troubling if they have the effect of redu-cing support for the constitutional court when it seeks to guard the consti-tution against the effects of party politics on constitutional structures and individual rights. An anti-corruption investigation in Ukraine in 2020 is sug-gestive of the problem, though, according to the account on which I draw, the constitutional court was already damaged when it intervened.[29] Corruption in Ukraine has been a central political issue for several years, to the point where it became a focus of contention in the 2020 U.S. presidential campaign. Anti-corruption prosecutors have been accused of corruption themselves, and have retaliated by investigating their accusers. In 2014, a comprehensive anti-corruption law was enacted. Among other things, it made it a criminal offense for public officials to knowingly provide false information on their annual income statements (or to fail to provide such statements). Judges were among those required to file those statements.

The constitutional court in 2020 held that applying criminal sanctions to judges who violated the disclosure requirements violated the principle of judicial independence, which required supervision of judges *by* judges, and was disproportionate in any event because the anti-corruption goals could be achieved equally well by administrative sanctions. In response, the nation's president proposed a law that would remove all the justices from the court, and – pending that law's enactment – publicly called on them to resign. I draw no strong conclusions from this truncated presentation but use it simply to illustrate a possibility – in this case, perhaps not troubling given the court's already low standing (apparently), but perhaps troubling in other cases.

Other concerns arise in connection with other fourth-branch tasks. Consider first anti-corruption investigations. Auditors and specialized prosecu-tors might be able to use "big data mining" techniques to focus in on suspicious transactions or contracts in ways that courts would find difficult to implement. Often investigations into possibly corrupt activities require tracing payments from one source to one recipient, then finding out that they were passed on to a corrupt official. Forensic auditors are trained to figure out how people conceal financial misconduct, constitutional lawyers not so much. A provision in the Constitution of Ecuador is instructive here. It authorizes the comptroller general, a financial expert, to demand information from third parties where there is evidence that a public official has engaged in

---

[29] My source is Andrii Nekoliak, "The Decision of Ukraine's Constitutional Court on the Anti-Corruption Reform," Verfassungsblog, Dec. 5, 2020, https://verfassungsblog.de/a-damaged-court-causing-a-constitutional-crisis/, archived at https://perma.cc/SFP7-MJVC. The source is openly partisan, and I have taken that into account in my use of the case.

"cover ups or the use of fronts."[30] Judges could do so as well, but their ability to detect a "cover up" or the use of a "front" might well be less than that of a forensic auditor.

Some constitutions entrench anti-discrimination agencies as fourth-branch institutions. We know, of course, that courts routinely deal with anti-discrimination law. Why then have a fourth-branch institution as well? First, constitutions often assign a wide range of investigatory and public-education roles to the anti-discrimination agency.[31] These are well outside the ordinary work of constitutional courts. More interesting is the possibility that courts and anti-discrimination agencies will develop different understandings of what constitutes discriminatory action. There seems to be a tendency among courts around the world to define discrimination in terms of what specialists in the field call "disparate treatment," with "disparate impact" law a distinct second choice.[32] That tendency might flow from a legalistic cast of mind associated with lawyers who deal with questions of individual fault across a wide range of their work (criminal law most notably, of course, but also contract, tort, and associated bodies of law). Anti-discrimination agencies, in contrast, might find it easier to define discrimination with reference to disparate impact and by paying attention to the ways in which organizations work independent of the intentions of those who staff them.[33]

"Carolene Products" accounts of constitutional review are generally taken to explain why the political branches confront problems of conflict and convergence of interest and therefore why constitutional courts should intervene.[34] These additional considerations about expertise count in favor of supplementing a Carolene Products–focused constitutional court with a specialized human rights institution. Mario Gomez emphasizes the "institutional flexibility" of human rights agencies. He offers brief case studies illustrating

---

[30] Constitution of Ecuador, art. 231.

[31] See Chapter 5.

[32] Hugh Collins and Tarunabh Khaitan capture the reluctance to disparate-impact doctrine in asking, "[H]ow can a rule or practice that treats people equally be regarded as an instance of discrimination or unequal treatment?" Hugh Colins and Tarunabh Khaitan, "Indirect Discrimination Law: Controversies and Critical Questions," in FOUNDATIONS OF INDIRECT DISCRIMINATION LAW (Hugh Collins & Tarunabh Khaitan eds., Hart Publishing, 2018), at 4.

[33] In the United States, the disparate-impact approach was initially adopted (with respect to employment) by the Equal Employment Opportunities Commission, then endorsed by the U.S. Supreme Court. For a description, see ROBERT BELTON & STEPHEN L. WASBY, THE CRUSADE FOR EQUALITY IN THE WORKPLACE: THE GRIGGS V. DUKE POWER STORY (University Press of Kansas, 2019).

[34] For a more skeptical view about the scope of Carolene-Products accounts, see MARK TUSHNET, RED, WHITE, AND BLUE: A CRITICAL ANALYSIS OF CONSTITUTIONAL LAW (Harvard University Press, 1988), at ch. 2.

these commissions' ability to hold hearings based upon complaints, engage in independent research resulting in reports, and hold "public inquiries" on matters the commissions themselves identify as important.[35]

My judgment, though, is that the case for including human-rights agencies in the fourth branch is rather weak. Courts that have internalized the model of U.S. public law litigation or South Asian public interest litigation can do some of the work the commissions do, and there are no obvious systematic reasons to think that commissions subject to political control – pressures from the government in one direction, pressures from the opposition and civil society in another – could not perform the public education and monitoring functions constitutionally entrenched commissions do. The latter assertion of course has to qualified where there is a dominant party and a weak opposition; but in such cases, the commission itself is likely to come under the dominant party's control no matter what its constitutional status.[36]

We should not place too much weight on the proposition that constitutional courts cannot call upon expertise when it is required. Public-law litigation in the United States and public interest litigation in India have shown that courts have the capacity to do many things that fall outside what Lon Fuller called "the forms and limits of adjudication."[37] They can appoint experts to provide advice,[38] and special hearing officers to obtain case-focused information, for example. So, concerns about expertise need not preclude assigning fourth-branch tasks to the constitutional court – with one important caveat: the U.S. and Indian legal cultures turned out to be reasonably receptive to augmenting the courts with ad hoc "institutions" to provide the courts

---

[35] Mario Gomez, "Advancing Economic and Social Rights through National Human Rights Institutions," in RESEARCH HANDBOOK ON ECONOMIC, SOCIAL, AND CULTURAL RIGHTS AS HUMAN RIGHTS 327, 335–43 (Jackie Dugard et al. eds., Edward Elgar Publishing, 2020).

[36] "Likely," not "inevitably." For a case study of how an actor with constitutional status can function effectively in a dominant-party nation, see Chapter 6 (on the South African Public Protector). I believe that right-to-information commissions can be analyzed in roughly similar terms. In some configurations of party power, the political branches may have incentives to conceal information to a degree that impedes good governance without advancing other valuable goals. Yet, there appear to be no special concerns requiring expertise unavailable to the courts that counsel in favor including right-to-information commissions in the fourth branch. For an optimistic view of the contribution that such commissions can make to good governance, see Mario Gomez, *The Right to Information and Transformative Development Outcomes*, 12 L. & DEVELOPMENT 837 (2019).

[37] *See* Lon L. Fuller, *The Forms and Limits of Adjudication*, 92 HARV. L. REV. 353 (1978); Abram Chayes, *The Role of the Judge in Public Law Litigation*, 89 HARV. L. REV. 1281 (1976).

[38] This appears to be the main function of the "public hearings" conducted by the Brazilian constitutional court. For an overview of these hearings, see "Public Hearings of the Federal Supreme Court (Brazil)," Participedia, https://participedia.net/method/4395, archived at https://perma.cc/ED4C-X6PV.

with expertise; other legal systems might be much more resistant to doing so. In such cultures, constitutional courts may find themselves authorized to deal with problems as to which they lack sufficient expertise and yet reluctant to augment their capacity. So in such cultures, creating additional fourth-branch institutions might be particularly desirable.

The conclusion here is that constitution designers need not create a fourth branch composed of several institutions. In some settings, authorizing the constitutional court to perform all the tasks identified by the logic of conflicts of interest might be sufficient, even as qualified. In other settings, though, creating several fourth-branch institutions might well be the more sensible choice.[39]

Tarun Khaitan offers a conceptual analysis of the idea of constitutional branches that serves as a useful summary of the characteristics of IPDs understood as a fourth branch.[40] They have the function of guarding the constitution (Khaitan refers to them as the "guarantor branch"). In contrast to the other three branches, which are generalists, fourth-branch institutions are specialists. Unlike administrative agencies whose jurisdiction is defined in somewhat specific terms, though, fourth-branch institutions are charged with enforcing relatively general principles. And, finally, fourth-branch institutions are not supposed to make all-things-considered judgments or narrowly legal ones; rather, they are to make decisions with reference to the specialized norms that define each one. Though I believe that Khaitan is mistaken to formulate these as *conceptual* criteria for identifying fourth-branch institutions, the descriptions he offers captures a great deal about the function and operation of fourth-branch institutions.

What, finally, is the relation between the constitutional court and other fourth-branch institutions? In principle, constitution designers could treat all fourth-branch institutions on the same plane – independent of all the others. Specifically, the constitutional court could not review decisions by the anti-corruption agency or the electoral court.[41] Michael Pal argues that, just as

---

[39] Fuller argued that disputes that he called "polycentric" were generally unsuitable for ordinary adjudication, and that were courts to attempt to dispose of them they would, as he put it, depart from "the judicial proprieties." Writing in the 1950s, Fuller had what we now can see as an essentialist view of courts as institutions, but we can also use his terminology to describe the conclusions reached in the text. IPDs are institutions that constitution designers use to off-load some polycentric problems away from the courts, and when courts attempt to deal with such problems, they experience stresses because of features that make the problems polycentric.

[40] Tarun Khaitan, "The Guarantor Branch," draft paper presented at Democratic Constitutions and Electoral Commissions Workshop, University of New South Wales, Dec. 7, 2020.

[41] Brown, *supra* note 7, discusses the position taken by Justice William Gummow of Australia's High Court, that in principle the constitutional court should be charged with protecting

each of the Montesquian branches is subject to some sort of check by another Montesquian branch, so too should fourth-branch institutions be subject to some sort of check.[42] Review by the constitutional court is one possibility, but – as with the other branches – so are Madisonian checks.

In practice, review by the constitutional court is quite likely to occur, and the real questions will be about the scope of that review. People who lose in the electoral court will seek review by the constitutional court, and that court's independence and stature will almost certainly induce its judges to take up such cases.[43]

Review by the constitutional court can take the usual two forms, procedural and substantive. The constitutional court will ask whether the procedures used in the corruption investigation or in resolving factual disputes in election controversies satisfied basic constitutional principles. This seems unexceptionable, but sometimes the fourth-branch institutions will use procedures different from – and seemingly inconsistent with – those required by the constitution in "ordinary" proceedings. Anti-corruption investigators might seize materials that would be protected by privacy guarantees in ordinary criminal cases, for example. Or, as we will see in the case study of Brazil in Chapter 6, the investigators might innovate in the use of coercive pretrial detention. The investigators might think, and sometimes correctly, that the

---

integrity. Brown disagrees, *see id.* at 317, but perhaps Justice Gummow is better understood as insisting that, as Brown puts it, the constitutional courts is "the *ultimate* overseer" of integrity (emphasis added), meaning that it will supervise the work of integrity institutions according to some standard of review.

[42] Pal's work is forthcoming.

[43] Constitutional courts have almost always won the well-known "battle of the courts" between them and apex ordinary courts, which provides an analogy. A typical version of the battle is this: The constitutional court holds that a statute administered by the ordinary courts would be unconstitutional were it interpreted as the apex court interpreted it, and therefore holds that the statute should be interpreted different. The apex court objects, observing correctly that the constitutional court has jurisdiction only over constitutional matters and has no authority to interpret statutes. In the end, constitutional courts figure out ways to ensure that their interpretations prevail. For an overview of the issues, see Lech Garlicki, *Constitutional Courts versus Supreme Courts*, 5 Int'l J. Const. L. 44 (2007). The only prominent exception appears to be an unusual decision by the Czech constitutional court, where that court adopted an interpretation inconsistent with European Union law (holding ultra vires the relevant EU law), and the apex court continued to insist on adhering to the EU interpretation. The story wandered on for many years until the Constitutional Court lost enthusiasm for the conflict, and the precise question at issue (discrimination against citizens of Slovakia in administering the Czech pension system) was mooted by time and an apparent though undisclosed settlement. For a description, see Zdenek Kühn, *Ultra Vires Review and the Demise of Constitutional Pluralism: The Czecho-Slovak Pension Saga, and the Dangers of State Courts' Defiance of EU Law*, 23 Maastricht J. Eur. & Comp. L. 185 (2016).

nature of their task requires these procedural innovations. A constitutional court's procedural review might struggle with such innovations: Should they assess them as if they occurred in ordinary criminal investigations – and perhaps hold them unconstitutional? Will they be able to uphold the techniques with respect to a limited domain of corruption investigations without enabling prosecutors to use them in ordinary cases?

The case of substantive review is similar, though the risk of improper extension to other domains may be small. As we will see, one risk associated with fourth-branch institutions is that those who staff them may take their missions "too seriously."[44] Charged with rooting out corruption, for example, investigators might escalate ordinary patronage into corruption. Or, as in Brazil, prosecutors will seek expansive interpretations of the criminal law imposing liability on superior officials for wrongdoing committed by their subordinates. Or, as I've suggested, the anti-discrimination agency will use a disparate-impact theory to impose liability more broadly than the constitutional court would on its own. Yet, as with procedural innovations, substantive innovations like these might be necessary if the fourth-branch institution is to perform is function effectively.

Conflicts between constitutional courts and fourth-branch institutions might arise when the institutions rely upon expertise that the courts lack and the courts fail to grasp the significance of their relative disadvantage. Simon Butt and Fritz Siregar describe several Indonesian decisions that "create[d] significant practical difficulties" for the nation's electoral commission. The court, for example, invalidated a requirement developed by the electoral commission that only those who had previously registered to vote could cast their ballots, and prescribed guidelines for ensuring that those who voted were eligible to do so – guidelines that, when complied with, would slow down the voting process in a nation where citizens regularly complained about how long they had to wait on line before they could vote.[45]

Considerations like those enumerated here suggest what Richard Stacey and Victoria Miyandazi describe as an "administrative law" model for review by the constitutional court.[46] Where fourth-branch institutions rely upon their

---

[44] For a discussion of the issue of "mission creep" in the context of South Africa's Public Protector, see Stu Woolman, *A Politics of Accountability: How South Africa's Judicial Recognition of the Binding Legal Effect of the Public Protector's Recommendations Had a Catalysing Effect That Brought Down a President*, 8 CONST'L CT. REV. 155, 168–69 (2016).

[45] Simon Butt & Fritz Siregar, "Indonesia," draft paper presented at Democratic Constitutions and Electoral Commissions Workshop, University of New South Wales, Dec. 7, 2020.

[46] Richard Stacey & Victoria Miyandazi, "The Regulative and Constitutive Components of Protecting a Democracy: Kenya's Electoral Commission and the Courts in the 2010s," draft

distinctive expertise (in making what Stacey and Miyandazi call "regulative" decisions), their decisions should receive deferential review.

Stacey and Miyandazi suggest, though, a different standard of review where the fourth-branch institutions engage in what they call a constitutive function. By that term, they refer to the core aspects of democracy the institutions are charged with protecting: for electoral commissions, the very idea of free and fair elections; for human rights agencies, the very idea of equality. Stacey and Miyandazi argue that these actions make the democracy what it is – constitute it – and thereby should be treated as constitutional courts treat other aspects of fundamental national identity: the constitutional court should not hesitate to replace the fourth-branch institution's understanding of these constitutive matters with its own understanding (plenary review, in short).

The category of "constitutive" decisions is, in my view, more porous than Stacey and Miyandazi suggest. What an "election" is, for example, is a matter of social no less than legal construction, as the case studies in Chapter 7 show. Similarly with corruption and equality. To adapt a term from Jürgen Habermas, social practices, decisions by fourth-branch institutions, and decisions by constitutional courts seem co-constitutive of the terms to which Stacey and Miyandazi refer. And, as with the idea of co-constitution in Habermas's original version, so here: it appears to counsel in favor of a rather more fluid relation between the fourth-branch institutions and the constitutional court than is captured by the idea of plenary review.

How constitutional courts respond to procedural and substantive innovations is of course an empirical question, and I know of no systematic studies on it. My intuition is that the best accounts of the relation between constitutional courts and other fourth-branch institutions will be driven largely by how each institution is located within the nation's party-political system, by the degree to which the constitutional court and the other institutions are more or less independent of the governing coalition in place when the questions arise, and by the constitutional court's members' confidence – warranted or not – in their ability to determine what is most likely to protect constitutional democracy.

Here and in Chapter 2, I have laid out the theoretical and functional logics of fourth-branch institutions. Those logics can help us understand what the institutions might do if they function well. But the logics have only a loose relation to both the origins and the actual performance of their functions.

paper presented at Democratic Constitutions and Electoral Commissions Workshop, University of New South Wales, Dec. 7, 2020.

Consider origins first: Heinz Klug has described how the Chapter Nine institutions came to be included in the South African Constitution.[47] According to Klug, during the negotiations over the transition to democracy, several parties proposed establishing an ombuds office, already a well-established institution in many constitutions. There were concerns as well about the fairness of the first elections, which were going to be conducted by the apartheid-favoring government in place. Negotiators for the African National Congress proposed, and the government accepted, that three independent commissions be established to ensure that the elections would be free and fair: an electoral commission, an "independent media commission," and an independent Broadcasting Authority. These institutions in turn became the models for the Chapter Nine institutions. Notably, though, of the three, only the Electoral Commission survived into the final constitution, along with the Public Protector/ombuds office. Chapter Nine was thus shaped by a combination of functional logic – the concern for election fairness – with the contingencies of the negotiating process.

And, with respect to performance: How well (if at all) will the real-world institutions that constitution makers put in place to deal with the problems they identify perform the posited functions is a separate matter? As the case studies presented in Chapters 6 and 7 show, and as a skeptical view of constitutional design would suggest quite generally, design and performance may be quite loosely correlated, or even unrelated. As I will argue, perhaps the best we can do is to build redundancy into the overall system, hoping that often enough some institution will step up and do what is needed in the circumstances at hand – even if no single institution can reliably do what is needed in all relevant circumstances.[48]

---

[47] Heinz Klug, *Transformative Constitutions and the Role of Integrity Institutions in Tempering Power: The Case of Resistance to State Capture in Post-Apartheid South Africa*, 67 Buff. L. Rev. 701 (2019).

[48] For a related observation, see Tom Ginsburg & Aziz Z. Huq, How to Save a Constitutional Democracy 196 (University of Chicago Press, 2019) ("A broad set of accountability institutions means that a putative autocrat must capture more of them in order to achieve total control over a political system .... Simple arithmetic implies that multiple and overlapping accountability institutions are more difficult for a backsliding leader or party to capture tha[n] one or two such bodies.") Note that Ginsburg and Huq limit their attention to situations of potential autocratic takeover rather than considering the accountability problem more generally, and that they focus on takeover of institutions rather than their mere ineffectiveness even when not captured. In addition, redundancy creates the possibility of jurisdictional conflicts that might produce gridlock and ineffectiveness.

4

Design Issues in General

Constitution designers can identify from local and worldwide experience some general threats to constitutional democracy: conflicts over election outcomes, for example, or corruption at high and low levels.[1] Their local knowledge can give them some sense of how important each type of threat might be for the systems they are designing. Variations in the types and severity of threats mean that designers must make *choices*: there is no one-size-fits-all "fourth branch" or any of its components. (That point should be obvious when we note the rather wide range of choices made in designing constitutional courts.)

Consider, for example, contests over election outcomes. We might expect them to be frequent in societies with persistent socio-economic-ethnic-political divisions, rare in more homogeneous societies. System designers might conclude that a permanent election court is appropriate in the first type of society, and that a more ad hoc system for resolving election contests appropriate for the second.

This chapter canvases some of the design choices available for fourth-branch institutions.[2] I assume that the choices are made at the constitutional level, though one available choice is to leave to the legislature some matters

---

[1] Taking a forward-looking perspective, I frame my discussion in terms of constitution design. The considerations I identify, though, can be used to analyze constitutional systems in place. For that reason, it is appropriate to draw illustrations on occasion from design choices already made.

[2] Michael Pal, in a forthcoming work, describes a design principle I don't take up here. Focusing on election commissions in federal systems, Pal argues that a single national commission "is appealing where the likelihood of capture of a sub-national election commission or abuse on minority political rights at the sub-national level is deemed a greater threat than the capture of a single, national election commission." This principle is consistent with those developed in this chapter.

that could be dealt with in the constitution.[3] The inquiry is largely normative, aimed at identifying principles of "good" design.

Yet, as already suggested, design choices are necessarily made behind a veil that is not entirely opaque: system designers have some sense, sometimes rough and sometimes more precise, about what politics will look like – at least for a while – after the constitution comes into effect. They will know, or have a good sense, that the first president will be the leader of the national liberation struggle (George Washington and Nelson Mandela as positive examples, many other African leaders as negative ones), or that the party system will have a dominant party (Singapore, South Africa, and India) or a well-organized multiparty system (Germany after 1945, the Icelandic revision process in the 2010s).

The partially opaque, partially transparent veil of ignorance has additional effects. Constitution designers will know precisely what problems have been thrown up by the existing constitutional provisions, and they will direct their attention to addressing them but at the cost of downplaying problems that they can imagine occurring, for example, because they have recently arisen in other seemingly similar nations. And, of course the designers' time horizons will matter: they will make one set of choices if all they care about is getting over the hump of an ongoing or recent crisis, another set if they expect their choices to affect policy over the next few decades, and yet another set if they imagine (unrealistically) that they are making choices that will bind the nation into the remote futures.

Further, politics affects *how* designs are actually implemented. This implies that real historical examples do not show how something like a "logic" of institutional design works itself out. These examples may be quite helpful in illustrating design possibilities, but they should always be understood as "infected" by their political surroundings.

4.1 A NOTE ON STATUTORY VERSIONS OF FOURTH-BRANCH INSTITUTIONS

Anti-corruption investigators can be ordinary prosecutors who have corruption investigations within their regular jurisdiction, or prosecutors within the

---

[3] I do not discuss except in this footnote the possibility that constitutions could require that some fourth-branch institutions be created by so-called organic laws, that is, by laws enacted according to some special procedure (typically a requirement of a majority of the body as a whole rather than a majority of a quorum, or some supermajority requirement), while allowing others to be created by ordinary laws.

ministry of justice specially charged with anti-corruption.[4] Auditing agencies can be formally located within the executive or legislative branches. Similarly with other institutions charged with protecting constitutional democracy: statutes can place them within one of the three Montesquieian branches. Why? And what are the consequences of doing so?

Sometimes decisions to create statutory versions of fourth-branch institutions occur because the perceived need for them arises after a classic Montesquieian constitution has been adopted, and the constitution is difficult to amend. So, for example, the U.S. Congress has created inspectors general for executive branch agencies, whose charge includes identifying and publicizing mismanagement, waste, fraud, and abuse. Corruption falls within these broad categories. The U.S. Government Accountability Office is an audit bureau, statutorily defined as part of the legislative branch. The structural and functional logics described in Chapters 2 and 3 explain why such institutions are created, and the rigidity of the U.S. Constitution explains why they are statutory rather than constitutional.

The account of fourth-branch institutions given in Chapters 2 and 3 suggests that the effectiveness of statutory institutions might be limited by the problems of conflicts and convergence of interest that make such institutions necessary in a party-political world. The statutes creating the agencies *can* provide guarantees of tenure that conduce to independence. But, again for the very reasons that such institutions are needed, political actors have incentives to limit those guarantees in practice. Inspectors general are typically removable by the president, for example, and there is a substantial constitutional argument for the proposition that the president's discretion to remove an inspector general she or he regards as overly aggressive cannot be limited. And even the possibility of removal might induce some IGs to see themselves as primarily employees of the president.[5] Similarly, heads of the Government Accountability Office must retain the confidence of legislators – and when control of Congress changes so can the person heading the GAO.

Put in general terms: statutory design choices occur without any veil of ignorance, even a somewhat opaque one. Legislative majorities in parliamentary systems and parties that control both the legislature and the executive in

---

[4] For a discussion of how the South African Constitutional Court converted the latter kind of investigator into one with constitutional status, see Chapter 6.

[5] Some IGs are nominated by the president and confirmed by the Senate, others are named by the heads of the agencies over which they have jurisdiction.

separation-of-powers systems can modify an IPD's structure and mandate to advance immediate partisan goals.[6]

There is, though, one important qualification. Sometimes legislators may believe that the statutory institutions they are creating will have a "quasi-constitutional" status. They expect the institutions to persist over a reasonably long period, and the extended period leads to some degree of uncertainty about the political context within which the institutions will operate. And, in an important addition, they believe that as a practical political matter it will be difficult for future legislatures to change the fundamental structures of these statutory institutions.[7]

We should acknowledge, though, that this partial veil of ignorance might not be enough to insulate the institutions from significant change in their actual operation as political conditions change. Politicians might be able to figure out ways in which what they can fairly present as mere "tinkering" with design details can have significant effects on the statutory institutions' ability to perform well. This observation too should be qualified: the same can be true of constitutionally entrenched institutions whose *general* contours are specified in the constitution with mere details to be left to legislation.

One constraint on political control of statutory fourth-branch institutions rests on two kinds of norms. First, if the public believes that these institutions should be independent of political control, political actors may incur political costs if they attempt to exercise control. Put another way, even statutory fourth-branch institutions might play something like a Madisonian role. But, of course, their ability to do so rests upon public perceptions of independence – and, at least at the formal constitutional level, statutory institutions cannot have the same degree of independence that the classic branches have. Statutory guarantees of independence, for example, can be repealed or modified by ordinary legislation. And, as just noted, politicians may be able to come up with ways of tinkering with design that the public won't understand to be as significant as they actually are, thereby reducing the political costs of interfering with the institutions.

---

[6] Michael Pal offers an instructive short case study of the statutory Canadian electoral management system, illustrating this sort of partisan modification. Michael Pal, *Electoral Management Bodies as a Fourth Branch of Government*, 21 REV. CONST. STUD. 85, 90–93 (2016).

[7] The account in the text is a version of "insurance" accounts of creating constitutional courts, modified to deal with the fact that statutory IPDs can be modified by ordinary legislation when one party replaces another as the majority in the legislature. For a discussion of insurance accounts, see Chapter 2.

The second kind of norm is internal to the fourth-branch institutions: the staffs of those institutions might have commitments to their professions – criminal prosecution, accounting, and the like – that offset, at least to some degree, the effects of political control, which is by definition not within the proper scope of the staffs' activities as professionals.[8]

From the perspective of constitutional design, statutory fourth-branch institutions are probably best understood as a second-best solution to the problems of conflicts and convergences of interests. Such a solution might be appropriate when, at the constitution-framing stage, designers are uncertain about the likely prevalence of one or another of the problems that arise from conflicts and convergences of interests. Statutory fourth-branch institutions might also be necessary when the constitution itself cannot easily accommodate constitutionally grounded fourth-branch institutions.

4.2 AD HOC, INCIDENTAL, AND PERMANENT INSTITUTIONS

I begin with three examples of different ways of resolving election disputes.

(1) The U.S. presidential election of 1876 resulted in a near tie under the counting rules.[9] The outcome depended on the resolution of claims about election fraud in three states. Congress created a special statutory commission to investigate the facts and draw conclusions. The commission had fifteen members, five senators, five members of the House of Representatives, and five Supreme Court justices. The Republican-controlled Senate named three Republican senators and two Democrats; the Democratic-controlled House reciprocated, naming three Democrats and two Republicans. Four of the Supreme Court justices were understood to be partisans, two Democrats and two Republicans. David Davis, chosen by the other justices, was thought to be politically independent and it was widely expected that he would cast the deciding vote.

Democrats in Davis's home state of Illinois came up with a strategy that they thought would incline him to resolve the voting disputes for Democratic presidential candidate Samuel Tilden: they named him to the Senate, expecting that he would take the position after completing his service on the commission. Davis surprised the Democrats by resigning from the commission upon accepting the appointment. The remaining

---

[8]   I discuss issues associated with professional norms in more detail in Chapters 6 and 7.

[9]   For a study of the events, see MICHAEL HOLT, BY ONE VOTE: THE DISPUTED PRESIDENTIAL ELECTION OF 1876 (University Press of Kansas, 2008), at 210–24.

justices had to choose a replacement, with no clear independents available. They did what they could by selecting Joseph Bradley, a Republican who Democrats hoped (without much basis) would be nonpartisan. Predictably, the Commission awarded all the disputed votes to Republican Rutherford B. Hayes, with Bradley casting the deciding vote.

(2) When the 2000 U.S. presidential election generated a similar controversy about how ballots should be counted, the parties turned to the Supreme Court. By a vote of five-to-four, tracking assumed partisan inclinations, the Court in effect awarded the contested ballots to George W. Bush. The Court's decision generated sharp partisan division, with critics emphasizing how innovative the Court's constitutional analysis was, and how its legal conclusion was undermined by the Court's emphasis that the principle it articulated arose from, and was limited to, the peculiar set of unlikely to be repeated facts of the case before it.[10]

(3) Mexico has a Federal Electoral Tribunal (TRIFE), located within the judicial branch, with seven judges nominated by the Supreme Court and confirmed by the upper legislative house by a two-thirds majority. For decades before 2000, the Party of the Institutionalized Revolution (PRI) dominated Mexican politics. In July 2000, that dominance ended with the election of Vicente Fox of the opposition Alliance for Change party (PAN) as president. In September, there was an election to choose the governor of the state of Jalisco. Initially, the PRI candidate had a narrow lead over the candidate of the left-wing Democratic Revolutionary Party (PRD). The PRD brought a challenge to the election that ended up in the Electoral Tribunal, which voided the election on the ground that widespread fraud had occurred. TRIFE reached the same result in the next few years in connection with elections for governor in Yucatán and Colima.[11]

---

[10] *Bush v. Gore*, 531 U.S. 98 (2000).

[11] For a discussion, see José María Serna de la Garza, The Constitution of Mexico: A Contextual Analysis (Hart Publishing, 2013), at 28–30 (describing TRIFE), 33–34 (describing the cases of the early 2000s); Kevin Sullivan, "Fraud Is Alleged in Tabasco Election: PRI Candidate Holds Slim Lead for Governor," *Washington Post*, Oct. 17, 2000, p. A16. A constitutional amendment adopted in 2007 limited the grounds for invalidating an election to specific constitutional violations, eliminating the basis upon which TRIFE had acted. TRIFE continued to invalidate elections by finding that such specific violations had occurred. Serna de la Garza, at 34. Todd A. Eisenstadt, Courting Democracy in Mexico: Party Strategies and Electoral Institutions (Cambridge University Press, 2003), at ch. 3, describes how Mexico's electoral courts gained legitimacy with opposition parties during the period of PRI dominance.

These examples illustrate three design choices, which I call *ad hoc, incidental* (to the ordinary work of existing institutions), and *permanent*. Each choice has characteristic advantages and disadvantages.[12]

4.2.1 Ad hoc Institutions

Suppose one thinks that election contests or high-level corruption or any other threats to constitutional democracy are probably going to be rare. Creating a permanent institution to deal with these occasional problems would be wasteful and perhaps counterproductive (the latter because the staff of the permanent institution would have incentives to go out and find problems – to justify their salaries – even when none really existed). Authorizing the legislature or executive to create ad hoc institutions to deal with problems when they arise – and possibly defining in the constitution the requirements for staffing the institution and its guarantees of independence once created – is an attractive option.[13]

The U.S. Electoral Commission for the 1876 election shows us the downside of ad hoc institutions. Every aspect of the Commission's design and, most important, its membership was dictated by the immediate political circumstances. By definition, ad hoc institutions are created after the fact, that is, after a problem has emerged. The veil of ignorance that is placed over decisions made at the constitution-drafting stage is removed. Further, the institution is designed to have a short lifetime, going out of existence as soon as it resolves the immediate controversy. The uncertainty introduced by a long time-horizon is absent.

Political actors can assess such matters as the ad hoc institution's terms of reference or jurisdiction and the appointment of the institution's head and staff with some awareness of the likely political consequences of their decisions. For an ad hoc investigation of corruption, for example, a narrow

---

[12] For a related taxonomy, see Adrian Vermeule, *Intermittent Institutions*, 10 PHIL., POL. & ECON. 420 (2011). For Vermeule, intermittent institutions "have a discontinuous existence" and come in two types, "periodic," which come into existence at regular intervals, do their work, and then disappear, and "episodic," which come into existence when some triggering condition is satisfied. (Vermeule notes that these distinctions are not hard-edged.) Most ad hoc fourth-branch institutions appear to be episodic.

[13] As discussed in Section 4.5, Commonwealth nations inheriting Montesquiean constitutions have used ad hoc commissions of inquiry to deal with corruption, police misconduct (which might otherwise fall within the jurisdiction of an ombuds office), and other matters.

definition of the institution's jurisdiction can predictably limit the exposure political actors have to prosecution.[14]

Or consider an institution with characteristics defined in the constitution that comes into existence when triggering conditions obtain. Strategic political calculations can affect the determination *that* those conditions are satisfied.[15] Examples are simultaneously too easy and too difficult to come by, for they include every instance in which political leaders decide that the political pressures they face from reaction to some scandal – corruption, law enforcement, or otherwise – are insufficient to force them to pull the trigger (or, perhaps more accurately, when they calculate that the balance of political costs and benefits favors using standard procedures in place over using the ad hoc institution).[16] Factors in this calculation include the possibility that the standard procedures will indeed lead to enforcement of sanctions against some wrongdoers (those "thrown under the bus," in pejorative terms) but not against others (the government's political friends), and the possibility that the ad hoc institution might impose sanctions more broadly (sometimes appropriately, and sometimes – both from the government's point of view and on the merits – inappropriately).

When a constitution constrains commissions of inquiry, the constraints can provide opportunities for political calculations in front of the veil. Croatia offers an interesting example. In 2020, a controversy erupted implicating high political officials in corruption and apparent sexual and other personal improprieties. The opposition proposed a wide-ranging commission of inquiry. The background law allowed commissions of inquiry, but barred them from addressing matters subject to pending criminal investigations. Likely to be

---

[14] An example: The letter appointing Robert Mueller as "Special Counsel" to the Trump campaign's contacts with Russia directed him to investigate: "[A]ny links and/or coordination between the Russian government and individuals associated with the campaign of President Donald Trump; and (2) any matters that arose or may arise directly from that investigation." A letter written two months later specified that the scope of the investigation covered specific allegations of criminal activity by Carter Page, Paul Manafort, George Papadopolous, Michael Flynn, and one other as-yet-unidentified individual. A third letter added a number of other individuals to the list.

[15] This means that defining an ad hoc institution's characteristics in a constitution is insufficient to create a full veil of ignorance.

[16] For a recent example, see William Booth & David A. Fahrenthold, "Scottish Lawmakers Decline to Call for Probe of Trump Golf Course Finances," *Washington Post*, Feb. 4, 2021, p. A22 (describing a parliamentary vote against a commission of inquiry after the first minister "said that [the relevant] decisions should be made by law enforcement officials").

damaged by the inquiry, the government insisted on imposing narrow terms of reference on the proposed commission.[17]

The veil of ignorance's absence can also affect the choice of an ad hoc institution's leader. Most crudely, the political actors whose behavior is to be investigated might be in a position to select an investigator they believe likely to be sympathetic to them – in the common phrase, to produce a report whitewashing their actions.

The force of this "veil of ignorance" account should not be exaggerated. Sometimes, perhaps often, constitution drafters have a decent sense of the likely contours of post-constitution politics. As already noted, when the participants in a successful national liberation movement succeed, for example, they are likely to know, with reasonable certainty, how large a margin they will have in the post-liberation legislature and even who the chief executive and leading parliamentarians are going to be. Constitutions drafted by dominant political parties will be shaped by party leaders' expectations about the course of action they expect to take.

The time-horizon here matters. With ad hoc institutions, the time-horizon is quite short – *this* investigation until it ends. Constitution drafting has two time-horizons. The first is the relatively short run: what is likely to happen in the first few years after the constitution goes into effect. The second is longer run: drafters might not be able to anticipate well the contours of politics in one or two decades.[18] The effects of the longer time-horizon can be unclear. Drafters might not expect the constitution they are drafting to persist into the long run, for example.[19] In short, constitution drafting is not always behind a completely opaque veil of ignorance, and some of the considerations that affect choices made in connection with creating ad hoc institutions can affect the very provisions authorizing their creation.

---

[17] The background is described in Zeljko Trkanjec, "Croatia's 'Secret Club' Scandal Exposes Cronyism, Corruption," Euractiv, Sept. 30, 2020, https://www.euractiv.com/section/justice-home-affairs/news/croatias-secret-club-scandal-exposes-cronyism-corruption/, archived at https://perma.cc/VQ3A-M797; Branko Lozančić, "Opposition Demands Founding of Commission of Inquiry with Broad Powers," HRT: The Voice of Croatia, Oct. 6, 2020, https://glashrvatske.hrt.hr/en/news/politics/opposition-demands-founding-of-commission-of-inquiry-with-broad-powers/, archived at https://perma.cc/G99T-YKH8. I thank Matija Milos for these references.

[18] This can be affected by the drafters' age. Sometimes the leaders of national liberation movements are quite young and they can expect to lead the nation until they become elderly. Notably, every South African president since 1994 – a period of more than twenty-five years – participated in the South African liberation struggle.

[19] Their choices about amendment rules might affect their expectations about the constitution's likely life span.

4.2.2 *Incidental Institutions*

Constitutions can assign several functional aspects of the protection of constitutional democracy to one institution. The most common choice is to give the constitutional court jurisdiction over election contests.[20] As noted earlier, the Supreme Federal Court in Brazil has jurisdiction over criminal trials, typically involving corruption, where sitting parliamentarians are defendants. Ombuds offices, which ordinarily have power only to make reports, might be given the power to enter enforceable orders in corruption cases.[21]

The reasons for these choices are ordinarily straightforward, combining concerns about staffing with reliance upon the core institution's prestige and trustworthiness. A nation might have relatively few people who can be trusted to handle fairly the questions associated with protecting democracy, and staffing the constitutional court with them is likely to have high priority. Once they are in place, the court's judges can do the additional work. They already have the kinds of guarantees of independence that, as we will see, are desirable for IPDs, and, as noted, they might be the most trustworthy people available.

Here too there are downsides. The additional tasks assigned to the core institution are almost by definition likely to be quite controversial politically. Constitutional courts' core work already implicates them in matters of high politics, and giving them additional work with strong political valences might erode their capacity to make effective their decisions in their core domain: a court that has disqualified a major political candidate from running, for example, might find itself under further attack if it later holds unconstitutional a program supported by that candidate's party.

A second concern is subtler. Recall that Lon Fuller suggested that courts assigned non-judicial tasks (polycentric tasks, in his terms) might adjust their behavior in two ways. They might depart from the judicial proprieties, which in this context is tied to the concern about weakening the court's prestige by

---

[20] Tom Ginsburg & Zachary Elkins, *Ancillary Powers of Constitutional Courts*, 87 TEX. L. REV. 1431 (2008). For an interesting study of how human rights monitoring became an incidental power of the State Comptroller's office in Israel, see Elie P. Mersel, Matan A. Guttman & Alon Rodas, *From State Comptroller to National Human Rights Institution – A Short but Necessary Path*, 48 ISRAEL Y'BOOK ON HUMAN RTS. 161 (2018). These authors use the terms "implied and overt models" to describe what I call an incidental IPD. As the terms indicate, in the overt model the designer expressly authorizes the audit body to do human rights monitoring, while in the implied one the audit body takes on the role on its own.

[21] *See* Chapter 6 for a discussion of a South African example.

forcing it to resolve electoral contests. Second, because the polycentric problem is not amenable to ready solution according to existing legal standards (on
Fuller's account), constitutional courts might transform the problem into a
more legally tractable one. In short, they convert a political problem into a
legal one.

The U.S. Supreme Court's decision in the 2000 election controversy
illustrates this. The dispositive issue at the dispute's final stage was whether
Florida's method of counting contested ballots violated the constitutional
guarantee of equal protection of the laws, meaning in this context that every
voter's ballot would count as much as any other's. The Florida system had
local election officials count the votes initially, with substantial discretion
about how to determine for whom an ambiguous ballot was cast, with subsequent review by the state supreme court under standards that the litigation had
left unclear. The Supreme Court held that this combination of features
denied equal protection. But, aware that the holding was innovative and
relied upon a perhaps unusual combination of facts, the Court's opinion
stated, "Our consideration is limited to the present circumstances, for the
problem of equal protection in election processes generally presents many
complexities."[22] Though unusual, the equal protection holding might be
defensible, but it shows the Court transforming a complex problem into one
that fit, however awkwardly, into an existing doctrinal box. The sentence
specifically raising the possibility that the decision's precedential effect would
be quite limited shows how the case placed pressure on the judicial "propriety" of giving precedential effect to Court holdings.

Striking the right balance among these considerations will of course vary
according to context. As we will see in Chapter 5, the use of the "incidental"
mechanism is widespread with respect to election contests. Only actual
national experience can tell us whether that choice is optimal.

4.2.3 *Permanent Institutions*

The Kelsenian constitutional court is the most familiar IPD. The general issue
associated with design is well-known, and it arises with respect to other IPDs:
how to best balance independence, accountability, and expertise. We can
describe this as a problem of joint (or multiple) optimization. For each institution, what is the best mix of independence, accountability, and expertise?

---

[22] *Bush v. Gore*, 531 U.S. 98, 109 (2000).

We can break that issue down further, again in familiar ways: choosing appropriate qualifications for selection for the institution, and choosing appropriate methods of appointment, defining the tenure of the offices' occupants, including the provisions for their removal from office for misconduct, and determining the range of functions the institution can best serve. For most of these matters, the options are well-known, principally from discussions of the design of constitutional courts, and canvassing them would not tell us anything special about fourth-branch institutions.

Consider, for example, a controversy in 2020 about the Bulgarian General Prosecutor Ivan Geshev's investigation of the nation's president. Disinterested accounts are hard to come by, and I rely on one that seems partisan,[23] simply to illustrate the possibility that an IPD can be too independent and insufficiently accountable – a point that we have known for a long time about constitutional courts, of course.

Investigating purported leaks of classified information, the prosecutor raided the president's office and arrested his legal secretary. According to the prosecutor's critics, this was inconsistent with a constitutional provision prohibiting criminal prosecutions of the president; they relied upon the idea that to be effective such immunities must extend as well to activities associated with the ordinary operation of the presidential office. The general prosecutor has a high degree of independence: his term is relatively long and he can be removed only by a two-thirds vote of the Supreme Judicial Council. And, notably, the prosecutor called himself "an instrument in the hands of God."

Bulgaria has a parliamentary system, with a weak president elected for a five-year term. Among the president's powers, though, is that of formally appointing the general prosecutor. President Rumen Radev opposed Geshev's appointment, taking to heart public criticism that Geshev would run the office as an arm of the prime minister and his party. When the Supreme Judicial Council nominated Geshev, Radev vetoed the appointment, as the constitution allowed. The nomination went back to the Supreme Judicial Council, which stuck to its guns and renominated Geshev. And, under the Bulgarian constitution, Radev had no power to veto the renomination. Geshev retaliated (in his critics' eyes) by targeting Radev with an aggressive investigation. The raid on the president's office occurred shortly after the president had publicly criticized as corrupt some actions taken by Geshev's political sponsors.

---

[23] Theodora Petrova, "The General Prosecutor Unbound," July 20, 2020, https://verfassungsblog .de/the-general-prosecutor-unbound/, archived at https://perma.cc/B6X9-NGGJ.

In this telling, Geshev was simultaneously too independent, which allowed him to investigate aggressively and perhaps unconstitutionally, and too accountable, to the prime minister. This illustrates why system designers seek to balance independence and accountability in IPDs, and why the design issues are difficult.

Two matters specific to IPDs and not constitutional courts require modest attention here. First, the interaction between expertise and design details: IPDs can be headed by a single person or they can have several members who decide either by consensus or majority vote. Similarly, and as we will see for similar reasons, a multimember body's members might have staggered terms or terms that end simultaneously. Choosing to have a multimember IPD and staggered terms might be affected by the strength of the expertise available to the IPD. Suppose the IPD is concerned with a matter as to which there is strong and reasonably objective expertise. Consider a census bureau. The only thing that matters to the bureau's head is getting the numbers right. Strong and objective expertise transcends party politics. In such cases, the reason we have IPDs – to address problems of constitutional preservation posed by party politics – can be served by an institution headed by a single person. In contrast, where expertise is weaker and less objective, we might be concerned that a single agency head would be "too partisan" in her deployment of expertise. That would lead to a choice of a multimember agency and, to ensure continuity as party power shifts, staggered terms.

Second, the jurisdiction of individual IPDs: What tasks should each IPD perform? Should central banks be given the narrow though of course important task of ensuring fiscal responsibility over the long run, or should they also include within their remit avoiding unacceptable levels of unemployment? This might be described as a choice between delegating precisely defined authority to the central bank and giving the bank broader discretion. The issue of range will come up differently for other IPDs. Should an electoral commission be charged solely with determining constituency boundaries, or should it also resolve disputes over which votes should be counted, or should it also be in charge of actually administering elections?

I doubt that there are general design principles bearing on the proper jurisdiction of specific IPDs, but there might be some. The example of central banks suggests one. All central banks have wide authority over the national economy, but Paul Tucker suggests a different definition of breadth: an IPD's jurisdiction is broader the more *separate* criteria there are for it to apply.[24] As

---

[24] Paul Tucker, Unelected Power: The Quest for Legitimacy in Central Banking and the Regulatory State (Princeton University Press, 2018).

Tucker points out, broad jurisdiction means more discretion. And, in the present context, the more discretion an IPD has, the more independent it will be of political control. That, in turn, suggests that IPDs with broad jurisdiction (as defined here) ought to have stronger accountability mechanisms.

Another suggestion is that an IPD's jurisdiction might be larger in nations where the number of persons qualified to sit on the IPD is relatively small. The thought is that such nations might not have enough qualified people to staff a boundary-setting commission, a commission for administering elections, and a commission for resolving post-election disputes.

Two issues are worth discussing. First, permanent institutions ordinarily have to allocate work among various possibilities. Consider the U.S. Supreme Court in its guise as a constitutional court. As a generalist court, it has to decide both which specific cases to take up and, more important, the composition of its docket (as between statutory and constitutional cases, for example). It has essentially complete discretion with respect to both types of decision.[25] Or consider a constitution that assigns anti-corruption investigations to a prosecutor-general. That official might have jurisdiction over a wide range of crimes, of which corruption is a subset, and will make choices about allocating resources to corruption investigations as against investigations, for example, of widespread activity by ordinary criminal gangs. The usual concerns about independence and accountability come into play here: To what extent will accountability lead the prosecutor to make allocation decisions based upon party politics, for example? On the independence side, to what extent will such decisions be made according to professional criteria?

That question brings us to the second and more important issue: expertise. Begin with constitutional courts. Kelsen had the last word in the exchanges with Schmitt because Kelsen understood that ordinary judges applying ordinary law nonetheless had to make some policy-based decisions. That was enough to justify calling the functionaries staffing constitutional courts "judges." But Kelsen appears to have understood as well that the policy-based decisions constitutional court judges would make were different from those made by ordinary judges. That is why he removed the constitutional court from the system of bureaucratic promotion prevailing in the civil law nations with which he was concerned. "Mere" legal expertise was not all that the work of a constitutional court judge required. Something more, some additional forms of expertise, were required. That was why Kelsen, or at least those who followed him in creating constitutional courts, insisted that those courts be

---

[25] Specialized (Kelsenian) constitutional courts can face the first choice if they have large caseloads.

staffed by lawyers with experience beyond that of ordinary judges – in particular, by academic lawyers whose studies gave them a synoptic view of the political-legal system and by lawyers with some political experience.

The argument here is that the democracy-protecting function the constitutional court served required a distinctive expertise tailored to the institution's function. The same is true of other IPDs.

Consider first districting commissions charged with drawing constituency boundaries in ways that satisfy demands of electoral fairness, which include substantial compliance with a one-person, one-vote principle.[26] Modern technologies make it easy to draw boundaries that comply with a quite rigid specification of that principle. We know, though, that a large number of different maps can be drawn each of which has constituencies drawn to comply with a rigid one-person, one-vote requirement (at least when the number of constituencies is more than a handful). Important political consequences flow from the choice of one or another map.

In addition, many theories of democratic representation hold that the one-person, one-vote principle can properly be tempered by a desire to respect what are known in U.S. voting rights jurisprudence as "communities of interest." That is, we can have two maps, each of which satisfies one-person, one-vote, but one map groups farmers in a single constituency while the other divides farmers among several constituencies each of which is dominated by urban voters.[27]

Choosing among available maps requires the exercise of some sort of political judgment – an expertise about politics. For that reason, boundary commissions are often designed with an eye to politics: some members will have political experience, others will have academic backgrounds, and others will be representatives of civil society. Note as well the contrast between boundary commissions and courts as supervisors of boundaries. Constrained to operate as courts of law under an obligation to explain their actions (or at least under an obligation to be able to explain when called upon for an explanation), courts will ordinarily invoke only the one-person, one-vote principle, then acknowledge the need for some flexibility, then set an arbitrary limit on deviations from one-person, one-vote.[28] This is another example of

---

[26] *See* Lisa Handley, "A Comparative Survey of Structures and Criteria for Boundary Delimitation," in REDISTRICTING IN COMPARATIVE PERSPECTIVE (Lisa Handley & Bernard Grofman eds., Oxford University Press, 2008), at 265–83.

[27] The example is obviously stylized because farmers rarely reside directly next to truly urban communities, but the analytic point should be clear.

[28] This is the account of U.S. apportionment jurisprudence offered in JOHN HART ELY, DEMOCRACY AND DISTRUST (Harvard University Press, 1980).

why institutions other than courts might be preferred to deal with polycentric problems.[29]

Electoral courts charged with determining whether a political party should appear on the ballot, or whether a particular candidate should be disqualified from running, face related problems of expertise. The German theory of militant democracy authorizes ballot exclusion for parties whose programs are fundamentally inconsistent with the nation's constitution.[30] Aimed at preventing constitutional subversions from within the system itself, the militant-democracy principle clearly raises delicate definitional questions. All constitutions can be amended, but the militant-democracy principle requires electoral courts to determine whether a party's program, if implemented through constitutional amendment or otherwise, would be incompatible with the constitution's "basic structure," as it is sometimes put, or with the nation's unchangeable constitutional identity.[31] Often that determination will be highly contestable, and not only by the parties subject to ballot disqualification.

Further, ballot-disqualification bumps up against another fundamental constitutional principle, what Alexander Hamilton called the basic principle "that the people should choose whom they please to govern them."[32] This is perhaps even more dramatic with ballot-disqualifications of individual candidates. Consider a common example. A number of constitutions provide that people subject to an undischarged bankruptcy judgment are disqualified from office.[33] The justification is clear. Such people might be vulnerable to bribery, either by those who threw them into bankruptcy and might forgive the debt in exchange for the legislator's vote or by others who would pay off the debts in exchange for that same vote. The provision is subject to abuse, though. A candidate's opponents might find plausible grounds for beginning a bankruptcy action – or, more dramatically, might begin legally justified actions

---

[29] I think it instructive that Fuller's central example of a polycentric problem was one involving the division of discrete goods between two claimants, which is structurally the same as the boundary-drawing problem for voting constituencies.

[30] For a collection of essays, see THE "MILITANT DEMOCRACY" PRINCIPLE IN MODERN DEMOCRACIES (Markus Thiel ed., Ashgate, 2009).

[31] Cases decided by the Supreme Court of Israel, discussed in SUZIE NAVOT, THE CONSTITUTION OF ISRAEL: A CONTEXTUAL ANALYSIS 100–108 (Hart Publishing, 2014), illustrate the phenomenon.

[32] Quoted in *Powell* v. *McCormack*, 395 U.S. 486, 547 (1969).

[33] For an overview of candidate disqualification rules, see Joseph Jaconelli, *Constitutional Disqualification: A Critique of English and English-Derived Law*, 14 VIENNA J. INT'L CONST'L L. 167 (2020).

resulting in monetary awards that force the potential candidate into bank-ruptcy.[34] Judges focused on legality are likely to apply the disqualification rule formalistically: the potential candidate is truly an undischarged bankrupt, and the constitution flatly disqualifies him or her from the ballot. An electoral court or commission with experts in politics on it might be willing to temper that formalism with something that lawyers might call equitable consider-ations. They might be willing to look into the circumstances creating the bankruptcy and, specifically, might be willing to waive the constitutional disqualification when they conclude that the bankruptcy was induced by strategic manipulation of the formally applicable rules of bankruptcy law.[35]

A distinctive form of expertise might be needed to detect corruption. At the most mundane level, audit bureaus charged with ensuring that money is spent for the purposes for which it was appropriated must have the expertise to read invoices and expense accounts sensitive to the ways in which people can manipulate those documents. Ezequiel Gonzales-Ocantos and Viviana Baraybar Hidalgo describe some of the more general difficulties of anti-corruption investigations:

> Criminals leave behind very opaque evidence trails and use the state appar-atus to mount sophisticated cover-ups. Corruption crimes also tend to be transnational in nature, involving the use of figureheads in multiple coun-tries, secret off-shore accounts in safe financial havens, and intricate asset-ownership structures. The mechanisms used to camouflage and launder the proceeds of corruption are indeed extremely convoluted. Uncovering these schemes requires highly technical financial investigations .... The political figures under investigation also may rely on special benefits, including parliamentary immunity to block the disclosure of evidence, enlist skilled

---

[34] The most dramatic example of which I am aware occurred in Singapore, whose libel laws have been interpreted to impose substantial liability on critics who use heightened political rhetoric that the courts are willing to characterize as false imputations about facts. In one widely known case, a leading figure of the political opposition went into bankruptcy because he faced high monetary awards in such cases. *See* Mark Tushnet, *Authoritarian Constitutionalism*, 100 CORN. L. REV. 391, 402–3 (2015). I note of course that even an "expert" election commission would be likely to be captured by the dominant party in Singapore, and that the expertise to which I refer in the text would be unlikely to help dissenters there.

[35] A recent study finds that, in one setting, nonlawyers tend to reason more formalistically than lawyers. Julian Nyarko & Jerome Hsiang, *Conforming against Expectations: The Formalism of Nonlawyers at the World Trade Organization*, 48 J. LEG. STUD. 341 (2019). It would be interesting to know whether the finding could be generalized to other settings, and, in particular, whether decision-makers chosen because they are experts in a field other than law are formalistic when law comes within their purview.

lawyers who are well-versed in the use of stalling tactics, and exploit their institutional prerogatives to weaken the legislative framework that governs criminal prosecutions.[36]

Just as electoral commissions need a kind of expertise about the political effects of their decisions, so too with anti-corruption investigators. Gonzales-Ocantos and Hidalgo make the obvious point that investigations in varying configurations of political power can produce dramatically different political effects. Most obviously, investigations that target members of the current political opposition can weaken the opposition; investigators might find it easier to target *former* power-holders, even those nominally aligned with the current administration, than to go after current power-holders.[37] They also point to "the absolute failure" of investigations into Odebrecht's Mexican corruption activities as showing that investigations by prosecutors aligned with those holding power into their political allies are unlikely to be effective.[38]

We now can see why the functional logic underlying the creation of IPDs might counsel in favor of creating *several* such institutions, and not merely a constitutional court. Some of the tasks associated with protecting constitutional democracy require the deployment of a kind of expertise different from and sometimes in tension with legal expertise. But, even putting aside the persistent question of the availability of sufficient numbers of qualified people to staff multiple institutions, we have learned that Fuller's vision of judicial capacity was too constricted. Implicit in his idea was a distinction between problematic stresses upon judges and permissible judicial creativity, and that distinction might sometimes be quite thin.[39] Courts can call upon outside experts to assist them, for example, without departing from the judicial proprieties.[40] Of course,

---

[36] Ezequiel Gonzales-Ocantos & Viviana Baraybar Hidalgo, Lava Jato *Beyond Borders: The Uneven Performance of Anticorruption Judicial Efforts in Latin America*, 15 TAIWAN J. OF DEMOCRACY 63, 68 (2019).

[37] Gonzales-Ocantos and Hidalgo offer the interesting case of Ecuador, where new President Lenin Moreno, the protégé of former President Rafael Correa, sought to create his own independent political identity by breaking with Correa and supporting investigations into corruption of the Correa administration, of which Moreno had been a part. *Id.* at 74–75.

[38] *Id.* at 85–86. *See also* Pablo Echeverria, *The Last Grand Inquisitor*, 88 UMKC L. REV. 575 (2020) (describing actions by the Colombian inspector general to remove Bogotá's mayor, and asserting that the result was "political chaos").

[39] EZEQUIEL A. GONZÀLEZ-OCANTOS, SHIFTING LEGAL VISIONS: JUDICIAL CHANGE AND HUMAN RIGHTS TRIALS IN LATIN AMERICA (Cambridge University Press, 2016), provides a valuable study of how what he calls "traditional legal preferences" can be transformed, though there the focus is on expanding specifically legal definitions of substance and procedure. *Id.* at 269.

[40] The classic work on this is Abram Chayes, *The Role of the Judge in Public Law Litigation*, 89 HARV. L. REV. 1281 (1976).

they must know when they should do so, and their legalistic cast of mind might lead them to under-use outside expertise. The final observation, which I described in Chapter 3, is that constitutional courts are almost certain to reserve to themselves the power to review decisions by IPDs – ballot disqualifications, the definition of corruption, and more. The review they conduct will be affected by the fact that they might lack relevant expertise – and might not fully appreciate either that fact or its implications.

4.3 INTERROGATING THE IDEA OF EXPERTISE

One reason for creating fourth-branch institutions is that they deal with problems of preserving democracy in a party-political world. As Kelsen and Schmitt argued, they should be "above" party in some important sense. Giving the institutions an appropriate degree of independence aims at satisfying that design requirement, as do criteria for appointment. Experience with constitutional courts shows, of course, that independence is not the only requirement – so is an appropriate degree of democratic accountability. And, as is also well-known, calibrating the mix of independence and accountability is quite difficult. In particular, "too much" accountability can eliminate the "above politics" character of a fourth-branch institution.[41]

Here I note a subtler problem in effectively placing fourth-branch institutions above politics. The positive argument for creating several fourth-branch institutions rather than assigning everything to a single one (typically the constitutional court) is that their different tasks require the deployment of different kinds of expertise: legal expertise for constitutional courts, expertise in political fairness for electoral commissions, expertise in investigating financial accounts for anti-corruption agencies and audit bureaus. And associated with each of these forms of expertise are professional norms guiding the experts. Lawyers, election experts, and auditors all work in professions one central norm of which is impartiality in the deployment of the expert's abilities. In our context, impartiality means indifference to the party-political implications of one or another action. Boundary commissioners should draw lines solely with reference to the criteria set out in the constitution, and should not take the party-political implications of the lines into account to any greater degree than the constitution authorizes. Lawyers staffing IPDs, including anti-corruption prosecutors, might be said to be partial to their client, with the client understood to be the nation; but on any account, the professional norm

---

[41] Section 4.4 examines some aspects of this difficulty in more detail.

of impartiality means that they should be indifferent to the party-political implications of prosecuting or refusing to prosecute individual cases.

Expertise and norms, though, are not above politics.[42] As Annelise Riles puts it in a related discussion of central banks, "There is no such thing as a culture-free bureaucracy," nor a politics-free one either. To the same effect, one of her sources says, "It is a political act to claim you are acting apolitically!"[43] Typically, the politics of a specific form of expertise is merely correlated, though sometimes strongly, with party-political positions. Take the (problematic) case of central banks. They are usually charged with guaranteeing price stability by acting to offset the systematic political inclination to incur excessive debt in pursuit of immediate electoral gains.[44] Accomplishing that requires the deployment of expert judgment about what steps should be taken and technical expertise in selecting among available measures. Yet, though the goal of price stability might be thought above party politics, the precise choice of means is almost always coded as "conservative."[45]

Other forms of expertise have their own political codings.[46] Anti-corruption specialists are inclined to see many forms of political patronage – "clientelism," pejoratively – as corrupt. And, as we will see in Chapter 6, there is reason to think that left-wing parties are systematically inclined to use patronage and more

---

[42] The argument developed here is different from the classic one offered by Harold Laski, who argued that expertise should not completely *displace* democratic decision-making, which Laski described as statesmanship guided by "supreme common sense," because of the expert's limited range of knowledge. HAROLD LASKI, THE LIMITATIONS OF THE EXPERT 10 (Fabian Society, 1931). *See, e.g., id.* at 4 ("it is one thing to urge the need for expert consultation at every stage in making policy; it is another thing, and a very different thing, to insist that the expert's judgment must be final"). IPDs are not vulnerable to Laski's critique because they combine expertise with democratic accountability, but they are nonetheless vulnerable to the critique offered here, that expertise itself has a political content. (I note that the latter critique might perhaps be teased out of Laski's observation about the "caste-spirit" of experts.).

[43] ANNELISE RILES, FINANCIAL CITIZENSHIP: EXPERTS, PUBLICS, AND THE POLITICS OF CENTRAL BANKING 27, 34 (Cornell University Press, 2018).

[44] *See id.*, at 10–11 (describing this rationale).

[45] Probably the most dramatic illustration of the conservative inclination of central bankers comes from the United States. Since the 1940s, the Federal Reserve has been charged with achieving both price stability and "maximum" employment, but after achieving functional independence in the 1950s, it has generally subordinated the "maximum employment" goal to price stability, often by implicitly interpreting "maximum" to mean "the highest level compatible with price stability." (I thank Daniel Tarullo for relevant discussions.).

[46] Cost-benefit analysis is a common target for those who believe that expertise is politically coded (here, generally, in favor of limits on command-and-control regulation), because, in their view, many public values are at best not easy to monetize. For a comprehensive critique of cost-benefit analysis along these lines, see FRANK ACKERMAN & LISA HEINZERLING, PRICELESS: ON KNOWING THE PRICE OF EVERYTHING AND THE VALUE OF NOTHING (New Press, 2004).

blatant forms of corruption to secure the political support they cannot get from wealthy political sympathizers. If so, "financial impropriety" is coded as politically conservative as well.

Legalism, the courts' domain, is "conservative" in many jurisdictions. Interestingly, though, legalism in the United States historically was conservative but is today liberal. Lawyers are systematically more devoted to the rule of law and constitutionalism than lay people, but the lawyers' understandings may have political colorations. Lawyers are likely to see institutional innovation, particularly large-scale innovation, as a threat to the rule of law or constitutionalism, for example. Innovators who propose a shift from one method of judicial selection to another or term limits for judges in jurisdictions without them will be met with the charge that the innovation threatens judicial independence, no matter how widely it is used elsewhere and no matter that the proposal comes with well-known "good governance" justifications. And, of course, in some local circumstances, the charge will be well-founded. Innovators sometimes seek to change the court's composition because they hope to alter its jurisprudence. Sometimes, but not always – and the near universal deployment of the language of threat to judicial independence suggests that lawyers' commitments to the rule of law and constitutionalism does have an institutionally conservative cast.

"Electoral fairness" has a political valence as well. The experts on boundary commissions typically regard one-person, one-vote as *the* goal, to be compromised only when small deviations can be justified by strong considerations of preserving communities of interest. Often, though, groups that we might think of as such communities are not treated as such by boundary commissions: today, in many jurisdictions, identity-based communities of interest – ethnic minorities for example – are taken into account but interest-group communities of interest such as farmers are not. The case of party-based boundary drawing is especially interesting because it directly implicates the role of election commissions in a party-political world. "Expertise" in political fairness today means ensuring that constituencies are drawn so that the party composition of the representative legislature is proportional to the distribution of party support in the jurisdiction as a whole. This is one sensible specification of political fairness, but it is not the only one – and today it is coded as politically liberal.

An additional difficulty is that in some contexts the professional norm of impartiality might actually undermine rather than protect democracy. For example, the Brazilian case study in Chapter 6 can be read to support the proposition that an impartial pursuit of corruption wherever it occurred contributed importantly to destabilizing the Brazilian party system, and that

that destabilization led to the election of Jair Bolsonaro.[47] As I argued in Chapter 2, Kelsenian constitutional courts should be designed to ensure that its members are sensitive to the political implications of their actions – and in that rather abstract sense to ensure that the judges are not impartial as the lawyers' professional norm would have it. More generally, the expertise and associated norms that justify the creation of IPDs must be tempered by some degree of political sensitivity – and that tempering might be inconsistent with professional norms of impartiality.

Treating the permanent civil service as a stabilizing force – and so in some sense as an institution protecting democracy – brings out yet another difficulty. Consider a nation where a set of policies – social welfare, national security, whatever – has been in place for a long time. The civil service has been administering those policies faithfully, without regard to their party-political implications. Then a new political majority takes control of the government on a platform that rejects many of the prior policies. Experience around the world shows that the permanent civil service will not rapidly shift away from the prior policies. This is well-known as the "Yes Minister" effect, after the British television program in which a high-level permanent civil servant nominally acquiesced in his political superior's policies but actually thwarted them.[48]

"Yes Minister" offers a comic version of civil servants' commitments, but recharacterizing the effect as the "Deep State" reveals its darker side. Civil servants accustomed to one policy for a long time might see that policy as by definition impartial, and so see the newcomers' innovations as "merely" partisan politics of a sort the civil servants are told to ignore. And, where the new government was elected to destabilize preexisting policies across the board, civil servants may see their resistance as protecting democracy.[49] Sometimes that will be true, sometimes not; and in the latter event, the norm of impartiality interferes with democracy.

One more general point: As Paul Tucker observes with respect to central banks, directing institutions to advance multiple goals – for electoral agencies; one-person, one-vote, and respecting communities of interest – inevitably

---

[47] That case study also discusses the possibility that the anti-corruption prosecutors there were not in fact impartial.

[48] For a discussion of the "Yes Minister" effect, see STEVEN FIELDING, A STATE OF PLAY: BRITISH POLITICS ON STAGE, SCREEN AND PAGE, FROM ANTHONY TROLLOPE TO THE THICK OF IT 189–95 (Bloomsbury, 2014).

[49] The original "Deep States" were the militaries in Turkey and Egypt, who (as Deep States) exercised power behind the scenes to prevent political Islamists from taking power, because they believed that political Islamists were anti-democratic. For a recent discussion dealing with the United States, see JOHN A. DEARBORN, STEPHEN SKOWRONEK & DESMOND KING, PHANTOMS OF A BELEAGUERED REPUBLIC (Oxford University Press, 2021).

gives them more independence from the body that created them.[50] The institution can defend *any* action it takes as striking the appropriate balance among the various goals under the circumstances at hand.

The party-political correlations of expertise and professional norms complicate the problem of calibrating independence and accountability. In the United States today, the correlation between party politics and the politico-legal expertise associated with constitutional law is quite strong – less so elsewhere. In other fields, the correlation between party politics and the field's expertise is probably weaker, though not absent. My sense is that constitution designers do not take these correlations into account, which if true means that it is even less likely than otherwise that the fourth-branch institutions they create are truly above party politics.

4.4 THE RELEVANCE OF PARTY STRUCTURES

No matter how good the constitutional design, once implemented a constitution operates in a party-political context. The extent to which IPDs can actually protect democracy depends only in part upon their design, and perhaps more upon the party structure in which they operate.

I offer a quite schematic outline of some possibilities, aware that analysis of individual IPDs in different nations will require nuances that the outline omits. I divide party structures into four broad groupings: (1) A dominant party or leader around whom a party is organized (Venezuela under Hugo Chávez, Singapore under Lee Kuan Yew);[51] (2) a dominant party with enduring factions, some of which might be centered on individuals and others centered on ideological differences, with some overlaps within those subgroupings (South Africa post-Mandela, perhaps Singapore post–Lee Kuan Yew); (3) a system with real party competition, whether among a relatively small number of parties or with multiparty coalitions whose composition shifts periodically (the United States, Germany, Great Britain);[52] and (4) a chaotic party system (Colombia in the 2000s, Brazil in the 2010s).[53]

---

[50] TUCKER, *supra* note 24, at 121–26.

[51] The parenthetical examples are only suggestive and nothing turns on whether I have accurately allocated a specific nation to a particular grouping.

[52] Two- or three-party systems differ from multiparty systems in some ways, but it is not clear that those differences are reflected in the relation between the IPDs and the party structures (except perhaps with respect to the ability to choose IPD members based on their party affiliation – easier in a two-party system than in one where the choice involves selecting a member of a multiparty opposition).

[53] For a discussion of Brazil's party system, see Chapter 6.

IPDs are probably unlikely to be of much use in the first and fourth cases. The fact that there is a dominant party and leader means that the dominant party will select the IPDs' members, and will try to choose members who will do the party's bidding. The IPDs will be independent to the extent that, and for as long as, the dominant party wants them to be independent. As one study puts it, in such systems independence is "a matter of political will."[54] There are two qualifications to this, though. Sometimes the party will make an essentially random error, which in some circumstances can be quite consequential. For example, in South Africa, the president chose someone he believed to be a party loyalist to serve as ombudsperson, but she turned out to have an independent streak that ultimately brought the president down.[55] And, perhaps more important, if the dominant party makes and sustains a choice to stay its hand with respect to some matter, whether it be fiscal policy, the conduct of elections, or combating corruption, the chosen IPD might be *more* effective than one in a competitive party system.[56]

More systematically, there is some evidence that IPD members can occasionally spot the impending end of "their" party's dominance.[57] Seeking to preserve their reputations, their jobs, or the reputation of their institution, these members can anticipate the future – that is, begin to act independently even while the dominant party retains its dominant role.

Where the party system is chaotic, the problem with IPDs is different. They might well do a good job at identifying corruption, noting the existence of unconstitutional actions, and the like. Having done so, however, they will find their orders unimplemented or at best imperfectly implemented because the political system as a whole lacks the resources to pursue *any* program systematically.

---

[54] Lance Ang & Jiangyu Wang, *Judicial Independence in Dominant Party States: Singapore's Possibilities for China*, 14 Asian J. Comp. L. 337, 344 (2019).

[55] For more detail, see Chapter 6.

[56] The best examples here are anti-corruption efforts in Hong Kong and Singapore, whose anti-corruption institutions are generally regarded as the gold standard in the field. The Hong Kong effort began under British rule and has continued since; the Singapore effort was a project of the dominant PAP. In both cases, the motivation was to ensure that the cities would be attractive venues for investment, a policy commitment that the regimes have sustained over generations. It may be, though, that these examples come close to exhausting the universe of IPDs sustained over a long period in dominant-party regimes.

[57] This is my interpretation of Lisa Hilbink, Judges beyond Politics in Democracy and Dictatorship: Lessons from Chile (Cambridge University Press, 2007). *See also* Sergio Verdugo, *How Can Judges Challenge Dictators and Get Away With It?*, 59 Colum. J. Transnat'l L. (forthcoming) (using the Chilean case to describe strategies available to judges where the authoritarian coalition includes some elements committed to at least nominal adherence to their constitution's limits of executive power).

IPDs are, I suggest, most likely to be successful in protecting democracy in the second and third cases – dominant parties with organized factions, and well-organized party systems. Strikingly, though, the Madisonian argument has its strongest purchase in precisely these cases, because the programmatic factions within the dominant party in the second case and the opposition parties in the third have political interests in challenging other factions or parties. Put a bit more strongly than is appropriate, IPDs are most likely to be successful just in the situations where they are least needed.

If the foregoing argument gets at something important about the relation between IPDs and party systems, we might want to look for ways in which IPDs can move systems from the outlier categories to the middle ones. Samuel Issacharoff has argued, for example, that constitutional courts have the ability to develop a law of politics that will shore up what he calls fragile democracies.[58] They can find unconstitutional rules that prevent – or allow – "aisle crossing," a practice that allows legislators elected as representatives of one party to defect to another after they have taken their seats. Depending on circumstances, aisle crossing can strengthen a dominant party by allowing it to offer to the defector some benefits the dominant party controls – or it can weaken a dominant party by allowing dissidents to break off and appeal to the people. In a nation with proportional representation, the constitutional court or perhaps the electoral court can move up or down the threshold a party must cross to obtain seats in the legislature, with higher thresholds producing fewer parties.

These are indeed possibilities, but the evidence Issacharoff presents is quite discouraging. Indeed, one conclusion that can be drawn from his study is that constitutional courts typically fail to grasp the opportunities they have to move their systems from the outlier categories to the more central ones. And the reason is clear. The people staffing the IPDs are the products of the very systems that we would like them to reform. They might choose to try to improve their nation's party systems, but, with the qualifications noted above about random errors and spotting impending change, they aren't likely to make that choice. And, indeed, the legalism associated with judicial expertise might actively impede them from doing so.

Another possibility would be to examine whether the desired party structures – dominant parties with stable programmatic factions and competitive party systems – could be *outcomes* of constitutional design. We do know some things about the relation between constitutional design and some kinds of

---

[58] SAMUEL ISSACHAROFF, FRAGILE DEMOCRACIES: CONTESTED POWER IN THE ERA OF CONSTITUTIONAL COURTS (Cambridge University Press, 2015).

party systems.[59] Proportional representation with a moderate threshold for entry into the legislature promotes a multiparty system with a reasonable number of parties, which can make it easier to form a coalition government.[60] Different forms of majority or plurality rules for elections from single-member districts promote the creation of two (sometimes three or four, but rarely more) parties. And, by the logic first explored by Anthony Downs, where such parties are led by those who take their goal to be winning office so as to carry out programs to which they are committed solely because the programs will attract support from voters, those parties will move toward the middle of the political spectrum.

Examining this last example in a bit more detail might be helpful. For present purposes, the question is whether we can use constitutional design to encourage parties to conform to the Downsian logic. And the answer is, Maybe, a bit, but doing so will put such design provisions in severe tension with principles of freedom of association.

Start near the end, with party leaders who develop platforms on which their candidates will run. To simplify the account, assume that there are two kinds of party platforms. One consists of policies flowing from ideological principles – social democracy for traditional social democratic parties, relatively laissez faire principles for traditional conservative parties, and the like. Sometimes these platforms will be electorally attractive, but that is not the reason party leaders develop them. The second kind of platform consists of policies chosen solely because they are electorally attractive.

The Downsian logic suggests that constitutional designers should try to find rules that encourage parties with the second kind of platform. Two constitutional rules might seem helpful: parties should be internally democratic, so that they respond to the preferences of party members rather than party leaders alone, and, probably more important, the parties should be open to essentially everyone in the nation. Under these conditions, the Downsian logic will reproduce itself within the parties and the parties will choose the "right" kind of leaders.

---

[59] I draw upon some aspects of a large literature here, and do not take up a great many details that scholars examining the relation between constitutional provisions and party structures have dealt with. For a helpful taxonomy that indicates some of the complexities, see Cindy Skach, "Political Parties and the Constitution," in THE OXFORD HANDBOOK OF COMPARATIVE CONSTITUTIONAL LAW (Michel Rosenfeld & Andràs Sajo eds., Oxford University Press, 2012).

[60] A low threshold generates a large number of parties, some of which can be personalistic and/or ephemeral, which in turn may make it difficult to form a governing coalition that holds together long enough to accomplish anything.

Both rules, but especially the second, are in some tension with other, probably more basic, constitutional principles – freedom of association and freedom of expression. Freedom of association would seem to prohibit governments from denying political status to parties with ideologically driven platforms. As already noted, the principle of "militant democracy" controversially does so by imposing various forms of legal disability upon parties whose platforms are found to be inconsistent with democracy itself, and upon members of those parties. Recognizing the tension between the principle of militant democracy and principles of freedom of association, constitutional courts have insisted that only a quite narrow category of parties can be subjected to those disabilities.[61] Notably, no one, as far as I can tell, argues that the fact that a party has an ideologically driven platform is sufficient to put it within the reach of the militant-democracy principle – and properly so, because doing so would violate even the most minimal understanding of freedom of association. That same understanding casts doubt on requiring open membership. Such a requirement means that a party could not exclude people who were not committed to its ideologically driven platform.

I forgo treatment of additional party-related constitutional provisions such as those providing that opposition parties have certain rights,[62] because such provisions presuppose that we are dealing with a roughly competitive party system already in place. They do not encourage the emergence of such a party system. Nor do they – or any other constitutional provisions of which I am aware – do anything to encourage the emergence of stable programmatic factions within a dominant party.

---

[61] *See* DONALD KOMMERS & RUSSELL A. MILLER, THE CONSTITUTIONAL JURISPRUDENCE OF THE FEDERAL REPUBLIC OF GERMANY 286–92 (3rd ed., Duke University Press, 2012) (discussing the basic German cases); National Democratic Party II, 2 BvB 1/13 (2017) (the most recent German case, refusing to disqualify the National Democratic Party from the ballot even though its program was anti-constitutional, because there was insufficient evidence that it had a realistic chance of electoral success). For an Israeli decision refusing to disqualify parties, see 2/84 *Neiman v. Chairman of the Central Elections Committee for the Eleventh Knesset*, 39(2) PD 225 (1985) (summarizing earlier opinions), https://versa.cardozo.yu.edu/sites/default/files/upload/opinions/Neiman%20v.%20Chairman%20of%20the%20Central%20Elections%20Committee .pdf. The narrowness of the category makes evasion by re-branding relatively easy, as shown by the reinvention of the Turkish Welfare Party (Refah Partisi) as the Justice and Development Party. The example also suggests another difficulty: the principle of militant democracy will reach small parties, but once an anti-democratic party becomes politically salient it will be difficult to suppress it – and yet that is precisely when the principle would be most useful. Of course, the principle might stifle an anti-democratic party in the womb, so to speak, and then we would never see it approach the threshold of political success that it might have achieved.

[62] For an examination of such provisions, see David Fontana, *Government in Opposition*, 119 YALE L. J. 548 (2009).

The design efforts I have sketched are doomed to at most modest success. With principles of freedom of expression and association taken as given, parties win elections because they persuade voters that their platforms are better than the alternatives. Institutional design choices of the type considered here can do relatively little to influence the preferences voters have. I return in the conclusion (Section 4.6) to other design choices that might shape voter preferences – noncoercively, as democracy requires.

The foregoing observations about the relation between party structures and IPDs' performance can be flipped around, shifting our focus from the way in which party structures can affect the way in which IPDs operate once created to the political story underlying the very creation of such institutions. Here too the story probably has two poles, defined principally by the expectations of how party systems will operate under the new constitution. At one pole, constitution framers expect the new system to be dominated by a single party for the foreseeable future. Here they might well adopt a panoply of IPDs, perhaps to satisfy international "best practices" standards, expecting however that the IPDs in operation will be relatively ineffective. At the other pole, the framers expect vigorous two-party (or similar) competition. They might create IPDs, but the real work will be done by Madisonian mechanisms, sometimes operating through the IPDs but sometimes through the standard Madisonian institutions. To complete the story, we have to add the effects of uncertainty about these and similar predictions. Perhaps, for example, a dominant party drafting a constitution will be unsure about how long its dominance will last, in which case it might be reluctant to write IPDs into the constitution. And perhaps drafters working in a reasonably competitive political environment might fear the emergence of a dominant party, in which case they might believe it necessary (not merely convenient) to supplement Madisonian mechanisms with IPDs.

4.5 COMMISSIONS OF INQUIRY: A BRIEF CASE STUDY

Domestic legal systems use commissions of inquiry (CoIs) for two purposes, which sometimes blend together.[63] Some commissions develop recommendations about policy matters such as revising the system of providing water or health care. Others investigate particular instances of government behavior,

---

[63] Commissions of inquiry are employed quite extensively in the international human rights system, where of course their design and operation are quite different from what occurs in domestic systems. I do not discuss these international commissions. For a collection of relevant essays, see COMMISSIONS OF INQUIRY (Christian Henderson ed., Hart Publishing, 2017).

typically some form of misconduct; these commissions make findings of fact and offer recommendations, sometimes regarding the specific incident and sometimes addressing the conditions that generated the incident.[64] Policy-oriented CoIs are not generically institutions for protecting constitutional democracy. They are more like experts assembled to inform a legislature about a policy problem. Incident-oriented CoIs, in contrast, resemble ombuds offices and anti-corruption agencies when, as is often the case, the incidents suggest some malfunctioning in the constitutional system.[65]

Although a general statute often gives the legislature or executive authority to convene a CoI and prescribes some of the procedures that CoIs must use (often dealing with the privileges available to and protections afforded witnesses who might face criminal charges or civil actions for defamation based upon their testimony),[66] incident-oriented CoIs are by definition ad hoc bodies.

The officials creating them make three decisions at the outset.

First, they decide to use a CoI rather than any other institution for examining the incident. Here it is important to remember that CoIs are created by the executive branch itself. It has investigative resources in the police, prosecutors' offices, sometimes legislative committees, and other bodies. A CoI comes on the list of possibilities when the government calculates that the likely (though of course not guaranteed) outcome of the inquiry will be better politically than the outcome of investigations using those other resources.[67] So, for example, facing suspicion that an "inside the government" investigation will be biased in favor of the government, officials might create a CoI headed by a retired

---

[64] For this distinction, see, e.g., J. Sarma Sarkar, Commissions of Inquiry: Practice and Principle with Up to Date Case Laws and Commentaries (Ashish Publishing House, 1990), at 3. For another version, see Gregory J. Inwood & Carolyn M. Johns, "Why Study Commissions of Inquiry?," in Commissions of Inquiry and Policy Change: A Comparative Analysis (Carolyn M. Johns & Gregory J. Inwood eds., University of Toronto Press, 2014), at 13 (quoting another scholar describing "the unique non-recurring issues which are the product of a particular event or set of circumstances, and ... the recurring issues of general social, economic, and cultural matters").

[65] It is widely understood that the distinction between the two types of CoIs can be blurred. Inwood and Johns quote an informed insider: "Virtually every commission turns into a policy commission because, with investigative commissions, not only are the specific questions responded to, but most investigative commissions place their answers in a broader policy context." *Id.* at 14.

[66] No general statute authorizes CoIs in the United States, where they are created by executive order.

[67] As Gregory Inwood and Carolyn Johns put it, CoIs "are established ... when the regular machinery of government or policy process is broken or fails." Inwood & Johns, *supra* note 64, at 8. Here "broken or fails" must be understood, as explained in the text, as likely to produce outcomes the executive branch's leaders will find less satisfactory than they expect from a CoI.

judge who, as we will see, can sometimes give the inquiry an air of impartiality. CoIs are "technically a part of government, [but] can be seen as independent of it and ... conferred with a legitimacy denied to regular executive and legislative bodies."[68]

Officials making this calculation must have a sense of the outcome or outcomes they desire. These may range from actually finding the facts and generating serious proposals for reform to whitewashing government actions, locating scapegoats within the government who can be dismissed without weakening the government's overall position, and discrediting opponents. Note that designing a CoI to achieve any of these last goals is in tension with the fact that provokes the creation of the CoI in the first place – suspicion about the bona-fides of a government-directed investigation.

Second and third, the government defines the commission's terms of reference and chooses the head (and other members, if any) of the commission. And, as noted earlier, it does so with full knowledge of the social, economic, and of course political context in which the commission will operate. For this reason, one former commissioner head from India describes commissions as often "motivated, ... appointed to allay agitation, to delay unpleasant truths or to discredit public servants or political opponents."[69]

---

[68] *Id.* at 10.

[69] SARMA SARKAR, *supra* note 64, at 1. A major study of policy-oriented CoIs in Canada begins by quoting an engaging ditty about CoIs:

> If you're pestered by critics and hounded by faction
> To take some precipitate, positive action
> The proper procedure, to take my advice, is
> Appoint a Commission and stave off the crisis.
> By shelving the matter you daunt opposition
> And blunt its impatience by months of attrition,
> Replying meanwhile, with a shrug and a smile,
> "The matter's referred to a Royal Commission."
> Thus, once a Commission in session commences,
> All you have to do is to sit on your fences
> No longer in danger of coming a cropper,
> For prejudging its findings is highly improper.
> When the subject's been held for so long in suspension
> That it ceases to call forth debate and dissension,
> Announce without fuss "There's no more to discuss.
> The Royal Commission's retired on a pension."

COMMISSIONS OF INQUIRY, *supra* note 63, at 3. In more formal tones, the Law Reform Commission of Canada made much the same points: "[C]ommissions may be established to stave off pressure, to postpone an awkward issue, to back up (hopefully) a government decision already made, or to make the man-on-the-street so sick of a particular issue that he will accept

Terms of reference and naming members are ex ante methods of shaping a commission's work. As such, they give their creators some chance at controlling the outcome, but only a chance. As Carolyn Johns and Gregory Inwood carefully put it, the "challenge" of naming commissioners "is complicated by the delicacy of finding commissioners whose backgrounds do not *overtly suggest* preordained conclusions" (emphasis added).[70] They note the common practice of using judges or retired judges as commission heads, because such people bring an "aura of objectivity and independence" that can "add[] credibility to the undertaking."[71] This may be especially valuable in incident-oriented CoIs, where concerns about procedural fairness to witnesses, victims, and suspects/targets are common.[72]

The terms of reference might allow a commission to range beyond what its creators thought was its remit, for example. Consider the famous incident-oriented Stephen Lawrence inquiry in Great Britain.[73] Lawrence was a young black man murdered in 1993 by a group of white racists.[74] His family believed that the police and prosecuting authorities had done a bad job of investigating the murder because no one had been charged with committing the crime.[75] A CoI was appointed, headed by Sir William Macpherson of Cluny, who had retired a year earlier from his position as a High Court judge; one commentator described Macpherson as a "quintessentially establishment personality – an elderly, white, Scottish aristocrat."[76]

The commission's terms of reference were "[t]o inquire into the matters arising from the death of Stephen Lawrence on 22 April 1993 to date, in order particularly to identify the lessons to be learned for the investigation and prosecution of racially motivated crimes." The great bulk of Macpherson's report dealt with the particulars of the incident and its investigation. But, the report said, "It soon became apparent that a narrow interpretation of our terms of

---

any resolution so long as the subject ceases to appear in the pages of this favourite newspaper." Quoted in *id.* at 17.

[70] Carolyn Johns & Gregory J. Inwood, "Theories of Policy Change and a Four-Part Theoretical Framework for Comparative Analysis," in COMMISSIONS OF INQUIRY, *supra* note 63, at 36.

[71] *Id.* at 36.

[72] Choosing between a sitting judge and a retired one might matter where the commission deals with a politically sensitive incident. The inquiry's result might implicate the commissioner – and indirectly the judicial system – in controversial political findings and recommendations.

[73] I do not argue that the Lawrence commission expanded its inquiry beyond what its creator intended, but use the example to show only that expansive interpretations of terms of reference by an aggressive inquiry head are possible.

[74] BRIAN CATHCART, THE CASE OF STEPHEN LAWRENCE (Viking, 1999), describes the events up to the date of publication.

[75] In 2011, more than a decade after the commission's 1999 report, two men were charged and then convicted for the murder.

[76] CATHCART, *supra* note 74, at 312.

reference would have been pointless and counterproductive. Wherever we went we were met with inescapable evidence which highlighted the lack of trust which exists between the police and the minority ethnic communities."[77] Macpherson took what the report described as the second part of the terms of reference – "to identify the lessons learned" – as authorization for a wide-ranging inquiry into how police and prosecutors dealt with racially tinged crimes. The report concluded that "[t]he investigation was marred by a combination of professional incompetence, institutional racism and a failure of leadership by senior officers."[78] It provided a definition of "institutional racism," and the report's discussion of that phenomenon was its most important contribution.

The commission was created to fulfill a campaign pledge by the Labour Party. Home Minister Jack Straw described the terms of reference as "narrowly focused,"[79] though it seems clear that Macpherson's expansive interpretation of "matters arising" was not unreasonable (and might have been anticipated by Straw despite his characterization of the terms of reference).

Another example is the Kerner Commission in the United States, officially the "National Advisory Commission on Civil Disorders." Its charge was to "investigate and make recommendations with respect to:

(1) The origins of the recent major civil disorders in our cities, including the basic causes and factors leading to such disorders and the influence, if any, of organizations or individuals dedicated to the incitement or encouragement of violence.

(2) The development of methods and techniques for averting or controlling such disorders, including the improvement of communications between local authorities and community groups, the training of state and local law enforcement and National Guard personnel in dealing with potential or actual riot situations, and the coordination of efforts of the various law enforcement and governmental units which may become involved in such situations;

(3) The appropriate role of the local, state and Federal authorities in dealing with civil disorders; and

(4) Such other matters as the President may place before the Commission."[80]

The first paragraph shows the incident-oriented component, and the others move to an orientation to policy. The Commission's most noted statement fell into the second, policy component: "Our nation is moving toward two

---

[77] The Stephen Lawrence Inquiry: Report," Feb. 1999, ¶ 45.6.
[78] *Id.* at ¶ 46.1.
[79] CATHCART, *supra* note 74, at 311.
[80] Executive Order 11365 (July 29, 1967).

societies, one black, one white – separate and unequal."[81] Its report contained an extensive list of new and expanded education, employment, social welfare, and similar programs to address what the Commission concluded were the causes of the tensions leading to urban disorder. President Lyndon Johnson probably expected the Kerner Commission to make recommendations of that sort, and almost certainly did not believe that the Commission had reached beyond its terms of reference.

Like all IPDs, incident-oriented commissions of inquiry have had varying results. Sometimes they "succeed" by providing an authoritative account of the incident; sometimes they succeed by inducing other political actors to do something – either to institute a prosecution or a civil action against wrong-doers, or to put policy changes in place that aim at reducing the chance that similar incidents will recur. And sometimes they have no evident effects.[82]

These categories are useful but incomplete. Consider a commission appointed to whitewash government action. Is it successful if its report finds no grounds for disciplining any government official? What if large segments of the public are skeptical about that conclusion? One would think that here success has to be measured in comparative terms: Would an internal investigation reaching the same conclusion have been received even more skeptically? Similarly with respect to scapegoating CoIs and of course opponent-targeting ones.[83]

The Kahan Commission in Israel offers a useful example of these complexities. The Commission was named to investigate "the facts and factors connected with the atrocity carried out by a unit of the Lebanese Forces against the civilian population in the Shatila and Sabra [refugee] camps." The chair was Yitzhak Kahan, then the president of the Supreme Court; the other members were Aharon Barak, then a member of the Supreme Court, and Yona Efrat, a retired army general. The commission concluded that, although no Israelis were "directly responsible" for the massacre, defense minister Ariel Sharon had "personal responsibility" for "ignoring the danger of bloodshed and revenge" and recommended that he be dismissed as defense minister. Sharon and Prime Minister Menachem Begin resisted the recommendation, but ultimately Sharon resigned that position while remaining in the cabinet as minister without portfolio.

---

[81] Report of the National Advisory Commission on Civil Disorders 1 (1968).

[82] COMMISSIONS OF INQUIRY, *supra* note 63, at 47, describe three types of outcomes: "[T]ransformative and direct," "transformative but diffuse," and "marginal and limited." Their focus is on policy-oriented CoIs, but the categories seem useful with respect to incident-oriented ones as well.

[83] I have not discovered systematic research identifying the conditions under which one or another of these effects are more likely.

Critics treated the report as a whitewash. Yet, there appears to be reason to think that the inquiry helped repair to some degree the damage the massacre had done to Israel's reputation in the international arena. *Time* magazine's report on the report's release offered this instant summary:

> It was hailed in the U.S. and Western Europe as a remarkable example of self-criticism by a democratic society. Said the New York Times: "How rare the nation that seeks salvation by revealing such shame." In France, Interior Minister Gaston Defferre remarked, "This report is the honor of Israel. It gives the world a new lesson in democracy." The Italian Communist paper L'Unita called the report "a turning point for Israel," while Italian journalist Arrigo Levi wrote in La Stampa of Turin: "It would be difficult to find any other nation at war that would let itself be subject to such an open and hard self-criticism."[84]

Evaluating the Kahan Commission's performance obviously turns on one's views about its purposes and how effectively it achieved those purposes: Can a CoI created to whitewash behavior or to find scapegoats ever be regarded as successful? If so, was a specific CoI with one of those goals successful on its own terms? Suppose the inquiry identifies wrongdoers who are then punished. Does that show that it was an honest inquiry, or were the targets scapegoats? And – truly unknowable – what would have happened had the government used its ordinary investigative tools rather than a CoI to address the incident?

A case from India shows a CoI apparently used for blatantly political – though in the case also apparently highly individualized – purposes, as well as what courts sometimes do when confronted with CoIs.

One commentator describes *P.K. Kunju* v. *State of Kerala*[85] as "a classic case of the use of a Commission of Inquiry as a political weapon."[86] The political context was quite complicated. Elections in Kerala in 1967 produced a "United Front Ministry," with members from seven parties. The chief minister was a member of the Marxist-Communist Party (MCP), and P. K. Kunju, the minister of finance, was from the Samyuktha Socialist Party (SSP). In 1969, a member of the Congress Party (which was not part of the United Front) and a member of the SSP (which was), alleged that Kunju had had some of his debts corruptly paid off, and had engaged in unlawful nepotism. A retired judge was appointed to conduct the inquiry, but before the investigation began,

[84] William E. Smith, Harry Kelly & Robert Slater, "The Verdict Is Guilty," *Time*, Feb. 21, 1983, p. 36.
[85] AIR 1970 Ker 252 (High Court of Kerala).
[86] A. G. Noorani, "Commissions of Inquiry," in CORRUPTION IN INDIA: AGENDA FOR ACTION 233 (S. Guhan & Samuel Paul eds., Vision Books, 1997).

Kunju sought to enjoin it, asserting that the allegations of corruption were made in bad faith.

The High Court described the basis for that assertion: According to Kunju, he and the chief minister were at loggerheads. Kunju described himself as "seething with resentment" against the chief minister, and the chief minister and the MCP "had come to regard him as a thorn by [sic] their side." The attempt to begin a commission of inquiry was, again according to Kunju, "a sinister device to weed him out of office." The High Court agreed that Kunju's assertions, if true, would entitle him to relief: "[T]he exercise of a statutory power for an unauthorised purpose, or even professedly for an authorized purpose, but in fact for a different one with an ulterior object, would vitiate the exercise of power." Notably, the conflict appears to have been personal rather than policy-motivated. The High Court counted it against the government that it had not pursued an action against another minister, also a member of the SSP, against whom quite similar corruption charges had been leveled.

On the facts before it, the High Court first discovered that the original order providing public notice that a commission would be convened had never been validly signed, which seems to have led the court to take a skeptical view of the government's position. Even assuming the order had been properly issued, it had some "strange" features. And even more, the government had presented the commission with only "certain points" and "certain facts," not with "other facts to complete the picture." According to the High Court, "It is not an improper inference that this was an improper attempt to [load] the dice against [Kunju] and to foul the mind of the Commission against him." Further, the chief minister "adopted a somewhat devious course": rather than providing official documents regarding Kunju's actions, he relied upon newspaper accounts. The High Court concluded that the record as a whole supported a finding of mala fides, and barred further action by the commission.[87]

---

[87] Derek O'Brien, The Constitutional Systems of the Commonwealth Caribbean: A Contextual Analysis 201 (Hart Publishing, 2014), describes a somewhat similar incident from St. Lucia. A commission of inquiry was to be convened to investigate land deals in which two former prime ministers had been involved. They objected to naming a retired judge to head the inquiry. In St. Lucia, prime ministers have discretion to extend the terms of judges beyond the retirement age specified in the constitution, and doing so is common. The targets of the inquiry noted that one had been prime minister, the other an important official in Caribbean affairs, when the designated judge had reached retirement age. The target had not recommended extending her term and both claimed that circumstance "gave rise to the risk of bias" on her part. The Eastern Caribbean Court of Appeal upheld the objection. O'Brien observes that the incident "dramatically highlights the difficulty in small island states of separating the judicial and executive spheres," *id.*, having already noted that the nations' small populations means that there is a limited number of people qualified to perform public service.

The conclusion seems inescapable: determining whether a CoI is successful requires an essentially political evaluation of the outcome. Put into the theoretical and structural frameworks developed in prior chapters, CoIs cannot systematically stand outside the party-political system as guardians of the constitution. We probably should bear this in mind in evaluating all IPDs.[88]

4.6 CONCLUSION

Putting everything together suggests one conclusion: constitutional design can contribute something to the effective operation of fourth-branch institutions, but the size of that contribution will be affected in significant ways by the party structure both immediately after the constitution goes into effect and in the longer term. Skepticism is probably warranted about the ability of these institutions to provide stable solutions to the problems they are supposed to address: overall, they will sometimes do something valuable, but probably not much and not often. Of course, this is an empirical question. As I indicated in Chapter 1, this study is a preliminary attempt to identify some questions, including empirical ones, for future investigation.

---

[88] Including constitutional courts.

5

Design Principles in Practice
A *Survey*

What design choices do constitutional framers actually make? Of course, one could simply compile constitutional provisions to find out, but it would be helpful to have some sort of classification. The functional argument for IPDs suggests some possibilities, allowing us to distinguish among IPDs and identify choices made about their powers, methods of appointment, required qualifications, and the like.

Any such classificatory exercise must be done cautiously, though. Consider a seemingly obvious category – the constitutional court. Sometimes our assessment of the extent to which a constitutional court's design comports with the conceptual and functional cases for IPDs will depend upon whether the court is a "pure" Kelsenian constitutional court or a general apex court whose jurisdiction includes constitutional matters. Classifications become even more complex with other institutions: Are ombuds offices in some places more like general prosecutors' offices or human rights agencies? How to we characterize officials designated as Defenders of the People (Argentina), compared to ombuds offices or prosecutors elsewhere?

More, lurking in the background and sometimes emerging openly as we examine how IPDs actually operate is the persistent question in comparative constitutional studies of the relation between a constitution's verbal description of an IPD and the institution's actual functioning. Anti-corruption agencies, we know, can themselves be corrupt institutions for attacking a regime's political opponents, yet that possibility can only sometimes be teased out of verbal formulations describing an agency's method of appointment and removal – and even then sometimes only if we know the actual configuration of party power.

With these cautions in mind, this chapter offers a modest survey of design choices actually made.[1] I offer some guesses about "predominant" or "common" choices, but my primary focus is on design possibilities that constitution framers have actually made, and in particular on some non-standard choices that some designers have found appropriate for their circumstances. The thought is that those innovative choices might be adapted elsewhere – or, put another way, the survey may provoke thinking "outside the box" in constitutional systems that might have become institutionally fossilized.

We might capture the survey's results in an only slightly overstated form: someone somewhere has thought about and built into a constitution a response to essentially every structural concern one might have about devising IPDs – but no one anywhere has built into a constitution a response to every structural concern.

5.1 SOME PRIOR STUDIES

Prior surveys of constitutional provisions dealing with IPDs include an examination of "ancillary powers of constitutional courts" by Tom Ginsburg and Zachary Elkins.[2] As of 2006, 55 percent of constitutional courts had responsibility for supervising elections or resolving election controversies, and 29 percent had the power to exclude political parties from the ballot.[3] Ginsburg and Elkins see election management as following from the logic of Ginsburg's "insurance theory" of constitutional review: political parties framing a constitution believe that there may be election controversies in the future but do not know whether they will be in charge of resolving those disputes when they arise, and reduce their risk of losing by creating an impartial decision-maker.[4]

---

[1] Charles M. Fombad, "The Role of Emerging Hybrid Institutions of Accountability in the Separation of Powers Scheme in Africa," in Separation of Powers in African Constitutionalism (Charles M. Fombad ed., Oxford University Press, 2016), provides a similar survey limited to Africa but using many of the same analytical categories as I do here. See also Charles M. Fombad, "The Diffusion of South African Style Institutions," in Constitutional Triumphs, Constitutional Disappointments (Rosalind Dixon & Theunis Roux eds., Cambridge University Press, 2018).

[2] Tom Ginsburg & Zachary Elkins, *Ancillary Powers of Constitutional Courts*, 87 Tex. L. Rev. 1431 (2008).

[3] *Id.* at 1443. Ginsburg & Elkins do not distinguish between election management – supervising the conduct of elections – and resolving disputed elections. (Other ancillary powers include review of treaties for consistency with the constitution, reviewing declarations of states of emergency, and dealing with charges against the chief executive.)

[4] *Id.* at 1454. They argue that party exclusion is a rough ex ante substitute for ex post review of the excluded parties' enacted legislation. *Id.* at 1448. That is, the platforms of excluded parties if enacted would be unconstitutional. This seems rather overstated: not everything in an

Why give the constitutional court these powers rather than creating an independent election supervision body? Ginsburg and Elkins offer a reputational account: "[T]he global success of judicial review has given constitutional courts a reputation as effective institutions. Constitutional review creates a kind of stock of capital that designers seek to draw on to help resolve impasses in the political system."[5] We could wonder, though, whether a new institution in one nation can rely on the reputation of constitutional courts in other nations for this kind of capital. Much depends, I suspect, on local conditions, and it seems to me at least as plausible that assigning election supervision to the constitutional court reflects the choice of an off-the-shelf design rather than the kind of strategic calculation embedded in the reputational account – what Günter Frankenberg calls the IKEA-ization of constitutional design.[6]

In related work Ginsburg and Zachary Elkins are joined by Svetlana Chernykh and James Melton in examining "constitutions and election management" more generally.[7] Their survey shows that 34 percent of constitutions that deal with election management lodge the task in electoral commissions, 26 percent in ordinary courts, and 8 percent in specialized electoral courts.[8] They note that designers "seem to view commissions and courts as substitutes."[9] Electoral courts appear to be regionally concentrated in Latin America; their use might reflect the well-known phenomenon that a good predictor of one nation's constitutional provisions are provisions dealing with the same subject in countries with a similar "cultural geography" – nearby locations, common colonial pasts, membership in related legal "families."[10]

---

antidemocratic party's platform would be unconstitutional if enacted, and exclusion precludes the party from engaging in post-election bargaining over the constitutionally permissible portions of its program.

[5] *Id.* at 1458. They also note, as argued in Chapter 3, that giving constitutional courts these functions creates a risk that "as [constitutional courts] are drawn into *explicitly* political conflicts," they will "draw[] down this stock of capital." *Id.* (emphasis added).

[6] *See* Günter Frankenberg, *Constitutional Transfer: The IKEA Theory Revisited*, 8 INT'L J. CONST. L. 563 (2010).

[7] Svetlana Chernykh et al., "Constitutions and Election Management," in ADVANCING ELECTORAL INTEGRITY (Pippa Norris et al. eds., Oxford University Press, 2014). The theoretical frame Chernykh et al. use is much the same as the "conflict of interest" account offered in Chapter 3.

[8] *Id.* at 101–2.

[9] *Id.* at 101. Here the term "courts" seems to include both ordinary and specialized electoral courts.

[10] *See* Jai Kwan Jung & Christopher J. Deering, *Constitutional Choices: Uncertainty and Institutional Design in Democratising Nations*, 36 INT'L POL. SCI. REV. 60, 65 (2015) (using the term "cultural geography") (focusing on governmental structures). *See also* Benedikt Goderis & Mila Versteeg, *The Diffusion of Constitutional Rights*, 39 INT'L REV. L. & ECON.

That aside, Chernykh et al. do not offer an explanation for the choice among the three possibilities.

On a related topic, Lisa Handley examined national systems for determining constituency boundaries.[11] As of 2008, sixty nations used districting for national elections. About three-quarters used either a boundary commission or some other "electoral management body" to draw district boundaries, with one-quarter having the legislature draw lines, mostly in connection with either multimember districts, where, she finds, district boundaries are rarely changed, or mixed systems that combine proportional representation for the nation as a whole with some seats allocated to districts. According to Handley, "The United States and France are the only two surveyed countries dependent solely on single-member constituencies . . . that allow the legislature a dominant role" in drawing constituency boundaries.[12]

Boundary commissions are relatively small, and their members are "often" nonpolitical public officials such as statisticians and official geographers, as well as judges. There are two patterns with respect to party officials on commissions. One group of nations excludes people with party connections, although as we will see, defining what counts as not having such connections may be difficult. Others specifically include party officials, typically one representative from the government and one from the political opposition. Boundary commissions have final authority in about half the nations surveyed, sometimes with only limited judicial review of their decisions; in the other half, the legislature must approve the boundary commission's proposals. A few nations require the legislature to accept or reject the commission's proposal without modifying it; others allow legislative amendment.

Finally, commissions are universally directed to make a priority of creating districts that are roughly equal in population. Most nations do not specify how much variation from population equality is permissible; where deviation is specifically authorized, the range is from "virtually none" to 30 percent. Commissions are allowed to take geography – natural boundaries and

---

1, 14 (2014) ("Constitutional rights diffuse: where countries are connected through colonial past, common legal origin, common religion or common aid donors, their constitutions are interdependent. By contrast . . . countries with a common border do not appear to drive the diffusion of constitutional rights.").

[11] Lisa Handley, "A Comparative Survey of Structures and Criteria for Boundary Delimitation," in REDISTRICTING IN COMPARATIVE PERSPECTIVE 265–83 (Lisa Handley & Bernard Grofman eds., Oxford University Press, 2008). Handley's survey is largely narrative, as I think appropriate, and includes only national systems (and so excludes practices of boundary drawing in the U.S. states and Canadian provinces, for example), and of course excludes nations where national elections are conducted on a list- rather than a constituency-basis.

[12] *Id.* at 269.

accessibility, in particular – into account in drawing lines, and about one-fifth specifically allow "communities of interest" to be taken into account.[13]

The Australian political scientist A. J. Brown draws on Bruce Ackerman's brief discussion of the possibility of an "integrity branch" for his survey of fourth-branch institutions.[14] For Brown,

> The integrity branch ... consists of those permanent institutions ... whose function is solely or primarily to ensure that other governmental institutions and officials exercise the powers conferred on them for the purposes for which they were conferred, and in the manner expected of them, consistent with both the legal and wider precepts of integrity and accountability which are increasingly recognized as fundamental to good governance in modern liberal democracies.[15]

Note that this is primarily a normative definition, not a functional one, though Brown does try to locate these institutions in the interstices of the classic Montesquiean description of a tripartite government.[16]

Using Australia's statutory institutions as his template, Brown lists the auditor-general, the ombudsperson, the anti-corruption commission, the information commissioner, and the public sector commissioner (roughly, the management system for the permanent civil service) as core integrity-branch institutions. He examined the 100 most recently adopted constitutions as of 2017, finding that 83 percent had an audit commission, 52 percent an ombuds office, 37 percent a human rights commission, 34 percent a judicial/civil service commission, and 29 percent an anti-corruption agency. Further, 89 percent had at least one of the audit commission, the ombuds office, or the anti-corruption agency, a figure that rose to 93 percent when electoral commissions were added to the list.[17]

Brown's valuable work is the most comprehensive overview of fourth-branch institutions of which I am aware. I believe, though, that the "integrity branch" characterization, though understandable in light of the influence

---

[13] This is independent of specific provisions for minority seats.

[14] As noted in Chapter 3, Brown also discusses whether – in the Australian context – these institutions should be conceptualized as a fourth branch.

[15] A. J. Brown, "The Integrity Branch: A 'System,' an 'Industry,' or a Sensible Emerging Fourth Arm of Government?," in MODERN ADMINISTRATIVE LAW IN AUSTRALIA: CONCEPTS AND CONTEXT (Matthew Groves ed., Cambridge University Press, 2014), at 301.

[16] A. J. Brown, "The Fourth Integrity Branch of Government: Resolving a Contested Idea," paper delivered at World Congress of Political Science, Brisbane, Australia, July 2018.

[17] *Id.* at 11–12. Fifty-eight percent of the constitutions had an electoral commission. Brown's text suggests that some of the institutions he identified were statutory creations authorized by constitutions that specified some of their characteristics once they were created.

Ackerman's work has had on thinking about constitutional design, misses the theoretical core of the general idea of a fourth branch. Integrity as defined by Brown sometimes overlaps with the function of protecting constitutional democracy, as with anti-corruption efforts. The category of IPDs is both broader and narrower than integrity protection, though. Broader, as Brown implicitly acknowledges, by simultaneously including electoral commissions in his survey and excluding them from his list of core integrity institutions. And narrower, as the problematic inclusion of human rights commissions in the fourth branch suggests.[18]

5.2 A NARRATIVE SURVEY OF CONTEMPORARY CONSTITUTIONS

I begin with some "eyeball" impressions from the survey, which examined more than 150 constitutions in force in 2019, without attempting a serious statistical analysis. The choice results from my judgment, noted earlier, that institutional details matter even within a well-defined category ("constitutional court," "electoral regulatory body," "ombuds office"), which suggests that seeking correlations between a category and something else might be misleading.[19]

The "eyeball" survey does make it clear that many constitutions do not provide for IPDs. For many, the United States will be the most obvious example, but Canada, Australia, and Japan also do not have constitutional provisions dealing with IPDs. One might think that older constitutions lack provisions for IPDs for the reasons given in Chapter 2. Prior to the early twentieth century constitution drafters worked within the Montesquiean tradition and became aware of the need for IPDs as party politics became central to governance. This might be reinforced by the difficulty of amending these older constitutions, for formal reasons where the amendment rule is quite strict (the United States, Australia, and Canada) and for informal ones associated with the politics of constitutional amendment (Japan and to some degree Canada).[20]

Yet the overall picture of constitutions lacking provisions for IPDs is quite mixed. Quite a few recently adopted constitutions lack them (Ethiopia, with

---

[18] *See* Chapter 3 for a discussion of human rights commissions.

[19] I may have missed a small number of IPDs because of variations in names and because an institution's description might be buried within a constitutional provision that didn't catch my attention as dealing with IPDs.

[20] There are scattered examples of nineteenth century IPDs, such as the Dutch constitution's creation of an audit court.

an initial adoption date of 1995; Uzbekistan, 1992), and some older constitutions that have been recently amended do not (Germany, 1949, with recent amendments; Norway, 2018; Switzerland, 1999). I suspect that the reasons for these choices are grounded in local constitutional politics: amenders or drafters do not think that there is any strong need to constitutionalize IPDs, perhaps because their nations have reasonably well-functioning statutory analogues already or because other matters are more pressing. There does seem to be a mild tendency for newer constitutions to have more IPDs.

Borrowing is suggested by some modest "neighborhood" and "legal tradition" effects, though eyeballing the survey suggests that these effects are weak relative to the effects of recency. The most dramatic perhaps are the commissions, variously named, on telecommunications and the press. They exist in the constitutions of twelve African nations and in those of a handful scattered around the world (Armenia, Iraq, Kosovo, Malta, Poland, and Turkey). The likely mechanism by which borrowing occurs is legal training and experience and specifically the venue of legal training and experience among a constitution's drafters, in which neighborhood, legal tradition, and recency are all likely to be quite tightly bound together, sometimes in regional institutions for the exchange of information.

5.2.1 *Underspecification*

Constitutions underspecify IPDs in several senses. First, though most recent constitutions contain at least one IPD, the precise ones written into specific constitutions seem almost random. This might reflect a well-known drafting phenomenon: drafters know of a large number of problems that *might* arise. They also know that they have limited time for concluding the drafting process. And, finally, they have some sense from experience – primarily local but sometimes broader – of which of the many problems they can describe will actually materialize in their nation. They spend their time on drafting provisions dealing with the threats they think most likely to eventuate, and leave other problems to be dealt with through later processes, either constitutional amendment or, more likely, ordinary statute.

One particular form of underspecification is worth noting – the inclusion of provisions identifying one or more IPDs that are to be created or defined or more fully specified "by law." As already suggested, that some nations do not have constitutional provisions for IPDs does not mean they lack such institutions entirely, but only that if they exist they are established by statute. And, notably, a significant number of constitutions that *do* "create" IPDs say only that they are to be established "by law."[21]

The inclusion of such provisions in constitutions poses something of a puzzle. They might be thought to create either a political or even a judicially enforceable duty to enact provisions for the institutions. But, as Brown observes, "just being mentioned in a Constitution ... does not even always guarantee that such a body will be created," giving the example of the 1972/1986 Bangladeshi constitution's authorization of an ombuds office that had not been created as of 2018.[22]

Tom Ginsburg and Rosalind Dixon argue that "by law" provisions are a form of putting off decisions until some future date.[23] Yet it is unclear that they are necessary or even useful for that purpose, at least in a government of plenary powers. A "by law" provision might signal to future decision-makers that the constitution's writers believed that the provision dealt with something especially important as compared to other topics not so singled out. But, again, the utility of sending such a signal to the future might be questioned.[24]

Another form of underspecification occurs in connection with IPDs that are created in the constitution. We can bring it to the surface by recalling the not uncommon practice of using constitutional courts to do some functions performed elsewhere by IPDs, especially election supervision. To put the point more generally and dramatically, why not create a single IPD with jurisdiction over all the threats to the constitution posed by conflicts and convergences of interests in a party-political world? The functional argument for creating a separate electoral regulatory institution is that election supervision calls for a set of skills different from – or at least differently weighted than – the skills constitutional jurists possess. And similarly for other IPDS.

One might think, then, that drafters who create specific IPDs would say something about the distinctive qualifications members of the institution should have. And sometimes they do. For example, the Central African Republic's provision for a commission on communications requires that members have experience in journalism, the arts, communication, law, and

---

[21] There are too many examples to list. A sample: Barbados – the anti-corruption agency; Belgium – the Audit Court; Zambia – the human rights commission; Kosovo – the Independent Media Commission.

[22] Brown, *supra* note 15.

[23] Rosalind Dixon & Tom Ginsburg, *Deciding Not to Decide: Deferral in Constitutional Design*, 9 INT'L J. CONST. L. 636 (2011).

[24] Another function of a "by law" provision might be to ensure that the matter is regulated by legislated law rather than executive decree, though that does not appear to be the case for "by law" provisions dealing with IPDs.

"new technologies of information and communication," and in Chad, the similar commission must have three members from television and the press and one from the "world of culture, art, and letters" as designated by their peers.

More commonly, though, the provisions that create an IPD say nothing about distinctive qualifications. The effect is to leave the definition of qualifications to later specification through legislation. And then the difficulty becomes obvious: the IPD at issue is needed because of problems associated with party politics, and yet the institution's granular design is left to party politics. Underspecification, then, decreases the likelihood that the institutions once created will actually protect constitutional democracy in the way laid out in the functional case for IPDs. A cynic might say that that is precisely the point of underspecification: constitutional design does not occur under conditions that screen out party politics from the designers' view. The case studies provided below offer some opportunity to assess whether IPDs in practice do what the underlying theory says they should do.[25]

5.2.2 *Placing IPDs "Above" Partisanship*

Electoral commissions and similar bodies bring the theory that IPDs should be above partisanship to the surface. When constitution drafters create such bodies rather than designating the constitutional court (itself in theory above partisanship), they have two core strategies for achieving that goal: making the commission bipartisan (or, sometimes, multipartisan) or making it nonpartisan. The first strategy expressly *includes* party representatives in the commission, the second *excludes* them.[26]

Creating an electoral commission, though, is insufficient. The commission's decisions have to be taken seriously – in a setting in which at least one, and perhaps more, political actors are likely to be unhappy with the outcome. Giving the constitutional court power over elections enhances the possibility

---

[25] A related phenomenon occurs in connection with central banks. Only occasionally do they specify anything at all about the central bank (term lengths in Bosnia and Hercegovina, Colombia, and Uganda; term length for the chair in Albania, Lithuania, and Poland; the number of board members in Sweden and Uganda), and even more rarely do they specify the goals the central bank should pursue even though those goals provide the functional justification for creating the bank ("price stability" in the Czech Republic, a stable currency and promoting development in Ghana).

[26] I note a mixed strategy that blends some degree of partisan composition with some degree of political neutrality. In what follows, I classify constitutions that pursue this mixed strategy as nonpartisan or bipartisan with an eye to which component predominates, while noting the specifics about composition.

that a decision overturning an election or drawing district boundaries will be taken seriously – or at least places such decisions on a par with the constitutional court's other decisions.[27] Again, two core strategies arise: make the commission's decisions binding or require that they be ratified by the legislature. The goal would be to make it more likely that political parties would have "buy in" on the commission's decisions. Buy-in might occur either at the commission stage, with parties given a formal role on the commission, or afterwards, with legislative ratification required. This might suggest, for example, that we might expect to see nonpartisan commissions with power to recommend legislation for ratification, and bipartisan ones whose decisions are automatically binding.

A third core strategy should be mentioned, only to be put to the side. One might insulate electoral commissions from partisanship by giving them detailed guidelines for action. No system does so with respect to resolving election disputes, probably because detailed guidance is impossible. And even the guidelines given commissions charged with drawing district boundaries leave quite a bit of discretion.[28] So, in the end, it is the commission's design rather than the rules it is charged with enforcing that seeks to place the commission above partisanship.

5.2.2.1 Achieving Nonpartisanship

Election and boundary commissions can be made nonpartisan by *inclusion* and *exclusion*. Inclusion means filling up all or nearly all of the commission's slots with judges, technical experts, and members of NGOs. Note that these membership criteria do not mean that technical experts necessarily lack party affiliations. The assumption underlying the strategy is that a commitment to technical expertise or electoral fairness (in the case of NGO members) is thought likely to dominate the commission members' thinking.

Exclusion means denying seats to people with partisan affiliations. How, though, does one define the latter? Typically, by excluding those who currently

---

[27] The mere fact that a decision emanates from a court does not guarantee that it will be followed, but constitution drafters and observers rather clearly believe that compliance with court judgments is likely to be as high as compliance with any other politically salient decision.

[28] For example, in Lesotho, the guidelines on boundaries are equal population with a 10 percent margin, taking into account communities of interest, "means of communication," and geography. The provisions in the constitutions of Mauritius, Uganda, and Zambia are similar.

hold public office or are or have recently been candidates for public office, and those who hold official positions within their parties or have recently done so.[29] One thing jumps out from those criteria: "Mere" party membership is not a ground for exclusion.[30] The reason is obvious, I think. Making party membership a ground for exclusion would drastically reduce the number of eligible candidates for appointment in a party-political world, perhaps to the point where the commission would be seen as unrepresentative. The Venezuelan constitution, for what it might be worth, says that the Electoral Power shall have five members "not linked to organizations with political purposes," three members nominated by civil society, one member from law faculties, and one nominated by the Civic Power, another constitutional body dominated by members from civil society.

5.2.2.2 Bipartisanship

Bipartisan commissions typically have members appointed by the government and the opposition, with the government typically getting one more seat than the opposition.[31] This structure requires that there *be* an opposition, which is easier to find in two-party systems. Introduce even a single third party and the problem becomes more complicated. Sometimes multiparty systems do have an official position of "leader of the opposition," who is sometimes chosen by a coalition of minority parties, sometimes the leader of the largest party in the minority. In Botswana, five of the Electoral Commission's members are recommended by an "All Party Conference." And in Kosovo, six of the eleven members of the Central Election Commission are chosen from the "largest parliamentary groups."

---

[29] Examples include Gambia and Kenya (which exclude those who have been members of a party's governing body within the preceding five years). The provision in Uganda appears to be rather weak. It requires commission members who are members of parliament at the time of their appointment to resign their seats. Much here would depend upon the relative salaries and other benefits associated with membership in parliament and on the electoral commission.

[30] Exceptions appear to be Tanzania, which provides that members of the Electoral Commission cannot "join" a political party, and Korea, which provides that members of the National Election Commission cannot join political parties or participate in political activities.

[31] Examples include Antigua, Barbados, Belize, and St. Kitts and Nevis (with a chair who is not a member of parliament and two members each named by the government and the opposition). The Pakistani chief election commissioner is a judge, chosen as follows: the president sends three names to a twelve-member parliamentary committee, with six members from the government and six from the opposition.

Lying somewhere between nonpartisanship and bipartisanship are election commissions with equal numbers of members chosen by the president, the courts, and the parliament.[32]

5.2.2.3 Finality

A political analysis suggests that the commission's composition might be related to the bindingness of its actions. Underspecification means that explicit consideration of this question is unusual, but there are some examples. They do not conform to the political logic that would counsel political buy-in at only one of the two stages, commission composition and action on commission reports.

(1) Bipartisan commissions. In Botswana the boundary commission has five (out of seven) members recommended by an All Party Conference; it reports to the legislature, which must adopt its recommendations. In contrast, in both St. Kitts-Nevis and St. Lucia, the bipartisan boundary commission's recommendations are nonbinding.

(2) Nonpartisan commissions. The recommendations of the boundary commission in Trinidad and Tobago fit the political logic: its recommendations are freely modifiable by the legislature. Elsewhere, though, nonpartisan commissions do not appear to require partisan buy-in at the legislative stage. In Malta, the nonpartisan boundary commission's recommendations must receive "fast track" review by the legislature, but in the event of disagreement the commission's recommendations become law. A related version occurs in the Seychelles, where the nonpartisan boundary commission's recommendations are approved if not expressly rejected by the legislature. In Panama, the Electoral Tribunal, composed of three judges, makes final decisions, reviewable solely for constitutional claims.

5.2.3 *Reporting and Its Relation to Enforcement through Legal Sanctions*

Recall that one reason for supplementing a constitutional court with other IPDs is the judgment that courts have a limited repertoire of governance techniques. Here we should be careful in identifying what exactly is at stake. A common formulation might be that courts cannot do X – issue reports, develop programs of public education, and the like. We know, though, that

---

[32] Examples include Haiti and Korea. In Lesotho, the king chooses three members of the Electoral Commission from lists of five names for each position, compiled with input from political parties.

pretty much for whatever "X" we come up with we can find a court somewhere in the world that has in fact done it. Put another way, there are no
essential *limiting* characteristics of institutions labeled courts. So, in theory at
least, constitution designers could rely on courts to do everything.

Yet we know as well that judges and lawyers in individual legal cultures
have a culturally determined sense of what *their* courts can do. Perhaps the
most dramatic example is the judgment by Australia's High Court that a
statute authorizing an Australian court to issue a declaration that a statute is
incompatible with fundamental rights (with no accompanying coercive order)
is incompatible with the separation of powers because it assigns a non-judicial
task to the courts.[33] Contrast this with the well-known "epistolary" jurisprudence of the Indian Supreme Court and the related *su moto* jurisprudence of
the Supreme Court of Pakistan.[34] The latter courts engage in investigations
and issue orders in cases that would be summarily dismissed in the United
States on numerous justiciability grounds, which is to say that they would be
dismissed because they fell outside the U.S. constitutional grant of the
judicial power.

With this in the background, we can examine what non-judicial IPDs are
authorized to do, and their relation to judicial enforcement. As I have already
suggested, the typical functions IPDs perform, that courts in their jurisdictions
do not, involve investigating, reporting, and providing various forms of public
education, which I will collapse into the category "reporting." Audit bodies
and ombuds offices are typically charged *only* with investigating and reporting.
The instances where these and other bodies charged primarily with reporting
are authorized to do more – and, in particular, to impose sanctions
themselves, to initiate enforcement proceedings, or to refer matters for
enforcement – are the matters worth noting to suggest what the design
possibilities are.[35]

5.2.3.1 Audit Bodies

(1) Brazil – The Tribunal of Accounts, whose members are to have "notable
understanding of law, accounting, economic, and finance or public

---

[33] *Momcilovic v. The Queen*, [2011] HCA 34.

[34] For overviews, see ANUJ BHUWANIA, COURTING THE PEOPLE: PUBLIC INTEREST LITIGATION IN
POST-EMERGENCY INDIA (Cambridge University Press, 2017); Hamid Kahn, A HISTORY OF THE
JUDICIARY IN PAKISTAN (Oxford University Press, 2016).

[35] The catalog that follows does not specify that the institutions have the power to investigate and
issue reports.

administration," is empowered to impose sanctions for illegal expenditures.[36]

(2) Chad – The Court of Auditors, composed of experts in "management, economics, taxation, and accountancy," can sanction mismanagement.

(3) Senegal – The Court of Auditors "shall sanction errors of management."

(4) Swaziland – The auditor general may disallow expenses and "surcharge" the person responsible.

(5) Zimbabwe – The auditor general may "order the taking of measures to rectify any defects."

Perhaps the only matter worth noting here is that a criterion such as mismanagement might be thought inappropriate as a judicially enforceable standard, perhaps because of its inevitable entanglement with basic policy questions.

5.2.3.2 Ombuds Offices

At their origin, ombuds offices were designed as institutions to which ordinary citizens could bring complaints about inefficiencies or mismanagement in the ordinary operations of government bureaucracies, typically with respect to administration of social welfare programs.[37] They were often adjuncts to the legislature, which might be thought to have "outsourced" a form of oversight. The ombuds offices would report to the legislature about inefficiencies and the like, and the legislature would decide whether the problems were worth responding to by means of new legislation.

That remains the dominant model of ombuds offices. Sometimes the model is reinforced by specific *limitations* on the office's powers. In Guyana, for example, the ombuds office cannot investigate where a judicial remedy is available to the complainant.[38] A similar limitation in Mauritius is qualified: the office may not investigate if there is a right to judicial review or a

---

[36] It is worth noting that the qualifications for auditing bodies are more frequently specified than are qualifications for many other categories of IPDs. Examples include Bolivia (a professional degree in an area related to the office), Congo (competence in financial and accounting matters), the Dominican Republic ("preferably" with expertise in accounting, finance, economics, or law), Guatemala (having been a public accountant for at least ten years), Honduras (expertise in law, economics, or public accounting), Kenya (extensive knowledge of public finance or at least ten years' experience).

[37] For an overview of the history of ombuds offices, see Sabine Carl, "The History and Evolution of the Ombudsman Model," in RESEARCH HANDBOOK ON THE OMBUDSMAN (Marc Hertogh & Richard Kirkham eds., Edward Elgar, 2018).

[38] In Sudan, the Public Grievance Chamber, which I take to be an ombuds office, may act only after legal recourse is exhausted.

remedy at law, but the limitation is lifted if it is not reasonable to expect the complainant to use those alternatives.

Some, though, may do more – and almost certainly in response to specific local issues. The ombuds office in Colombia, for example, can bring habeas corpus actions. In Finland, the Parliamentary Ombuds office can charge judges with unlawful conduct. The office in Namibia can refer cases for prosecution, including those involving the misappropriation of public money. In the Slovak Republic, the ombuds office may "participate" in proceedings aimed at holding accountable those who violate basic human rights. We will see as well that in South Africa the Constitutional Court converted the ombuds office's power to issue reports into a power to make legally binding orders.[39]

What do these provisions suggest? Perhaps a not-so-obvious design decision: after designing one institution, one notices possible gaps in its coverage and, rather than patching the gap there, patches it by giving another institution the power to deal with the problem. This is constitutional bricolage at the granular level.

5.2.3.3 Human Rights Commissions

In addition to their reporting powers, human rights commissions are sometimes given a role in litigation.[40] They can litigate themselves (Argentina, Ghana) or refer complaints to litigating authorities (Afghanistan), or, more vaguely, "take steps to secure appropriate redress" (Kenya) or issue a "public censure" (Guatemala).[41] These provisions combine concern about the possibility of gaps in coverage with modest suspicion of the likelihood that other authorities will actually pursue human rights violations. We see a bit of redundancy here, which I will argue is an important feature in designing IPDs.[42]

---

[39] See Chapter 6.

[40] See Mario Gomez, "Advancing Economic and Social Rights through National Human Rights Institutions," in RESEARCH HANDBOOK ON ECONOMIC, SOCIAL, AND CULTURAL RIGHTS AS HUMAN RIGHTS (Jackie Dugard et al. eds., Edward Elgar Publishing, 2020), at 330 ("The modern NHRI tends to have a broad mandate combining a complaints resolution function, an educational function, an advisory function and a law reform function.").

[41] The commissions in South Sudan and Uganda are specifically authorized to visit jails and prisons, and the latter may order a prisoner's release and award compensation, subject to an appeal to the courts.

[42] David Bilchitz's examination of the South African Human Rights Commission focuses almost entirely on its complaint-processing role, which he contends is "relatively small." David Bilchitz, "Socio-Economic Rights and Expanding Access to Justice in South Africa," in THE

Finally, I note that almost without exception IPDs other than those specifically designed as multimember commissions are headed by a single person identified in the constitution: a general prosecutor or auditor general. Of course, these actors have staffs to assist them, but responsibility for decisions lies with a single person. Such a design obviously promotes accountability, because observers can fairly attribute decisions to a readily identified individual. Still, I think it interesting that constitution designers have not chosen to create multi-member anti-corruption prosecuting agencies to ensure nonpartisan operation (as they have created multimember anti-corruption policy-focused commissions), in light of the rather obvious risks of political bias in anti-corruption investigations.[43] Perhaps, though, the interaction between prosecutors and courts, especially investigating magistrates in the civil law tradition, gives some anti-corruption investigations some features associated with multimember bodies.

5.2.4 *Intertemporal Conflicts of Interest*

As discussed in Chapter 3, intertemporal conflicts of interest might justify creating an IPD when politicians' interests in short-term political advantage are likely to dominate the consideration of the long run *and* when phenomena that will be realized in the long run pose threats to democracy. Central banks are the most common institutions to deal with intertemporal conflicts. A few recent constitutions deal with similar threats. Tunisia's 2014 Constitution includes a "Commission for Sustainable Development and the Rights of Future Generations," and Algeria has a "Supreme Youth Council."

The social and political problems posed by climate change and age-skewed population numbers may induce constitution drafters to include similar

GLOBAL SOUTH AND COMPARATIVE CONSTITUTIONAL LAW 210, 220 (Philipp Dann, Michael Riegner & Maxim Bönneman eds., Oxford University Press, 2020). Bilchitz also points out that, despite the Commission's constitutional status, its budget is appropriated by the legislature, and the appropriations have limited its capacity.

43 For brief comments supporting this assertion, see Pablo Echeverria, *The Last Grand Inquisitor*, 88 UMKC L. REV. 575, 615 (2020) (describing actions by the Colombia Inspector General Alejandro Ordoñez, a well-known conservative who later sought a conservative party's presidential nomination, to remove two left-wing politicians from their offices); Michael Johnston, *Reforming Reform: Revising the Anticorruption Playbook*, 147 DAEDALUS 50, 59 (Summer 2018) (noting that "the excellent ICAC of New South Wales, Australia, has often had to fend off accusations of favoritism by one political party or another.").

provisions in future constitutions. Yet, we should at least put on the table the question of why constitution drafters might be able to see the need for institutions to address problems caused by intertemporal conflicts of interests when ordinary politicians do not (and, again, why the institutions are to be specified "by law," that is, by ordinary politicians). Here of course the Ackermanian account of constitutional moments may be useful: crisis conditions may push forward a new set of politicians not yet focused on short-term political concerns, or might elevate long-term considerations in the list of ordinary politicians' priorities because failing to address long-term concerns poses a short-term political threat.

5.2.5 *Anti-corruption Efforts: Locating an IPD as Part of a General Agency*

By the turn of the twenty-first century, students of democracy converged on the conclusion that corruption corrodes democracy. They offered numerous policy options for combating corruption. Constitutional designers developed two tools against corruption. The first was simple: create prosecuting offices independent of political control – that is, with constitutional guarantees of independence – to go after corruption.[44] This path was actually even simpler, because many constitutions already provided for independent prosecutors: attorneys-general who were not part of the executive cabinet, directors of public prosecutions, procurators, and the like.[45] Constitutions might clarify that corruption prosecutions fell within the ordinary prosecutorial remit. So, for example, the Colombian Constitution specifically singles out corruption as a target for the general prosecutor. In Mexico, the attorney general is to have had experience "in the field of . . . the fight against corruption."

Occasionally, prosecutorial independence is tempered by consultation requirements. The Botswanan director of public prosecutions is to consult with the attorney general before bringing "cases considered by the Attorney

---

[44] For an overview of anti-corruption agencies in Africa, see Nico Steytler, "Toward Understanding and Combating the Crime of Corruption in Africa," in CORRUPTION AND CONSTITUTIONALISM IN AFRICA 461–62 (Charles M. Fombad & Nico Steytler eds., Oxford University Press, 2020).

[45] This independence is typically assumed when the relevant official is given constitutional status. The Constitution of the Solomon Islands makes the assumption explicit: the attorney general is specifically said to be outside the Cabinet and Parliament, and the director of public prosecutions is "not subject to direction or control."

General to be of national importance." And in Rwanda the justice minister can instruct the National Prosecution Authority with respect to specific investigations.

The second path could be followed along with the first: create some sort of policy-oriented anti-corruption agency. Algeria has a National Council on Corruption, charged with proposing and facilitating relevant policy. Bhutan's commission is to issue reports that are supposed to lead to "prompt" action by the attorney general. Fiji's Constitution has quite detailed provisions describing its Independent Commission Against Corruption, which is to investigate *and* prosecute. Sri Lanka has a commission to "Investigate Allegations of Bribery or Corruption" (to be created "by law"). Finally, the Tunisian Good Governance and Anticorruption Commission has the power to investigate both public and private corruption and refer its findings to the "competent authorities."

I end with a description of the Zimbabwean anti-corruption agency. It has nine members who serve six-year terms, renewable once. One must be a public accountant; another must have ten years of experience in investigating crime. The members may not "act in a partisan manner" or "further the interests of any political party" or "prejudice the lawful interest of any political party," and they may not be "active" members of any political party. It is striking that, in moving away from underspecification, this provision expressly acknowledges the possibility that anti-corruption investigations might have partisan political effects.[46]

Notably, constitutional provisions dealing with anti-corruption agencies attempt to make the agencies independent of political control, but say relatively little about the agencies' accountability. The assumption appears to be that professional norms guiding these agencies build in accountability – if not to the public, then to the profession (the law, mostly) itself. That assumption, as the case studies in Chapters 6 and 7 show, may be too generous.

Yet, overall, the strongest impression one gets from constitutional treatment of corruption is that constitution designers generally do not think that corruption requires special constitutional attention. It is, for them, mostly an ordinary problem of enforcing the criminal law.

---

[46] The experience of Zimbabwe demonstrates that design and performance are not closely related. According to Nico Steytler, in 2018, the nation's president created an anti-corruption unit within his office, nominally to combat corruption but with the effect of "sidelin[ing] the 'independent' institution and plac[ing] anti-corruption measures firmly under political control." Steytler, *supra* note 44, at 481.

5.3 CONCLUSION

As I noted at the outset of this chapter, simply identifying constitutional provisions can give us a sense of design possibilities but provides little or no insight into how the institutions actually operate. Anti-corruption prosecutors can themselves be corrupt and electoral commissions can be toothless.[47] For that reason, I turn to several case studies of anti-corruption efforts and electoral commission activities in an attempt to see whether, or perhaps more accurately, the degree to which IPDs in the real world conform to and depart from the theoretical and functional logics that underlie their creation.

---

[47] Indeed, the general conclusion of the policy literature on corruption is that institutional design has essentially no relation to success or failure in reducing corruption; what matters is political will and leadership. *See,* e.g., Bo Rothstein, *Fighting Systemic Corruption: The Indirect Strategy,* 147 DAEDALUS 35, 38 (Summer 2018) (reviewing prior studies and reporting that "the importance of formal institutions has been much overrated"); ROBERT I. ROTBERG, ANTI-CORRUPTION x (MIT Press, 2020) ("institutions alone cannot counter corrupt practices unless leaders exercising political will have socialized their citizens to accept a political culture of probity"). For relatively recent summaries of the policy literature, see ROBERT I. ROTBERG, THE CORRUPTION CURE: HOW CITIZENS AND LEADERS CAN COMBAT GRAFT (Princeton University Press, 2017); *Anticorruption: How to Beat Back Political & Corporate Graft,* 147 Daedalus (Summer 2018) (Robert I. Rotberg, guest editor). Assessing the performance of IPDs in Africa, Fombad, "Diffusion," *supra* note 1, offers a generally pessimistic summary.

6

Anti-corruption Investigations

Case Studies from Brazil and South Africa

6.1 INTRODUCTION

During the late twentieth century, first policy-makers, then students of constitutionalism, came to understand that pervasive corruption undermines
constitutional democracy.[1] Corruption at the street level – police officers
who respond to complaints and civil servants who process claims only after
receiving bribes – undermines citizen confidence that their government can
deliver anything worthwhile.[2] Corruption at the highest levels, this chapter's
focus, breaks the connection between elections and policy outcomes. By the
late twentieth century, the project of fighting corruption had become an
important component in democracy promotion and, by extension, in
constitutional design.

Anti-corruption institutions take all the available forms: constitutionalized
and statutory, permanent and ad hoc, and so on down the list of possibilities.[3]

---

[1] There is a large literature on anti-corruption policy and enforcement. A great deal of the
literature is focused on how anti-corruption policies can best be implemented by designing
institutions well. A portion of *that* literature deals with constitutional design, but in my view
systematic exploration of that specific question is unusual (though I may have missed some
contributions).

[2] It is widely recognized that even authoritarian governments have an interest in combating
street-level corruption because it discredits their leadership (as is true for non-authoritarian
governments as well), and that authoritarian governments can use corruption investigations as a
weapon against factions within the ruling party as well as against the opposition. This is the
general conclusion of studies of the Chinese Communist Party's recurrent anti-corruption
crusades. For a now quite dated analysis whose conclusions seem still correct, see Alan P. L.
Liu, *The Politics of Corruption in the People's Republic of China*, 77 AM. POL. SCI. REV. 602
(1983); for a more recent account, see Minxin Pei, *How Not to Fight Corruption: Lessons from
China*, 147 DAEDALUS 216 (Summer 2018).

[3] For an illustration of the range, see Marina Matic, "Specialised Anti-Corruption Agencies," in
LEGAL MECHANISMS FOR PREVENTION OF CORRUPTION IN SOUTHEAST EUROPE: WITH

An important feature is that anti-corruption efforts often require coordination among institutions, beyond the obvious point that constitutional courts will typically review the actions taken by anti-corruption institutions to determine whether they comply with constitutional requirements. Prosecutors and judges must act together when the criminal law is the instrument for controlling corruption, for example. Coordination can multiply the difficulties associated with fourth-branch institutions.

Chapter 4 described some of those difficulties: the possibility that an anti-corruption agency might become overly committed to its mission and adopt unnecessarily expansive definitions of corruption and the possibility that a specialized agency will pursue its mission without taking its impact on the political system as a whole into account. As discussed earlier, Lon Fuller identified several additional problems in discussing what happens when courts attempt to solve what he called polycentric problems. Fuller's argument, though perhaps neither directly nor completely applicable to our topic, is suggestive.

One problem he identified is that courts will, as he put it, depart from the judicial proprieties when faced with a polycentric problem. Anti-corruption case studies may show unusual, arguably norm-transforming actions when traditional institutions – or even specialized anti-corruption prosecutors and courts – address high-level corruption.

Fuller also noted that standard legal doctrines are sometimes ill-suited to deal with polycentric problems. When courts are required to deal with such problems even so, Fuller argued, they will transform the problems into ones that are more tractable in traditional doctrine. This suggests that we might be alert to the possibility of doctrinal innovation when courts handle anti-corruption cases.

Fuller rather clearly thought that departing from the judicial proprieties and transforming problems into more tractable ones were normatively troubling features of the use of courts to deal with polycentric problems. We need not go that far. Rather than treating these phenomena as problems, we can see them as *innovations* or *developments* in the law elicited by the nature of the problem at hand, here combating corruption. Still, in some cases (though not in others) such innovations and developments might weaken rather than strengthen democracy.

The remainder of this chapter presents two case studies of anti-corruption efforts conceived of as actions taken to protect democracy. The first deals with

Special Focus on the Defence Sector (Aleksandra Rabrenovic ed., Institut za uporedno pravo, 2013).

Brazil. The case study involves traditional institutions: a number of ordinary investigators from the state and federal levels rather than investigators and prosecutors drawn from institutions specially designed to deal with high-level corruption, and a traditional investigating magistrate rather than a specialized anti-corruption court. The second involves South Africa, where several institutions – a specialized investigating unit that in the course of events was transformed from a statutory to a constitutional body, the ombuds office, and the constitutional court – interacted to address high-level corruption.

The narratives attempt to bring out features of the events that will deepen our understanding of how fourth-branch institutions can both promote and weaken democracy, and how ideas inspired by Fuller can enhance our understanding. In both, I begin by describing the events, then provide a legal and constitutional analysis of them, and offer some conclusions. Before launching into the case studies, I think it important to note a key feature that will play a large part in the narratives. That feature is the structure of party competition – in Brazil, basically disorganized, and in South Africa, with a single party, with internal factions, dominating the political system.

6.2 BRAZIL

One could tell the story of public corruption in Brazil starting at nearly any point.[4] As in many cultures, public corruption has been so pervasive as to give rise to adages such as, "For my family everything, for my friends justice, for my enemies the law."[5] To keep the story under control, I begin with the Brazilian dictatorship that lasted from 1964 to 1985. As the dictatorship progressed, its leaders created a simulacrum of a party system, consolidating their supporters in one party and creating a weak "opposition" party. The dictatorship's end led to the collapse of this sham party system. What replaced it was a world of small party groupings, some leaning to the right and some to the left. "By 1985, eleven parties were represented in Congress, and by 1991 the total had reached nineteen."[6] According to Thomas Skidmore, there was one exception to this incoherence. The Workers' Party (PT, for Partido dos Trabalhadores) was

---

[4] For an overview as of 2011, see CORRUPTION AND DEMOCRACY IN BRAZIL: THE STRUGGLE FOR ACCOUNTABILITY (Timothy J. Power & Matthew M. Taylor eds., University of Notre Dame Press, 2011).

[5] An internet search attributes a version of the phrase to Peruvian President Oscar Benavides, but I have seen versions in Italian (as a slogan describing the mafia) and in Portuguese (describing Brazil).

[6] THOMAS E. SKIDMORE, BRAZIL: FIVE CENTURIES OF CHANGE 183 (2nd ed., Oxford University Press, 2010).

"[b]orn in the labor union activism of the late 1970s" during the dictatorship, and "had become a genuine national party" as Brazil reentered a period of democratic government.[7]

Brazil's overall constitutional system is one of "coalitional presidentialism." A president is elected with the support of his or her party, but the president's party "has never held more than 20 per cent of the seats in the Chamber of Deputies." To govern, presidents must "build party coalitions,"[8] and those coalitions can readily become unstable – mostly because they contain too many parties. The parties are sometimes vehicles for the advancement of particular political leaders and are difficult to sustain once the leader leaves the scene. Such party systems are generally prescriptions for chaotic governance and often for the displacement of democratic rule, discredited by that chaos, by authoritarianism. And, as Virgilio Afonso da Silva puts it, "the price to pay for attaining stable coalitions was not always a political price [that is, the development of a compromise political agenda], but frequently also a monetary price, that is, the need to illicitly buy support from deputies."[9]

The Menselão scandal broke into public view in the late spring of 2005, peaked that fall, and remained a matter of public attention through the early 2010s. It illustrates the connection between the party system and corruption. The left-leaning PT led by Luiz Inácio "Lula" da Silva formed the government in 2003. The PT had fewer than 20 percent of the seats in the legislature, exemplifying coalitional presidentialism. The PT-led coalition included twelve parties. The scandal, which had many facets, involved among other things payments made by the PT to parliamentarians to retain them within the party or to ensure their continuing support for the coalition. The payments were concealed by taking them from advertising budgets of state-owned companies. Though clearly illegal and largely understood to be so by the participants, the payments also served a party- and coalition-maintenance function.[10]

---

[7] *Id.* at 203.

[8] VIRGILIO AFONSO DA SILVA, THE CONSTITUTION OF BRAZIL: A CONTEXTUAL ANALYSIS 42 (Hart Publishing, 2019).

[9] *Id.* at 52. Whether the connection between coalitional presidentialism and corruption is causal or merely coincidental is a matter of some controversy. For an overview, see Juliano Zaiden Benvindo, "The New Presidential Regime in Brazil: Constitutional Dismemberment and the Prospects of a Crisis," Int'l J. Const. L. Blog, Mar. 10, 2020, http://www.iconnectblog.com/2020/03/the-new-presidential-regime-in-brazil-constitutional-dismemberment-and-the-prospects-of-a-crisis/, archived at https://perma.cc/XKC7-V27D.

[10] Cf. Michael Johnston, *Reforming Reform: Revising the Anticorruption Playbook*, 147 DAEDALUS 50, 55 (Summer 2018) (noting that corruption sometimes "functions as a means of … maintaining social order"). See also Alina Mungiu-Pippidi & Michael Johnston, "Conclusions and

That large-scale corruption at high levels of government had been common was well-known among the Brazilian public. The Mensalão scandal occurred when it did because attacks on government corruption had become a priority in the international development and human rights community from the late 1990s, rising precisely at the time when the PT finally came into office in Brazil.[11] It focused almost entirely on parliamentarians, not the outside businesses implicated in some parts of the bribery scheme. Probably for that reason, congressional committees rather than fourth-branch institutions conducted the investigations. And, because the Brazilian Constitution specifies that members of parliament charged with criminal actions in connection with their offices may be tried only in the Supreme Federal Court, the scandal illuminates the background context of later corruption inquiries – for example, supporting narratives that routinely refer to the high number of parliamentarians currently under investigation or indictment.[12]

Many of these features of the Mensalão scandal support the observation that it casts little light on how fourth-branch institutions deal with high-level corruption. More recently, Brazil had a major anti-corruption investigation that simultaneously rooted out substantial corruption, devastated the leadership of one of the nation's leading parties, and contributed to the election of a president with clear authoritarian tendencies and himself tainted by corruption.

The Lava Jato (Car Wash) scandal began with an investigation of bribes paid by Odebrecht, a major construction company, in connection with valuable contracts, to high-level employees of Brazil's semi-public oil and gas company Petrobras.[13] The public corruption dimension of the scandal was in essence this: Members of the federal cabinet nominated Petrobras

Lessons Learned," in TRANSITIONS TO GOOD GOVERNANCE: CREATING VIRTUOUS CIRCLES OF ANTI-CORRUPTION (Alina Mungiu-Pippidi & Michael Johnston eds., Edward Elgar Publishing, 2017), at 249 (concluding from a large-N analysis that "legal restrictions on party finance do not reduce corrupt practices – they might even prompt more illegal behavior").

[11] *See* Fabio Sa e Silva, *From Car Wash to Bolsonaro: Law and Lawyers in Brazil's Illiberal Turn (2014–2018)*, 47 J. L. & SOCIETY S90, S92 (2020) (describing anti-corruption efforts as a "subset" of the "rule of law" industry in the 1990s); Fabiano Engelmann, *The 'Fight against Corruption' in Brazil from the 2000s: A Political Crusade through Judicial Activism*, 47 J. L. & SOCIETY S74, S78–82 (2020) (describing the connections between international and Brazilian anti-corruption efforts).

[12] Forty people were charged in the Supreme Federal Court in August 2007. The most important charges were resolved in October 2012 with convictions of three major figures – José Dirceu, who had been Lula's chief of staff, José Genoino, former PT president, and Delubio Soares, the PT treasurer.

[13] The scandal got its name from an early stage in the investigation, which revealed money laundering processed through a chain of car washing stations. In what follows, I rely heavily on

officials. Those officials in turn solicited and received bribes from construction companies (on an enormous scale). The officials then paid off the cabinet members. The cabinet members retained some of the money for their personal benefit and transmitted some of it to their party treasuries.[14]

Note the chain connecting the payment of money to public officials: construction company (Odebrecht) to Petrobras officials (where money actually changed hands) to cabinet members who nominated the Petrobras officials to Lula. Notably, there was only scattered and thin evidence that the cabinet members had appointed the Petrobras officials knowing that the latter would receive bribes from Odebrecht, and similarly thin evidence that the cabinet officials themselves received payoffs either from Odebrecht or the Petrobras officials who they had appointed. There was evidence that Lula had paid less than cost for a smallish apartment he maintained as something like a vacation home, that he ended up receiving a larger apartment, and that a construction company had made improvements within the apartment and charged Lula less than their cost. There was no evidence that the company making the improvements did so because it had benefited from specific decisions made by Lula's cabinet members (in a traditional quid pro quo sense), nor that Lula knew that the below-cost benefit he received resulted from his own choices.[15] At the same time, it was an open secret that private money flowed to public officials and their parties even when no one could identify either a specific individual or a specific payment that was openly corrupt.

The effect of the Lava Jato investigation on Brazil's political system was substantial. The PT had been leading the government since 2003. As a result, the politicians implicated in the scandal were from that party. Further, like many left-leaning parties around the world, the PT could not rely upon direct support from wealthy contributors who, of course, leaned to the right. Bribes and other forms of corruption were in part, though only in part, a means of filling the party's treasury and augmenting what some politicians might fairly have regarded as inappropriately low salaries. So, in addition to enriching public officials, the bribes had some effect in strengthening the PT within an overall political system of quite weak parties. Coalitional presidentialism

---

an unpublished paper by Mariana Mota Prado (University of Toronto) and Marta Machado (Fundação Getúlio Vargas, São Paulo) [Prado & Machado].

[14] Sometimes the construction companies and Petrobras officials cut out the middlemen and paid the money directly to the parties, but not as legal campaign contributions.

[15] Rumors circulated in the Brazilian political elite that Lula had in fact received more direct corrupt payments, but such payments were not part of the public case against him. (Here I rely upon conversations with Brazilians knowledgeable about Brazilian politics.).

meant in addition that the coalition would sometimes include extremely weak parties, who could benefit from the party-finance dimension of the Lava Jato scheme.[16]

The most dramatic effect the investigation had on Brazil's politics occurred as the 2018 elections approached. Because Lula's protégé Dilma Rousseff had been impeached for purely political reasons amid a serious economic downturn (and replaced as president by a representative of a coalition party that was ideologically remote from the PT), Lula was again running for president and appeared to be the leading candidate. The Lava Jato investigators charged Lula with corruption – accepting costly improvements in housing he used, to be paid for by one of the construction companies that had bribed Petrobras officials. Lula was disqualified from the ballot immediately after his conviction was affirmed by an appellate court, leading to the election of Jair Bolsonaro to the presidency.

The Lava Jato investigation was a coordinated effort by the Federal Public Prosecutors' Office, which is decentralized with substantial independent authority in state-level officials, and the Federal Police Department, under the control of the national Ministry of Justice. Judge Sergio Moro, a well-respected judge even prior to the investigation, was the supervising magistrate.[17] The investigation's official venue was the state of Curitiba, one of Brazil's more conservative states.

One member of Brazil's Supreme Federal Court called Lava Jato a "spectacular investigation," meaning that it was an investigation-as-public-spectacle.[18] In the name of transparency, the investigators maintained a website that was updated with information as it became available. Perhaps even more dramatic, Judge Moro authorized the investigators to make recordings of conversations between Lula and Dilma and then released them to the public. The most damaging of the recordings, from Lula's point of view, had actually occurred *after* the authorization to record had ended.[19] The recordings included a conversation about Dilma's planned appointment of Lula as her

---

[16] See George Mészáros, *Caught in an Authoritarian Trap of Its Own Making? Brazil's 'Lava Jato' Anti-Corruption Investigation and the Politics of Prosecutorial Overreach*, 47 J. L. & Society S54 (2020), especially at S58–59.

[17] Judge Moro served as an assistant at the Supreme Federal Court during the Mensalão episode.

[18] See also Mészáros, *supra* note 16, at S62–64 (describing the public relations campaign the Lava Jato prosecutors conducted).

[19] Judge Moro authorized the recordings on February 17, 2016. At 11:13 AM on March 16, 2016, he entered an order terminating the surveillance. The police and the telephone company received that order around noon. Recording continued, though, and a recording made at 1:32 PM covered a conversation about Dilma's intention to appoint Lula chief of staff the next day. Releasing unauthorized surveillance recordings is a crime under Brazilian law.

chief of staff, which would have transferred the investigation from Judge Moro to the Supreme Federal Court. The day after the recordings were released to the public, Judge Moro placed a note in the official file – itself publicly available – stating that he had not noticed that the conversation occurred after the surveillance was to be ended, and offering a legal justification for releasing the recording notwithstanding the termination of the authorization to record.[20]

The circumstances and targets of the investigation led PT supporters to suspect that it was politically motivated. The timing of the investigation into Lula himself, the quite indirect connection the payments for home improvements had to core examples of corruption, and particularly the concededly unlawful recording and then release of the Dilma–Lula recordings all contributed to the sense among those on the left that something more than pursuit of corruption was going on.

Each aspect of the investigation that critics wondered about could be given a charitable nonpolitical explanation. For example, PT officials were disproportionately targeted because the PT had formed the government during the period covered by the investigation. Yet, Brazil's culture of corruption was deep rooted, and PT supporters argued that corrupt conservatives had not been pursued nearly as aggressively when they were in power.[21] Similarly, Judge Moro defended the unlawful recording as an oversight that occurred under the press of time, and its release similarly innocent. Again, a charitable reading of the events is possible. But, critics suggested, the accumulation of actions too close to the margin of politically motivated investigation placed real pressure on charitable readings.[22]

---

[20] Cf. Ezequiel Gonzales-Ocantos & Viviana Baraybar Hidalgo, Lava Jato *Beyond Borders: The Uneven Performance of Anticorruption Judicial Efforts in Latin America*, 15 Taiwan J. of Democracy 63, 70 (2019) (noting that "judges and prosecutors may need to rely on unorthodox tactics to disclose key pieces of evidence that help them undermine the credibility of their attackers").

[21] Anti-corruption investigators did target some opposition politicians, notably Aécio Neves, who had lost the presidential run-off election in 2014 to Dilma Rouseff.

[22] A communication on July 28, 2016 from Lula's lawyers to the Office of the High Commissioner for Human Rights, under the Optional Protocol to the International Covenant on Civil and Political Rights, lays out many of the concerns these critics had. The case, No. 2841/2016, is described in "Brazil's Ex-President Appeals to UN over Abuses of Power in Corruption Case," *The Guardian*, July 28, 2016, https://www.theguardian.com/world/2016/jul/28/brazil-ex-presi dent-un-petition-luiz-inacio-lula-da-silva, archived at https://perma.cc/GWV9-QYP6. In this connection, I note that Judge Moro resigned his judicial post to take a position with the Bolsonaro government as minister in charge of anti-corruption. For Moro's critics, this served as a post hoc justification for their skepticism about his evenhandedness during the investigation. That justification might well survive Minister Moro's public claims that he would continue to

In a relatively straightforward scheme, Odebrecht and other construction companies handed money over to obtain favorable treatment in public contracts. Some of that money went to Petrobras officials as ordinary personal bribes. Other payments went to political parties, with the payments required as a condition for obtaining the contracts. Yet the simplicity of the scheme does not mean that the legalities of the investigation were equally straightforward. Some of the investigation's key facets required significant institutional innovation or improvisation, sometimes near and sometimes perhaps crossing the border of impropriety.

According to most Brazilian legal scholars, the Lava Jato investigation and ensuing prosecutions pushed the limits of the law as previously understood in ways that evoke Fuller's concerns. George Mészáros summarizes a widespread view: "Recent laws targeting corruption and other offenses were pushed to their limits and beyond."[23] Almost all the developments were legally defensible though often controversial; from Fuller's perspective, the developments might be understood as transforming the law under the pressure of the circumstances. It seems clear that prosecutors and judges believed that rooting out corruption was essential to ensuring that, as one judge put it, "judges will not let crime kill the renewed hopes of the Brazilian people."[24]

The prosecutors' and judges' innovations were both procedural and substantive. They expanded the use of plea-bargaining, which required that they "temper their prosecutorial zeal" in ways that might have run "against their professional ethos or deeply ingrained views about what the law requires from them as members of the judicial branch."[25] Further, prosecutors, with judicial approval, expanded the use of a process that compelled suspects to answer questions before being formally charged. Prior to the Lava Jato investigation, such questioning was authorized, though it rarely occurred, but only after the

---

be evenhanded as minister and Bolsonaro's claims on forming his government that it would be a government of technocratic experts, not politicians. Minister Moro resigned from the cabinet in April 2020 after President Bolsonaro fired the head of the national police. The *New York Times* story reporting the resignation described Moro as "one of Brazil's most popular *politicians*" (emphasis added). Ernesto Londoño, Letícia Casado & Manuela Andreoni, "Turmoil in Brazil: Bolsonaro Fires Police Chief and Justice Minister Quits," *New York Times*, April 24, 2020, https://www.nytimes.com/2020/04/24/world/americas/brazil-bolsonaro-moro.html?action=click&module=Latest&pgtype=Homepage, archived at https://perma.cc/SR4D-NXR5. Mészáros, *supra* note 16, at S73, refers to Moro, who has disclaimed interest in running for the presidency, as "a credible candidate for the 2022 presidential elections."

[23] Mészáros, *supra* note 16, at S69.

[24] Renan Ramalho, "STF confirma ordens para prender Delcídio Amaral e André Esteves," Globo, http://g1.globo.com/politica/operacao-lava-jato/noticia/2015/11/stf-confirma-ordens-para-prender-delcidio-amaral-e-andre-esteves.html, cited in Prado & Machado, *supra* note 13.

[25] Gonzales-Ocantos & Hidalgo, *supra* note 20, at 69.

suspects had refused a request to appear voluntarily and answer questions. The Lava Jato investigators questioned suspects without making such a request. Most notably, they descended upon Lula's house to conduct such questioning, having notified the press of their impending action. This might be seen as a departure from the proprieties of ordinary criminal investigations.

The investigators justified their actions by noting a concern about the possibility that suspects would destroy incriminating evidence between the time of a request and their appearance. Such a concern would seem to be present in nearly every case, though, and yet the courts had previously required strict adherence to the requirement of a prior request. In 2018, the Supreme Federal Court held that questioning without a prior request was unconstitutional, but it also allowed prosecutors to use material obtained in cases where the questioning had already occurred.

The substantive law of responsibility for corruption also developed during the Lava Jato scandal. Brazilian law clearly prohibited *giving* a bribe. Whether the person who received a bribe committed a crime was less clear, at least in cases where the person offering the bribe expected a return but where proof of a quid pro quo was weak or absent. And, even more murky was the status of the politicians in the Lava Jato scandal. The construction companies bribed Petrobras officials. The officials passed some of the money on to the politicians, but there was no evidence available that those transfers were explicitly in exchange for appointing the Petrobras officials to positions where they could get or even solicit bribes. Even more remote was the responsibility of the president: there was no evidence that Lula had done or even promised to do anything whatever, including appointing ministers who would appoint Petrobras officials who would solicit bribes, that led the construction company to pay for his home improvements.[26]

One could have a creative theory of "systemic" criminal responsibility: although the politicians did not know specifically which construction companies would bribe which Petrobras officials, they knew or must have known or should have known that such bribery was going on.[27] And, similarly, they must or should have known that some of the contributions the construction companies made to political parties resulted from compliance with the

---

[26] Andrea Scoseria Katz, *Making Brazil Work? Brazilian Coalitional Presidentialism at 30 and Its Post-Lava Jato Prospects*, 5 Revista de Investigações Constitutiocionais 77, 93 (2018), writes, "Some charges ... have been flimsy, hasty – especially, agrees the legal community, those against Lula himself."

[27] I note that Camila Vergara, Systemic Corruption: Constitutional Ideas for an Anti-Oligarchic Republic (Princeton University Press, 2020), develops a quite different notion of "systemic corruption," not focused on criminal responsibility.

unlawful conditions Petrobras officials imposed upon contractors who were awarded contracts. The overall system of contracting was in effect a criminal conspiracy. That theory, though, would have been a dramatic extension of existing theories of criminal liability.

Judge Moro instead developed two ideas in support of the lawfulness of the charges he brought. The seeds of each were latent in existing law. Existing statutes defined "passive corruption" using the phrase (translated), "in connection with [the official's] position ... even if it is to simply perform the obligations [of the office] ... but in connection with [the office]."[28] Judge Moro read this to authorize conviction for receipt of gifts without any showing that the recipient promised or did anything directly to benefit the person giving the "gift" as long, apparently, as the recipient exercised power associated with an office that had some connection to the donor.

He also developed the idea of command responsibility, familiar from international criminal law, to go up the chain of command from the actual recipients of bribes to the ministers who appointed the recipients and ultimately to the president who appointed the ministers.[29] Judge Moro's rulings were thus not unprecedented, but they extended previous decisions that had themselves been and that remained controversial among Brazilian legal scholars. Again, we might see this with a Fuller-ian lens, a transformation of the law to make an evident problem more legally tractable.

A final example of pressure on the law requires the presentation of some detail. In 2009, the Supreme Federal Court, relying on its understanding of the presumption of innocence, held that those convicted of crimes could not be imprisoned until all avenues of appeal had been exhausted. Critics noted that this holding disproportionately benefited white-collar criminals compared to those convicted of other crimes because the former had more resources than the latter to pursue appeals to the highest courts – whose dockets were so overloaded that deciding a criminal appeal might take several years during which the convicted person would remain free.

In February 2016, the Court changed the rule, by a vote of six-to-five.[30] The majority held that imprisonment could follow upon the affirmance of a conviction by an intermediate appeals court. Roughly a year later, one of the judges in the majority indicated that he had changed his mind: immediate

---

[28] 13ª Vara da Justiça Federal de Curitiba (J.F.) (Federal District Courts on Matters of Federal Interest), Ação Penal No. 5046512-94.2016.4.04.7000/PR, Relator: Sérgio Fernando Moro, July 12, 2017.

[29] Here Judge Moro built upon interpretations developed during the prior Mensalão scandal.

[30] S.T.F., HC 126.292 / SP, Relator: Min. Teori Zavascki, 17.02.2016, D.J.e., 17.05.2016 (Braz.) (discussing the 2009 case), discussed in Prado & Machado, *supra* note 13.

imprisonment should be allowed after the initial affirmance only if the defendant presented purely factual questions on appeal; if the defendant presented issues of law, imprisonment had to be deferred until after all appeals had been concluded.

That fit Lula's case precisely, so it would appear that he would not be sent to jail until his appeal to the Supreme Federal Court concluded – and that therefore he could appear on the 2018 ballot. The court took up Lula's challenge early in 2018, amid intense public attention. The case presented (for present purposes) two questions: Could he be imprisoned after the intermediate court affirmed his conviction, and were there legal questions that invalidated his conviction? On the face of it, there would seem to have been a majority favoring Lula on the first question – the five dissenters from 2016 and the judge who had changed his mind. That was not how things turned out, though. One of the dissenters voted to allow imprisonment after initial affirmance. She took the position that she was bound by the 2016 prece-dent from which she had dissented.[31] The result was that Lula was imprisoned and disqualified from the ballot.

In 2019, the Court revisited the issue and this time held that a person could be imprisoned after his or her appeal was rejected by the intermediate appeals court only if the court made an individualized determination that imprison-ment would "guarantee public and economic order, [promote] the conveni-ence of criminal proceedings or … ensure the application of the criminal law.[32] The Court again divided six to five, and it is perhaps worth noting that justices appointed by Lula and Dilma were found on both sides: two of Lula's appointees and one of Dilma's were in the majority, three of hers and one of his in the minority. The decision eliminated – far too late, of course – Lula's automatic ineligibility for office and opened up the possibility that he could run for the presidency in the election scheduled for 2022. That possibility, though, was subject to a decision by Brazil's electoral court, which was authorized to disqualify Lula on grounds other than his conviction alone.

The story continues to play itself out. In early 2021, a judge vacated Lula's conviction because it had been improper to investigate Lula in the Curitiba court. This left open the possibility that the prosecution could be renewed elsewhere, with Brasilia as the obvious candidate. Almost simultaneously, a divided panel of the Supreme Federal Court held that Judge Moro had been

---

[31] S.T.F., HC 152752, Relator: Min. Edson Fachin, 04.04.2018, 127, D.J.e., 27.06.2018 (Braz.), discussed in Prado & Machado, *supra* note 13.

[32] "STF decides that the enforcement of prison sentence should begin only after exhaustion of appeals," https://perma.cc/GWV9-QYP6.

biased against Lula, lending support to suspicions by PT supporters that the entire Lava Jato investigation had been politically motivated. The entire court immediately moved to take up the claim of bias, and no decision has been rendered at the time of writing.[33]

What general lessons about anti-corruption investigations can we draw from this case study? Anti-corruption investigations are not pure examples of polycentric problems, though their political implications give them some degree of polycentricity. Yet, Fuller's predictions about what happens when courts attempt to deal with polycentric problems have at least some resonance in the Brazilian case.

Fuller suggested, for example, that judges dealing with such problems would, as he put it, depart from the "judicial proprieties." Fuller held essentialist views about those proprieties, and much of what he thought propriety precluded has become commonplace in adjudication around the world. Even so, the actions taken together by Judge Moro and the prosecutors pushed beyond not uncommon but somewhat unusual methods of keeping the public up-to-date on the progress of ongoing investigations through press releases and (these days) a regularly updated website. Judge Moro's public defense of his role in releasing the Dilma-Lula recordings can fairly be described as extraordinary. And, more generally, Judge Moro invited public attention to his actions, becoming something of a celebrity judge in the process.[34] More generally, the "team," for so it should be thought of, sought not merely to inform the public about the investigation but to build public support for it by expanding the audience for claims about how corruption undermined democracy. That efforts along these lines might well be good policy does not mean, though, that courts (and prosecutors) should engage in them, even when other public bodies are silent. Here too we can reasonably think about the way in which the anti-corruption effort placed pressure to depart from judicial propriety.

The developments in substantive law, such as the expansion of the concept of "passive corruption" and the doctrine of willful blindness, might also have resulted from the pressures of pursuing high-level corruption. It was not

---

[33] On the decision about Judge Moro's bias, see Matheus Teixeira & Marcelo Rocha, "Moro Was No [sic] Impartial to Lula, Says Supreme Court," FOLHA DE S. PAOLO (English edition), Mar. 24, 2021, https://www1.folha.uol.com.br/internacional/en/brazil/2021/03/moro-was-no-impartial-to-lula-says-supreme-court.shtml?utm_source=newsletter&utm_medium=email&utm_campaign=newsen, archived at https://perma.cc/9KH4-A764.

[34] I thank Shrudhar Jaynathi, Harvard Law School '22, for pushing me to clarify the points in this paragraph. Judge Moro offered his view of the investigation in Sergio Fernando Moro, *Preventing Systemic Corruption in Brazil*, 147 DAEDALUS 157 (Summer 2018).

obviously mistaken to think that Lula's acceptance of home improvements was inconsistent with the ethical demands of public service. Without an expanded concept of passive corruption, though, his actions might have escaped sanction.

The Brazilian courts developed the law innovatively to deal with procedural and substantive problems associated with the Lava Jato investigation. Lawyers working in the common law tradition see such development as characteristic of law as such. Yet, though there appears to be nothing intrinsically wrong with that process, it does seem noteworthy that one matter played no articulated role in the judges' decisions: no one appears to have openly taken into account the potential disruption of politics the investigation caused. Or, perhaps more accurately: the judges and prosecutors appear to have believed that the benefits to democracy of an aggressive stance against high-level corruption outweighed the obvious disruption of ordinary politics – and especially the removal of Lula from the presidential ballot – that the investigation was causing.[35] We cannot know yet whether they were correct. But, when coupled with the effective (even if not intended) tilt of the investigation against a leftist party, I believe there is reason to be concerned about the course the Lava Jato investigation took.

6.3 SOUTH AFRICA

As noted earlier, Chapter Nine of the Constitution of the Republic of South Africa identifies a number of institutions supporting constitutional democracy. It does not include an anti-corruption agency. Initially, anti-corruption efforts were placed in the ordinary ministries concerned with justice and policing. Efforts by President Thabo Mbeki to exercise political control over corruption investigations led to an important Constitutional Court decision giving the anti-corruption effort constitutional protection against politically motivated interference, though the precise contours of that protection remain unclear. Corruption investigations eventually led to the removal of Mbeki's successor Jacob Zuma from office.

Two aspects in the background of all these developments frame the following discussion. First, since the end of apartheid, South Africa has been a "dominant party" state, with the African National Congress (ANC) having a substantial majority of parliamentary seats. Internally, though, the ANC was

---

[35] Cf. Matthew M. Taylor, *Getting to Accountability: A Framework for Planning & Implementing Anticorruption Strategies*, 147 DAEDALUS 63, 67 (Summer 2018) (observing that one major anti-corruption investigation in Italy left an "obliterated political landscape").

something like a coalition. Initially, the components derived from the nation's chief labor organization and the South African Communist Party, and the party was held together by the astute and charismatic Nelson Mandela. When he voluntarily left politics, leadership passed to factions centered on Thabo Mbeki and Jacob Zuma. These factions were partly personalistic, partly programmatic, the latter involving disagreements over the best policies to achieve economic growth and enhance the wealth of the nation's black population. To build support, both factions engaged in patronage politics, which sometimes were the vehicle not only for faction-building but straightforward individual-level corruption.

Second, the initial South African Constitutional Court was extremely strong and able. Its members were quite distinguished lawyers who had provided legal support to the ANC during apartheid or had led the legal opposition to apartheid. As presidents, Mbeki and Zuma weakened the Court, appointing less distinguished lawyers and hoping to increase their influence on it. As we will see, those efforts were partly, but only partly, successful.

The institutions leading anti-corruption efforts in South Africa were the South African Police Service (SAPS), the ordinary police force under the control of the minister of justice, and the National Prosecuting Authority (NPA), headed by a director of public prosecution who reports to the minister of justice as well. In 1999, parliament created a special unit, the Directorate of Special Operations (DSO), within the NPA, charged with investigating "national priority crime," defined to include corruption, organized crime, and financial crimes. Known as the Scorpions, the DSO was by all accounts a rather effective agency whose successes created bureaucratic tension with the SAPS.

Though President Mbeki was never accused of corruption himself, there is no doubt that corruption was widespread during his administration. One major example was the "arms deal." The deal combined hopes for investment in military modernization with kickbacks to influential ANC members. Zuma's chief financial adviser was prosecuted as part of the arms deal investigation. This led to a major confrontation between Mbeki, who as president was thought to control the Scorpions, and Zuma. Zuma won the intraparty fight and forced Mbeki out of his position as ANC head, and quickly out of the presidency.

The Scorpions figured in the factional conflict and Zuma's faction, and so the ANC in parliament, supported legislation dissolving the Scorpions and transferring its power to the SAPS, in a unit that came to be known as the Hawks. Businessman Hugh Glenister managed to get the Constitutional

Court to consider a constitutional challenge to the Scorpions' replacement by the Hawks, contending that the Scorpions had, but the Hawks lacked, the degree of independence of political control that, he contended, the Constitution required.

Dividing five-to-four, the Constitutional Court agreed with Glenister.[36] Controversially finding support from international commitments South Africa had made, the majority first found that the Constitution did indeed require that the anti-corruption agency have sufficient independence from political control despite the fact that there was no specific constitutional provision to that effect. Corruption, according to the majority, "blatantly undermines ... the institutions of democracy."[37] To combat it, the Constitution implicitly required an independent anti-corruption agency.

The majority found that the Hawks were not sufficiently independent. It examined both structure and what it called "operational autonomy," by which it appeared to mean the way in which the Hawks actually went about investigating and, importantly, refrained from investigating.[38] It also emphasized that the appearance of independence might be as important as actual independence. This mattered because, whatever the reality, the public appeared to believe that Zuma had reduced the unit's independence by replacing the Scorpions with the Hawks. Structural defects included the absence of special protections against removal beyond those available to all police officials and the possibility of reappointment as head of the Hawks, which might lead incumbents to curry favor in hopes of reappointment. Most important, though, was the fact that the Hawks' work would be coordinated through a cabinet committee, which nominally would be concerned only with general policy but which was likely to shape policy in light of specific investigations. The thought was that, having a specific investigation in mind, the committee could gerrymander the list of topics the Hawks were authorized to investigate to bar them from looking into individual targets the committee wished to protect.

The majority observed that any anti-corruption agency had to be subject to parliamentary oversight, but found that the oversight mechanisms for the Hawks were too intrusive. Dissenting Chief Justice Sandile Ngcobo disagreed. He concurred that the Hawks had to have some degree of independence from political control, but stressed, more than the majority did,

---

[36] *Glenister* v. *President of the Republic of South Africa and Others* (CCT 48/10) [2011] ZACC 6; 2011 (3) SA 347 (CC); 2011 (7) BCLR 651 (CC) (17 March 2011).

[37] *Id.* ¶166.

[38] *Id.* ¶ 206.

that accountability through oversight was required as well. Anti-corruption agencies "should not be a law unto themselves."[39] "What is required are legal mechanisms that will limit the possibility of ... interference in the operational decisions."[40] After outlining what he believed were some specific requirements, the chief justice found that the Hawks' structure had "important safeguards" against improper political control.

The government responded to this decision by making cosmetic changes in the legislation about the Hawks. Glenister and his allies were unsatisfied and again prevailed in the Constitutional Court. This time the decision was written by the new Chief Justice Mogoeng Mogoeng. Mogoeng's appointment had been controversial: he was the Court's junior justice when appointed chief justice, and many thought that he would be too deferential to Mbeki and the ANC. He was also a highly religious man who agreed with a skeptical interviewer's question that God wanted him to be chief justice.[41] His religious commitments to justice and honesty infused his views about what the law required. The opinions he wrote in major anti-corruption cases are filled with little essays on the importance of the rule of law and the separation of powers, and on the depth and importance of South Africa's commitment to democratic and accountable government. These essays create a rhetorical atmosphere pervaded by democratic ideals, though they seem at best loosely connected to the legal arguments Mogoeng made. Seen in their best light, the essays might be understood as a form of civic education for those who read or read about them; seen less generously, they are ways for Mogoeng to polish his reputation.

Chief Justice Mogoeng ruled against Mbeki in this iteration of the Hawks case. The majority went systematically through the changes the new legislation had made, and found that most of them enhanced the Hawks' independence. One key objection remained. The new statute continued to give the government the power to control the topics the Hawks could investigate, a power that the initial Glenister case feared could give the government the power to determine who the investigation would target. Having encountered what it clearly believed to be government obstruction, the Court "severed" the unconstitutional oversight mechanism, thereby in effect giving the Hawks' leader complete discretion to identify targets.

[39] *Id.* ¶ 123.
[40] *Id.* ¶ 120.
[41] "Mogoeng: God Wants Me to Be Chief Justice," Times Live, Sept. 4, 2011, https://www .timeslive.co.za/politics/2011-09-04-mogoeng-god-wants-me-to-be-chief-justice/, archived at https://perma.cc/XNQ6-J4XY.

Eventually, Zuma was forced to resign as president, as a result of an investigation by the Chapter Nine Office of Public Protector, whose responsibilities include investigation of "improper acts with respect to public money." Designed on the ombuds office model but with a larger remit, the public protector – a single person – was charged with making reports but seemingly lacked direct enforcement capacity. The opening paragraph of Chapter Nine imposed duties on other state agencies: "Other organs of state, through legislative and other measures, must assist and protect these institutions to ensure the independence, impartiality, dignity and effectiveness of these institutions."[42]

Zuma's forced resignation resulted from an investigation into spending on his family compound at Nkandla.[43] News reports revealed that Zuma had used more than a million dollars in public funds for home improvements, nominally to increase his personal security – though the improvements included a chicken coop and a swimming pool. Public Protector Thuli Madonsela investigated the matter.

Prior to her appointment in 2009, Madonsela had been a backbench ANC parliamentarian with an undistinguished career, and Zuma probably expected her to be a team player as public protector. That expectation was supported by an anodyne op ed column she wrote in 2011, in which she described her role as someone who "gives the people a voice while giving the traditional leader a conscience."[44] Nor was it weakened by her investigation into corruption charges against Jacob Malema, who had been the leader of the ANC's youth wing prior to his expulsion from the ANC for actions that could "sow division and disunity in the ANC." Stu Woolman describes Madonsela's early actions in the office as "erratic."[45] Zuma apparently did not take into account that, according to close observers of South African politics, she was quite strong-willed and became committed to the tasks she was given. After investigating the Nkandla matter, Madonsela issued a report saying that Zuma should repay the cost of home improvements that were unrelated to enhancing Zuma's personal safety. Zuma and the ANC, which he continued to dominate, refused to do anything in response.

---

[42] Constitution of South Africa, art. 181 (3).

[43] For an overview of the events, see Tom Ginsburg, Aziz Huq & David Landau, *Designing Presidential Impeachment*, 88 U. CHI. L. REV. 81, 105–9 (2021).

[44] Thuli Madonsela, "Way of the Makhadzi," *City Press*, June 4, 2011, quoted in THANDEKA GQUBULE, NO LONGER WHISPERING TO POWER (Jonathan Ball Publishers, 2017).

[45] Stu Woolman, *A Politics of Accountability: How South Africa's Judicial Recognition of the Binding Legal Effect of the Public Prosecutor's Recommendations Had a Catalysing Effect that Brought Down a President*, 8 CONST'L CT. REV. 155, 178 (2016).

A year later, the Supreme Court of Appeal – the highest general court – issued a decision in another case involving a report by the public protector about administrative failures by the chief operating officer of the South African Broadcasting Corporation. In language evocative of Kelsen's argument for a constitutional court, the Court described the public protector as an institution that "guards the guards." Giving the report *some* legal force, the Court held that the Corporation, a public agency, could not ignore the report's conclusions; doing so would violate the duty to "assist" the public protector. According to the Court, the SABC could disregard the report only if it provided "rational reasons" for doing so; otherwise, it had to implement the public protector's recommendations through its own processes, for example, by holding an internal disciplinary hearing on the charges against the report's target.[46]

Building on the SABC decision, the Constitutional Court held in 2016 that the public protector's report on Nkandla placed Zuma under a legal duty to repay the money, which he did.[47] Echoing Madonsela's imagery, Chief Justice Mogoeng described the public protector as "the embodiment of a biblical David, that the public is, who fights the most powerful and very well-resourced Goliath, that impropriety and corruption by government officials are."[48] After several paragraphs of "good government" rhetoric, the opinion continued, "If compliance with remedial action ... were optional, then very few culprits ... would allow it to have any effect." That would make it "incomprehensible just how the Public Protector could ever be effective in what she does."[49]

The chief justice then turned to constitutional text. Section 182 provides that the "Public Protector has the power, as regulated by national legislation ... to take appropriate remedial action." He continued, "The power to take remedial action is primarily sourced from the supreme law itself." Legislative regulations could not "eviscerat[e] their constitutional forebears into operational obscurity." So, the public protector's remedial order could have direct legal effect even without supplemental legislation. The opinion bolstered this conclusion with several textual references: that the public protector was to be impartial and exercise her powers without fear or

---

[46] *South African Broadcasting Corp.* v. *Democratic Alliance*, 2015 (4) All SA 719 (SCA). Note that the case was brought by the Democratic Alliance, the leading opposition party.

[47] *Economic Freedom Fighters* v. *Speaker of the National Assembly*, 2016 (3) SA 580 (CC). The Economic Freedom Fighters is a political party founded in 2013 by Julius Malema.

[48] *Economic Freedom Fighters*, ¶52. The chief justice also noted that the office's name itself reflected its important role, in contrast to the more neutral "Ombudsman." *Id.* ¶51.

[49] *Id.* ¶56.

favor, including power directed at "target[s] ... in the throne-room of executive raw power" and, even more, that other government actors had a duty to
assist the public protector so as to ensure her effectiveness.[50]

The steps other actors had to take might vary depending on circumstances;
sometimes, for example, mediation or conciliation would be appropriate.
Rejecting one possibility raised in the SABC case, the Court observed that
the addressees of remedial measures could not simply disregard them if they
had "a rational basis for doing so."[51] And, in the circumstances, the public
protector's order that the president repay the costs of the unnecessary improvements at Nkandla was appropriate.

The opinion went further, though. It stated that Zuma had "failed to
uphold, defend and respect the Constitution," the first constitutional obligation placed on the president, who, a subsequent provision states, can be
removed for "a serious violation of the Constitution."[52] Zuma's failure trig-
gered a duty in the National Assembly to "give urgent attention to or intervene
by facilitating his compliance" with the order to repay the expenses.[53]

Despite the little essays about the rule of law and the like, the chief justice's
opinion was less conclusory than those in the Scorpions/Hawks litigation, but
it was not without difficulties. The problem lay in treating the public protect-
or's "remedial" order – her direction that Zuma pay the non-security related
costs of the renovations – as legally binding on the president. The problem was
hidden in a paragraph late in the opinion. Zuma objected that the public
protector's order could not bind him because she was not "a Judicial
Officer."[54] Suppose she had investigated an ordinary bureaucrat, concluded
that the bureaucrat's action had damaged a citizen's business, and ordered the
bureaucrat to pay the citizen a specified amount in damages. Trace out the
ensuing litigation, and we would find eventually that a judge would enter an
order directing that the payment be made, giving some weight to the public
protector's conclusions but ultimately taking them on as the judge's own. That
is, there would be a judicial determination that wrongdoing had occurred,

---

[50] *Id.* ¶66.
[51] *Id.* ¶¶ 69, 70.
[52] Constitution of South Africa, §§ 83(b), 89 (a).
[53] *Economic Freedom Fighters,* ¶104.
[54] *Id.* ¶ 72. Aziz Huq describes this as a claim that the remedial order was merely a "recommendation[]," which is a slightly informal way of putting it. Aziz Z. Huq, A *Tactical Separation of
Powers,* 9 Const. Ct. Rev. 19, 35 (2019). He also describes the opinion as "arguably circular" in
its assumption, as he reads the opinion, that the public protector's recommended remedies
were "sanctioned by law," which "assumes the legal force of those recommendations." *Id.* at
35n87. For a contrary view, see Woolman, *supra* note 45, at 182 (describing the Court's "textual
arguments" as "persuasive").

albeit one that might rest to some degree on deference to the public protector's investigation.

Zuma sought exactly the same. The Constitution gave the Constitutional Court exclusive jurisdiction over complaints against the president, so it was in the position of the ordinary courts in the prior example. Zuma wanted the Court, not merely the public protector, to determine that his actions violated his constitutional duty. The chief justice's opinion circled around doing so, and some of its formulations might be taken as the Constitutional Court's agreement with the public protector's substantive conclusions. If that was indeed what the Court had done, a more transparent presentation would have been better.[55]

Zuma's troubles accumulated.[56] His opponents contended that the actions he had taken in connection with his house justified his impeachment. His allies in parliament blocked that effort, but the Constitutional Court held that the Assembly's speaker had the power to require that a motion of no confidence in the president be conducted by secret ballot,[57] and, by a sharply divided Court, that parliament had a constitutional duty to make rules governing the process of presidential removal and a constitutional duty to determine whether what Zuma had done satisfied the constitutional requirements for removal.[58] All this and more culminated in Zuma's resignation as president in early 2018.

As already noted, Lon Fuller was skeptical of courts' ability to deal effectively with "polycentric" disputes because, in his view, the conceptual tools of legal doctrine – of doctrine as such – were unsuited to such problems. He suggested, for example, that courts might transform otherwise intractable polycentric problems into ones they were comfortable dealing with, by squeezing them into familiar categories. The initial Glenister case provides support for Fuller's suggestion. The doctrines the courts deployed to move the anti-corruption investigations along were clearly problematic, as Chief Justice Ngcobo's dissent showed. And the ultimate conclusion, that the Constitution

---

[55] Woolman, *supra* note 45, at 176, argues that the Court's opinion shifts the burden of establishing wrongdoing in court from the public protector to the president (or, arguably, to every target of a remedial order from the public protector).

[56] For details of the ensuing events, see Woolman, *supra* note 45, at 183–88.

[57] *Economic Freedom Fighters* v. *Speaker of the National Assembly*, 2018 (2) SA 571 (CC).

[58] *United Democratic Movement* v. *Speaker of the National Assembly*, 2017 (5) SA 300 (CC). Chief Justice Mogoeng's dissent described the majority position as "a textbook case of judicial overreach," to which the judges in the majority responded that their position was "self-evidently serious, impartial, and future-directed." *Id.* at ¶¶ 223 (opinion of Mogoeng, C.J.), 286 (opinion of Froneman, J.).

itself protected a seemingly statutory investigatory agency from "interference" in the form of changes in its charge, is even more awkward.

The Nkandla case illustrates a related difficulty. Ombuds offices typically operate by making reports and recommending – rather than compelling – action. This is reflected in Chief Justice Mogoeng's enumeration of the ordinary actions an ombuds office recommends: mediation, conciliation, negotiation, recommending litigation, "referral of the matter to the relevant public authority."[59] Of course, the public protector was not called an ombuds office, but its proximate origin in the Interim Constitution clearly was modeled on ombuds offices (and, notwithstanding the chief justice's observation about the significance of the office's name, was also called the public protector) and had only reporting and recommending powers.[60]

Notably, in both cases, the Constitutional Court gave constitutional status to Chapter Nine institutions – in one by finding in the Constitution protections for an anti-corruption agency from legislated changes in its jurisdiction, and in the other by similarly finding in the Constitution a power to enter orders that a court would enforce. And, in both cases, doing so required some creative legal reasoning – not outside the bounds of what courts can do with language, but in some tension with the Constitution's words themselves.

At the most general level, the problems presented by both the Scorpions/ Hawks and the public protector show that designing anti-corruption agencies requires striking a balance between independence and accountability. One recent study suggests that the design choice is "between legal mechanisms, which involve apolitical expert bodies such as prosecutors' offices, political mechanisms, which run through elected bodies such as legislatures, or some mix of the two." The author observes that none of the options "is obviously optimal."[61] The reason is clear: anti-corruption investigations of high-level officials are deeply implicated in politics, and mere technical expertise is not the only qualification investigators should have.

Further, even the legalistic dimension of design poses difficulties. Courts assessing whether specific offices satisfy constitutional requirements for balancing independence and accountability necessarily must cast their arguments in doctrinal terms. Yet, the concepts of independence and accountability resist "doctrinalization." As the legislation adopted in the wake of the first Scorpions/Hawks case shows, it is extremely difficult to give a reasoned

---

[59] *Economic Freedom Fighters, supra* note 47, at ¶ 69.

[60] Interim Constitution of South Africa, Chapter 9, § 112 (c).

[61] Aziz Z. Huq, *Legal or Political Checks on Apex Criminality: An Essay on Constitutional Design*, 65 UCLA L. Rev. 1506, 1510 (2018).

explanation for why marginal changes in design details balance the competing concerns either appropriately or inappropriately. As events unfolded, it seems that the Court's decision to allow the Hawks' investigations to proceed unimpeded worked well, as did the public protector decision. The reason, though, may well have been that the justices understood in a way that could not be openly articulated that Mbeki and then Zuma were indeed deeply corrupt and that something had to be done about them. Fuller might describe what the Court did as forcing a desirable outcome into an ill-fitting doctrinal framework.

One important finding in studies of anti-corruption efforts is that institutional design is largely irrelevant: designs that seem good in the abstract work badly, and designs that seem bad (because, for example, they give one potential target of investigation an effective veto power) can work well. That finding is supported by the South African case studies. The precise details of institutional design – where the Scorpions or the Hawks were located within the nation's constitutional structure, the public protector's powers – appear to have had little to do with the successful outcome. One reason might be found in the complexities of the narrative or, put another way, in the pervasiveness of high-level corruption in South Africa. Public officials and private citizens, political parties and factions, and NGOs were investigating multiple instances of serious corruption simultaneously. The investigations interacted, mostly reinforcing the investigators' sense that something needed to be rooted out.[62] Different institutions had different designs along several dimensions, and complexity's effects might have reduced the importance of any individual design detail.

The South African case shows that investigations of high-level corruption can succeed even in a system with a dominant party. The Constitutional Court ruled consistently against Zuma (less consistently against Mbeki), and its decisions kept the issue of his corruption on the public agenda in the face of Zuma's efforts to ignore the allegations. And the public protector, a Chapter Nine institution, played an important role. One condition of success appears to have been the existence of reasonably stable intraparty factions, and perhaps the existence of an anti-Zuma faction that was not merely the vehicle for the personal advancement of another party leader. Another, though, was personality – of Public Protector Madonsela and of Chief Justice Mogoeng. Though both were thought initially to be compliant ANC supporters, both

---

[62] I note, though, that in other circumstances multiple investigations might cancel each other out, especially when some do not generate "successes," allowing targets to delegitimize other investigations by showing that it is not always the case that where there's smoke there's fire.

had an independent streak and both believed that their jobs placed them under special duties to the public and, at least in Mogoeng's case, to God.

6.4 GENERAL CONCLUSIONS: REDUNDANCY AND INNOVATION/STRESS

In both case studies, personalities – Moro, Mogoeng, Madonsela – appear to have mattered. And we will see that Madonsela's successor as public protector appears to have functioned as a pliant tool of one faction within the ANC.[63] This is consistent with the conclusion drawn by Robert I. Rotberg, a leading anti-corruption scholar, that political leadership matters more than institutional design.[64] Rotberg focuses on leadership by presidents and chief executives rather than by leaders of anti-corruption agencies. Where party systems are chaotic, as in Brazil, or where a dominant party is divided into relatively stable factions, space opens up for other leaders – specifically, those heading anti-corruption agencies – to push forward.[65]

These seemingly random personality factors, some of which might be catalogued under the heading of leadership, might be thought to suggest the importance of redundancy in designing the fourth branch.[66] The more

---

[63] Chapter 9.

[64] See especially ROBERT I. ROTBERG, THE CORRUPTION CURE: HOW CITIZENS AND LEADERS CAN COMBAT GRAFT (Princeton University Press, 2017). For present purposes (consideration of matters of institutional design), the observation that there is "an emerging skepticism regarding the effectiveness of anti-corruption agencies," coupled with the additional observation that "for a clear majority of commonly prescribed anti-corruption policies, the existing evidence is too thin to offer rigorous assessments," is sufficient. Jordan Gans-Morse, Mariana Borges, Alexey Makarin, Theresa Mannah-Blankson, Andre Nickow & Dong Zhang, *Reducing Bureaucratic Corruption: Interdisciplinary Perspectives on What Works*, 105 WORLD DEVELOPMENT 171, 183 (2018). See also Mungiu-Pippidi & Johnston, *supra* note 10, at 252 ("one reading of our cases might be that each story is unique, contingent upon a variety of factors both local and fortuitous"), 260 (referring to "the vagaries and importance of history and circumstance"). As Will Freeman pointed out to me, Rotberg might underestimate the degree to which individual leaders truly committed to stamping out corruption can succeed only if they are surrounded by other elite supporters. Perhaps, though, dynamic leaders *create* the coalitions of support that they then can use both against corruption and to defend themselves against the inevitable attacks. But see *id.* at 261 (suggesting that political leaders emerge from "[e]xpectations and demands flowing from major segments of society itself").

[65] I note in this connection that close observers of Brazilian politics speculate that despite his disclaimers, Judge Moro plans to run for president in 2022.

[66] Ezequiel Gonzales-Ocantos and Viviana Baraybar Hidalgo describe the importance of personality – and some institutional features – in affecting how the investigation of Odebrecht's corrupting activities in Peru proceeded. They argue that the investigation was ineffective when it was divided between one group investigating asset-laundering and another investigating corruption itself. The latter group's leader was reluctant to use the power to immunize

institutions there are in the fourth branch, the more likely it is that at least one of them will be run by someone with an independent streak in dominant-party states or states where the configuration of parties – chaotic in Brazil or in some party distributions of control in separation of powers systems – inhibits the operation of the Madisonian system of checking power. But, as noted earlier, using redundancy to capitalize on the possibility of randomly good outcomes might be a trap. It would have little downside if the alternative to random success was regular ineffectiveness.[67] But it might not be. In addition to hoping for a randomly good outcome, we should worry about the possibility of a randomly bad one – an anti-corruption investigation that goes so far off the track as to disrupt the political system quite severely. And proliferating anti-corruption bodies can create opportunities for targets to game the system by insisting that the institution that they expect will be least damaging to them is the only one with jurisdiction.[68]

I have emphasized as well the way in which anti-corruption efforts place Fuller-like pressures on what he called judicial proprieties. We can generalize the observation beyond the courts, though, by speaking of institutional routines or standard operating procedures.[69] In their comparative study of investigations in Latin America into the activities of Odebrecht and other companies, Ezequiel Gonzales-Ocantos and Viviana Baraybar Hidalgo observe, "In order to make breakthroughs, investigators must go an extra mile and *defy* their formal 'terms of reference.'"[70] Gonzales-Ocantos and Hidalgo give these and similar observations a normatively positive cast by recharacterizing the stresses as inducing "creativity," which "makes the attribution of individual criminal responsibility possible by enabling the disruption of investigative routines that are ill-suited for cases of macro-criminality, involving

---

defendants aggressively. The investigation became more effective when the two groups were unified under the leadership of the former, who was more aggressive. Gonzales-Ocantos & Hidalgo, *supra* note 20, at 80–81. Note that the problem they describe arose from the existence of two *nonredundant* investigations.

[67] Charles M. Fombad, "The Role of Emerging Hybrid Institutions of Accountability in the Separation of Powers Scheme in Africa," in SEPARATION OF POWERS IN AFRICAN CONSTITUTIONALISM (Charles M. Fombad ed., 2016), at 333, notes several costs: conflicts with other branches of government, unnecessary bureaucracy, and inefficiency due to cases falling between the cracks in turf identification wars."

[68] Dilma's failed attempt to name Lula her chief of staff illustrates the general problem: had she succeeded jurisdiction would have shifted from the Lava Jato investigators to the supreme court.

[69] See Gonzales-Ocantos & Hidalgo, *supra* note 20, at 69 (referring to "behavioral routines").

[70] *Id.* at 87.

powerful defendants and opaque evidence trails."[71] Lawyers know, though, that institutional innovators can be *too* creative. Their innovations might disrupt beneficial ways political systems have developed to cope with overall conditions: an innovation that on its own terms is extremely well-designed might disrupt other reasonably well-functioning parts of the overall system.

And, to close the circle, invoking Roberto Unger's large-scale interests in institutional redesign, we might say that such creative innovations fail because they are not creative *enough*. Perhaps combating corruption requires more than well-designed anti-corruption institutions; it might require quite large-scale institutional transformation.[72]

---

[71] *Id.* at 65. *See also id.* at 67 (referring to "judicial acumen, courage, [and] creativity"), 84 (referring to "an impressive display of media savviness on the part of the embattled prosecutors."). Cf. Rotimi T. Suberu, *Strategies for Advancing Anticorruption Reform in Nigeria*, 147 Daedalus 184, 185 (Summer 2018) (quoting political sociologist Larry Diamond's claim that "judicious institutional innovation 'can compensate for some of the weaknesses' in political economy and culture" with respect to corruption).

[72] *Cf.* Mungiu-Pippidi & Johnston, *supra* note 10 (identifying large-scale factors as perhaps the primary determinants of success in combating corruption).

7

Electoral Commissions

Case Studies from India, the United States, and South Korea

I begin with two mini-studies of election administration's political setting.

Malaysia 2018. From independence in 1957 until recently, Malaysia was a "competitive authoritarian" state whose political system was dominated by an alliance known since the 1970s as the Barisan National (BN). The BN controlled all national political institutions, including the national Election Commission. The Commission determines district boundaries and supervises the conduct of elections. By the early 2010s, the BN's dominance was fraying because of internal divisions and the increasing consolidation of a single opposition group.

The nation held a general election in May 2018. To increase the BN's chances of prevailing, the Election Commission set the election for a Wednesday. Doing so was thought likely to decrease turnout: even though the day itself was a national holiday, many Malaysians within the country would have to travel over several days from where they worked to where they had to vote (and back), and similarly for the large number of overseas Malaysians living in Singapore, where they were ineligible to vote by mail.[1] The Election Commission then refused to allow the national Human Rights Commission to monitor the election but allowed several recently formed groups, rather clearly BN-controlled, to do so.

In addition, anticipating the 2018 election, the Election Commission redrew constituency boundaries in ways that were thought likely to favor BN candidates. Malaysian law allows for wide discrepancies in constituency size and specifically authorizes drawing boundaries that favor rural districts (often

---

[1] There were also allegations that mail-in ballots were produced late and in smaller-than-required numbers, though those allegations are contested.

BN strongholds). The boundaries drawn for the 2018 elections resulted in more than one-half of the total numbers of constituencies with greater than 35 percent deviations from a one-person, one-vote standard. The Election Commission bolstered this BN-tilted malapportionment by gerrymandering numerous districts, again to improve the BN's chances of winning.[2]

The BN government used many other techniques to attempt to cook the outcome, but ultimately it failed, winning only 79 seats in parliament, to the opposition's 121.[3]

The United States 2000. Election administration in the United States is highly decentralized. Although the Constitution gives Congress the power to regulate the "Times, Places, and Manner" of electing national officials, it has done so in only two truly important ways, setting a uniform national election date and requiring that elections to the lower legislative chamber be done in single-member districts. Otherwise, election administration is left to state legislatures. And states typically decentralize further, leaving the details of election administration – designing and counting ballots, for example – to local election boards.[4] The election boards are typically supervised by state-level officials, usually called the secretary of state, who is, again typically, elected as a partisan.[5] And decisions by secretaries of state are usually subject to ordinary review – usually deferential – by state supreme courts.

The 2000 presidential election was extremely close. Its outcome turned on which candidate received more votes in Florida. Local "canvassing boards" began to recount the paper ballots that had been used. One common technology required voters to use a stylus to punch out a small square of paper next to their preferred candidate's name. The punched-out squares were known as

---

[2] For an overview of the Malaysia story, see Muhamad M. N. Nadzri, *The 14th General Election, the Fall of Barisan Nasional, and Political Development in Malaysia, 1957–2018*, 37 J. CURRENT SOUTHEAST ASIAN AFF. 139 (2018), especially at 154–56.

[3] The Istanbul mayoral election in 2018 offers another example of failed manipulation by a government-dominated election supervision body. The opposition candidate won an extremely narrow victory – the margin was certified as around 14,000 out of a total of more than 4.3 million votes cast. The governing AKP Party challenged the outcome, contending that more than 10,000 votes had been cast illegally in one of the city's districts. The election commission endorsed the challenge by a vote of seven-to-four, the division tracking party lines, and ordered a new election. The opposition candidate won a massive victory in that election, with an 800,000-vote margin.

[4] *See* Richard C. Schragger, *Reclaiming the Canvassing Board: Bush v. Gore and the Political Currency of Local Government*, 50 BUFF. L. REV. 393 (2002).

[5] For example, Kathryn Harris, Florida's secretary of state in 2000, was a Republican who had served as a cochair of candidate George W. Bush's presidential campaign in the state. Some secretaries of state do see their jobs as requiring nonpartisan administration of state election laws. See text accompanying notes 34–35.

"chads." For a variety of reasons – weakness in the voter's hands, an accumulation of built-up chads in the voting apparatus, and more – sometimes the chads were not fully detached, hanging by one or two corners, or even worse, not detached at all but only "dimpled," that is, the ballot showing pressure from the stylus but no detachment at all. How were "hanging chads" and dimpled ballots to be counted?

The partisan secretary of state set a firm deadline for completing recounts, too strict to allow full recounts in several major jurisdictions. Local boards did the best they could to determine voters' intent: some counted a ballot if the chad was hanging by one corner but not two, others refused to count ballots that did not have a fully punched chad, some counted dimpled ballots, others did not. The state supreme court extended the deadline the secretary of state had set and directed all the recounts then in process to count all ballots where the voter's intent could be determined. Litigation rapidly reached the U.S. Supreme Court, which held that the "intent of the voters" standard denied voters equal protection of the laws because a ballot hanging by one chad might be counted in one county but discarded in another, and because recounts were being conducted only in a handful of counties. And, because a majority believed that there was insufficient time to do a state-wide recount pursuant to some more precise standards that the state supreme court might come up with, it effectively terminated the recounts and awarded Florida's votes to George W. Bush.[6]

These vignettes show us how election administration can become a locus for political contestation. Indeed, election administration is always political. Election administration comes in many forms – distributing and counting ballots, maintaining electoral rolls, resolving election contests, and more – and politics can affect the performance of these tasks in varying ways.[7]

A nation could elect all its legislators with proportional representation from a single roster; no need to draw district lines here. And equally true, a nation could allow anyone to run for any office; no need to determine qualifications

---

[6] *Bush v. Gore*, 531 U.S. 98 (2000). A detailed account of the episode is HOWARD GILLMAN, THE VOTES THAT COUNTED: HOW THE COURT DECIDED THE 2000 PRESIDENTIAL ELECTION (University of Chicago Press, 2001).

[7] YONHYOK CHOE, HOW TO MANAGE FREE AND FAIR ELECTIONS: A COMPARISON OF KOREA, SWEDEN AND THE UNITED KINGDOM (Distribution, Göteborg Univ., Dept. of Political Science, 1997), at ch. 3, provides useful analytic categories, distinguishing among issues that arise before elections (drawing constituency boundaries and civic education), during elections (voter registration, preparing election places, party and candidate registration, election campaigns, advance voting procedures, and polling on election day), and post-election (counting, announcing a decision, and resolving disputes).

for office or for the ballot here. And true as well, a nation could allow every citizen to vote without even an age qualification. In such systems, one might see a lot of frivolous parties (the "Party All the Time Party") and frivolous candidates. Precisely because they are frivolous, they do little damage to a reasonably well-functioning democracy. And, indeed, the appearance of a frivolous party – Pirate Parties in Scandinavia or the "The Rent is Too Damn High Party" in New York State – can be a symptom of some failings of the overall political system.[8]

Even so, ballots must be counted to determine for whom they were cast and whether the people who cast them were citizens or foreigners. And of course, there are good-governance reasons for electing legislators at least in part from geographically (or functionally or linguistically) defined districts and for requiring that parties and candidates satisfy some conditions for appearance on the ballot. As far as I am aware, every constitution does at least one of those things, and most do many of them. When constitutions have these sorts of arrangements – districting or party or candidate qualification rules – again, some body has to decide where to draw the lines and whether the qualifications have been met.

That in turn creates the obvious possibility of abuse. As the survey in Chapter 5 showed, constitution designers have chosen to assign these tasks either to courts or to specialized election bodies (sometimes called commissions, sometimes "electoral courts").[9] As noted there, designers might choose courts either because they believe that the citizenry will be confident that the courts will decide the issues before them fairly or, more mundanely, because they believe that their nation does not have enough qualified (meaning at least in part, visibly fair) people to staff a separate election body. The survey also canvassed the possibilities for achieving fairness through institutional design.

Design cannot guarantee fairness, of course, especially but not exclusively in dominant party nations. For example, some national constitutions are

---

[8] The Pirate Parties started out as mostly jokes by devotees of modern technology, with a program of eliminating all restrictions on "piracy" of intellectual property. In some places, though, they have become regular features of the political scene. On the "Rent is Too Damn High" party, see https://en.wikipedia.org/wiki/Rent_Is_Too_Damn_High_Party, archived at https://perma.cc/9QTZ-E3Q8.

[9] Another term frequently used is "electoral management bodies." For a survey of East African institutions, see ELECTION MANAGEMENT BODIES IN EAST AFRICA: A COMPARATIVE STUDY OF THE CONTRIBUTION OF ELECTORAL COMMISSIONS TO THE STRENGTHENING OF DEMOCRACY (Alexander B. Makulilo et al. eds., African Minds, 2016). Nicholas Stephanopoulos, *Our Electoral Exceptionalism*, 80 U. CHI. L. REV. 769, 783 (2013), asserts, "The nearly universal answer [to drawing district boundaries] is ... [to] use independent redistricting commissions whose plans are subject to highly deferential judicial review."

committed to a theory of "militant democracy," a democracy that takes steps to preserve itself against internal subversion of the most serious sort.[10] One such step is the disqualification from the ballot of parties whose programs are anti-democratic or otherwise inconsistent with national self-preservation. It would not be surprising to find that members of a judiciary or of election-supervision bodies who are themselves deeply committed to the nation would have an unconscious bias that would lead them to find risks of subversion where others might not. And so experience suggests: courts clearly devoted to protection of fundamental rights have on occasion made rather questionable decisions implementing militant democracy.[11]

Even more than the risk of bias is the risk of mindlessness. Chapter 4 discussed the problem of candidate disqualification for having an undis-charged bankruptcy order against the candidate. According to Simon Butt and Fritz Siregar, the electoral management agency in Indonesia clashed with the nation's constitutional court over the eligibility of persons who had completed their sentences for criminal offenses. Apparently relying on the principle that the people should be allowed to choose whoever they want to represent them, the constitutional court allowed convicts to stand for office five years or more after completing their sentences, if they disclosed their criminal past and had been reintegrated into society. The election commis-sion persisted in refusing to allow such candidates to run for office, and prevailed when, in Butt and Siregar's words, "political parties succumbed to pressure from civil society groups."[12]

Another example comes from Australia. There, members of Parliament cannot hold dual citizenship – a sensible restriction though not one that every democratic regime would impose. Consider then a problem that arose in 2017.

---

[10] For overviews of militant democracy, see MILITANT DEMOCRACY AND ITS CRITICS: POPULISM, PARTIES, EXTREMISM (Anthoula Malkopoulou & Alexander S. Kirshner eds., Edinburgh University Press, 2019); THE "MILITANT DEMOCRACY" PRINCIPLE IN MODERN DEMOCRACIES (Markus Thiel ed., Ashgate, 2009).

[11] For reviews of the Israeli experience, see Raphael Cohen-Almagor, *Disqualification of Lists in Israel (1948–1984): Retrospect and Appraisal*, 13 L. & PHIL. 43 (1994) (concluding that the key decision as to the date of publication was "flawed"); Mordechai Kremnitzer, Disqualification of Lists (ha-Makhon ha-Yiśre'eli le-demokraṭyah, 2005) (concluding that the Supreme Court's decisions have "not demonstrated consistency or decisiveness"). The most recent decision in Germany discusses the problems associated with party disqualifications, National Democratic Party II, 2 BvB 1/13 (2017), https://www.bundesverfassungsgericht.de/SharedDocs/ Entscheidungen/EN/2017/01/bs20170117_2bvb000113en.html, archived at https://perma.cc/ W5G6-AHHC. Notably, the Constitutional Court refused to disqualify a seemingly neo-Nazi party that had already achieved a significant degree of electoral success.

[12] Simon Butt & Fritz Siregar, "Indonesia," draft paper presented at Democratic Constitutions and Electoral Commissions Workshop, University of New South Wales, Dec. 7, 2020.

In one of several related cases, the parents of a member of Parliament emigrated from Italy and had a child in Australia after arrival.[13] The parents became Australian citizens. But, under the Italian law of nationality, they remained citizens of Italy. Fine, they cannot serve in Parliament. Suppose, though, that the Italian law of nationality says that the *children* of Italian parents have Italian citizenship no matter where they are born or reside. Is the child a dual citizen disqualified from being a member of Parliament? Even worse, what if the child grows up knowing of her Italian heritage but completely unaware that under Italian law she is an Italian citizen? When the problem arose Australia's courts – well-known for their commitment to formalistic reasoning – concluded that the child was indeed a dual citizen and so disqualified from office, at least until she expressly disclaimed Italian citizenship (even if Italy itself would not give such a disclaimer legal effect).[14]

Like all IPDs, then, election commissions respond to obvious problems in a party-political world and have characteristic advantages and disadvantages. The case studies that follow explore some ways in which election commissions can work well or badly.[15] With anti-corruption bodies, the primary problem is that in a party-political world it is quite difficult for the investigators to get rid of corruption without appearing to be politically biased, with a secondary difficulty that judicial involvement appears to create some problems of policy wisdom and perceived fairness. With election commissions, the primary problems are similar. For example, in a party-political world, partisans may be skeptical about the effectiveness of structural provisions designed to support nonpartisanship. And professional standards for election administration place weak constraints on partisan administration – or, to give the point slightly different emphasis, professional standards are inflected by partisan concerns. As to the courts: bending over backwards to demonstrate their position above party politics, they might formalistically apply the rules in ways that do nothing to advance and that might even impede good democratic functioning.[16]

---

[13] I simplify the facts for expository purposes, but do not believe that I have distorted any essential feature of the problem.

[14] Re Canavan, [2017] HCA 45, (2017) 263 CLR 284.

[15] Michael Pal, *Electoral Management Bodies as a Fourth Branch of Government*, 21 Rev. Const. Stud. 85, 97–106 (2016), provides a good albeit selective overview of the design choices made in creating election commissions. For another survey, see Malcolm Langford, Rebecca Schiel & Bruce M. Wilson, "The Rise of Electoral Management Bodies: Diffusion and Effects," draft paper presented at Democratic Constitutions and Electoral Commissions Workshop, University of New South Wales, Dec. 7, 2020.

[16] If one defines one of the judicial proprieties with which Fuller was concerned as adopting the right mix of formalist and realist reasoning without regard to the surrounding political

With these considerations in hand, this chapter looks at how several election commissions have functioned in their political environments. It shows that the nominally technical and nonpartisan commissions have a politics associated with them. Sometimes that politics tracks conventional party lines, more interestingly, sometimes it does not. Constitutional courts interact with election commissions in developing competing or mutually supportive images of what they believe to be a normatively attractive form of politics. Those images are themselves political.

7.2 THE UNITED STATES: THE POLITICS OF NONPARTISANSHIP

As noted at the outset of this chapter, election administration in the United States is highly decentralized, with states having primary authority, much of which is in turn delegated to local election officials. The national constitution of course limits what states can do, for example, by requiring that constituency boundaries be drawn according to an interpretation of the "one-person, one-vote" principle that requires that the population of each district be roughly the same at that of every other district in the state or city. And an important federal civil rights statute requires that boundaries be drawn to ensure that voters of racial minorities have a reasonable chance to elect representatives of their choice (to simplify a complex statute and its judicial interpretations).[17]

A final provision is relevant to the case study presented here. Article I, section 4 states, "The Times, Place and Manner of holding Elections for . . . Representatives, shall be prescribed in each State by the Legislature thereof," although Congress has the power to "make or alter such Regulations."[18]

In 2000, Arizona held a referendum on creating an Independent Redistricting Commission. The referendum was approved by a 56.3-43.7 percent margin.[19] The Arizona Independent Redistricting Commission (AIRC) uses the "partisan balance" model described in Chapter 5. The majority and minority leaders in both legislative houses pick one member; those four pick a fifth, who becomes the commission chair. Members can't be public officials or candidates, and the chair can't be a member of either major

---

environment, excessive formalism to avoid the appearance of political bias would be a departure from the judicial proprieties.

[17] National statutes also affect the financing of local campaigns for national office.

[18] No such congressional legislation is relevant to the case study.

[19] For many of the details that follow, I rely on a memorandum prepared for me by Sebastian Spitz, Harvard Law School, 2021.

political party.[20] The Commission isn't a permanent election management body; its sole task is to draw the boundaries for legislative and congressional districts every ten years after the national census reports the state's population and its distribution. That task completed, the Commission dissolves. The Commission has six criteria for drawing boundaries: equal population; compactness and contiguity; compliance with the U.S. Constitution and the 1965 Voting Rights Act; "respect for communities of interest"; "incorporation of visible geographic features," which includes respect for city boundaries; and creation of competitive districts "where there is no significant detriment to other goals." The Commission's map is final.[21]

In a 1989 speech at Arizona State University, former president Ronald Reagan mentioned with approval the idea that district boundaries could be drawn by an independent commission. Believing that the 1980 district maps had placed them at a disadvantage, the state's Democratic leaders took up the idea. When Democrats won a majority of seats in the state's Senate in 1990, they were in a position both to prevent a Republican gerrymander and to push forward the commission proposal. The legislature and governor agreed on boundaries for state legislative districts because, observers believed, they protected incumbents. State politicians couldn't agree on congressional district lines, and those lines were drawn by a federal court following the established rules for getting the job done when state officials couldn't. The state legislative maps went to the Department of Justice in Washington for approval as required by then-existing law, and the Department rejected the map because it diluted the influence of Hispanic voters in one city. After a few additional iterations, the maps did get approved.

While all this was happening, proposals to create a redistricting commission moved forward fitfully. In 1992, the state Senate approved a "partisan balance" model by a vote of 19-10. Democrats strongly favored it, 13-3, and Republicans were basically evenly divided, 6-7 against. The idea was revived in 1995, with the bill's sponsor focusing not on gerrymandering but on the incumbent protection that had drawn attention in 1992.

---

[20] I elide some details that don't affect the basic account. For example, elected school board members or candidates can serve on the Commission.

[21] The 2000 map was challenged but upheld by the state supreme court in 2009. Treating the Commission as a legislative body, the court considered only whether it had followed "constitutionally mandated procedures," and concluded that it had. It rejected the lower courts' approach of asking whether the Commission's actions were arbitrary and capricious. *Ariz. Minority Coalition for Fair Redistricting* v. *Ariz. Indep. Redistricting Comm'n*, 220 Ariz. 587 (2009).

By 1997, the idea of a commission had become quite politicized. The state Democratic Party platform included a commission in its list of reforms to the political process; other items on the list were lobbying reform and campaign funding disclosure rules. After elections in 1998, the issue came before the legislature again. This time proponents said that they would sponsor a state referendum if the legislature failed to act. Republicans in the legislature opposed the commission idea, but the *Arizona Republic*, which had a generally quite conservative editorial orientation, strongly supported it, again invoking the incumbency-protection concern.[22]

Democrats and Republicans sponsored competing legislative proposals. Democrats had settled on a proposal with commission members appointed by legislative leaders from both parties with an additional member appointed by the legislators' choices. Republicans countered with a proposal that gave them a clear majority on the commission: the majority leaders of each house and the governor would have two appointments each for a total of six, and minority leaders and the state chair of the minority party one each, for a total of three. The Republican proposal passed the House but wasn't voted on in the Senate.

The legislative impasse energized proponents of a referendum. The referendum campaign gained wide support from "good government" groups and the *Arizona Republic*, as well as from liberal interest groups. Some prominent Republicans, including a former governor and a former state attorney general, also supported the referendum. In general, Republicans opposed it, as did the state Farm Bureau and Chamber of Commerce. The Republican Senate majority leader argued that an independent commission "would be just as political as the legislature but less savvy and knowledgeable about the state."[23]

After a somewhat bumpy start, the Commission drew maps based on the 2000 census. Hispanics appeared to be the major winners from the Commission's map, but Democrats gained less than they had hoped, particularly because they appeared to protect too many incumbents. The maps were "an unmitigated disaster for Democrats," in the words of one news story in the *Arizona Republic*.[24] Democrats tried but ultimately failed to block funding the Commission's defense of lawsuits against it.

The 2010 round of redistricting saw an escalation of contention over the AIRC, this time with Republicans in the lead. They charged the Commission

---

[22] The newspaper endorsed Republican presidential candidates in every election before 2016.

[23] Quoted in Nicholas Stephanopoulos, *Reforming Redistricting: Why Popular Initiatives to Establish Redistricting Commissions Succeed or Fail*, 23 J. L. & POLITICS 331, 369 (2007).

[24] "Change, Cheesy Remarks Doom '1-Term Wonder,'" *Arizona Republic*, Dec. 2002, p. B5.

and especially its (nominally) nonpartisan chair Colleen Mathis with corruption and bias in pressuring the Commission to hire a consulting firm that had worked for President Obama's 2008 campaign. Acting on a letter from Republican governor Jan Brewer, the state Senate impeached Mathis for neglect of duty and gross misconduct. The specific charges were that she had conducted some Commission business in meetings not open to the public and had "failed to adjust the grid map as necessary to accommodate all of the goals" set out in the constitution. The state supreme court held that these actions did not amount to neglect of duty and misconduct and restored Mathis to her position.[25]

The Commission ultimately approved new maps with Mathis and the two Democratic appointees in favor, the Republican appointees opposed. Republicans attacked the congressional districting boundaries, Democrats were at least somewhat uncomfortable with the state legislative ones because the Commission had not emphasized competitiveness enough – that is, had not drawn lines in ways that increased the chances of Democratic candidates.

The state legislature filed a federal constitutional challenge to the Commission contending that the U.S. Constitution required congressional districting be done by "the Legislature," which the AIRC was not. The case reached the U.S. Supreme Court in 2015. The Court divided five-to-four in rejecting the challenge. Four justices nominated by Democratic presidents were joined by Justice Anthony Kennedy, a Reagan nominee; the four dissenters were all nominated by Republican presidents.

The near-partisan voting alignment on the Supreme Court is more important for present purposes than the details of the arcane – and quite U.S.-specific – details of the disagreements among the justices. To summarize the opinions quite brutally: The question was whether the constitutional provision saying that "the Legislature" of a state determines the manner of congressional elections refers to the bodies called legislatures in 1789 and their lineal descendants (the dissenters' view) or instead refers to the entity, perhaps with several components, designated by a state's processes of constitutional lawmaking as a legislature (the majority view). These two definitions of "the Legislature" were extensionally equivalent, as scholars of language say, in 1789 but can today direct our attention to different entities.[26]

---

[25] *Ariz. Indep. Redistricting Comm'n v. Brewer*, 229 Ariz. 347 (2009).

[26] It should be clear that a legislature could create an independent districting commission. That would be one way for the legislature to determine the "Manner" by which districting should occur. The self-interest of legislators in determining district boundaries makes it unlikely that they would do this, though. (This is true at least for drawing boundaries for state legislative districts. Partisanship and personal ambition in the form of hopes to run for a congressional seat

The dissenters argued that the Constitution used the term "the Legislature" so often that departing from the definition of legislatures as 1789-type bodies would introduce a high degree of instability into the government structure overall. The majority responded that the processes of state constitutional lawmaking could slice, dice, and reconfigure the 1789-type legislature. A state's people certainly could convert a two-house legislature to a one-house one, and calving off a special subject such as districting into a new entity such as the AIRC stood on the same footing; it might be thought of as creating a third house of the legislature with a quite narrow jurisdiction and a special form of finality in its decisions.[27]

The story of the AIRC is one of partisanship deeply embedded in nonpartisanship – or, perhaps, of the inevitably partisan nature of at least some aspects of electoral management.[28] Partisanship shaped the AIRC's very adoption, infected the reception its 2010 maps received, and may have affected the division among the U.S. Supreme Court justices.

Were there avoidable features of the AIRC's design that promoted partisanship?[29] The "balanced partisanship" model might be flawed even or perhaps especially when the balance is achieved indirectly, through party-based appointment of commissioners who are not themselves public officials.[30] The AIRC commissioners in 2010 were not technocratic specialists trained

might make them reluctant to create a commission tasked with drawing only the boundaries of congressional districts.).

[27] The national power to regulate the "manner" of holding elections for members of Congress probably authorizes national legislation requiring states to use districting commissions, which would eliminate any definitional disputes over what constitutes the "legislature" for purposes for state determination of regulating the manner of elections.

[28] At the time of writing, the process for selecting members of the commission to be charged with redistricting after the 2020 census is underway. One initial report suggests that Republicans, having controlled the governorship and legislature for several years, have devised ways of ensuring that the commission will tilt in their favor. The techniques include controlling the nominating commission for the AIRC so that it nominates as Democrats only people with either weak or nominal affiliations to the Democratic Party, and characterizing as nonpartisan people who are nominally independents but actually have close ties to Republicans. For a clearly partisan (Democratic-leaning) account, see David Daley, "Arizona Republicans Make Sneaky Moves to Rig Redistricting Commission before Any Lines Are drawn," *Salon*, Jan. 14, 2021, https://www.salon.com/2021/01/14/arizona-republicans-make-sneaky-moves-to-rig-redistricting-commission-before-any-lines-are-drawn/, archived at https://perma.cc/DFS6-GBRU.

[29] The AIRC is an intermittent institution as defined in Chapter 4.

[30] The "balanced partisanship" model is the one most widely used in the United States. Iowa's districting commission is a permanent body, with members selected on the basis of their qualifications as experts. Other states supplement the "balanced partisanship" model by imposing some qualifications, technocratic in nature, on members.

to deal with elections. Chair Mathis was an economist working in a health care system; three others were lawyers with a real estate practice, a general practice, and a commercial and business-side litigation practice; the fifth was the chief executive officer of an evangelical Christian NGO and a conservative political activist.[31] Their lack of expertise on election matters might confirm the Republican criticism of a commission of "unsavvy" amateurs.

A better design might include qualifications for membership on a districting commission or other election management body. We have seen, though, that qualifications are typically quite underspecified in constitutional provisions creating IPDs. Even singling out a subset of NGOs from which commissioners must be drawn might not be sufficient. Consider faculties of law and political science, which are sometimes listed as sources for membership on some IPDs. Such faculties can be highly politicized, and whoever gets to choose the political scientist to serve on a districting commission might choose a partisan who knows international relations over a neutral who knows something about domestic elections.[32]

The criminal laws associated with anti-corruption efforts falls within the domain of the legal profession, and as we have seen, anti-corruption investigators can refer to professional norms that guide, however loosely, their actions. Election administration, in contrast, has no well-defined profession associated with it.[33] Even "neutral" appointees come from the permanent civil service or are designated ex officio, meaning that they might have professional expertise in some other domain such as accounting. Election administrators might develop a sense of professionalism, reinforced in part by the fact that sometimes the facts compel them to act in ways that favor one, then another, party, and in part by face-to-face meetings with their counterparts in other jurisdictions. But, as noted earlier, their professionalism is quite likely to be inflected by partisan concerns.

---

[31] *See* https://azredistricting.org/About-IRC/Commissioners.asp, archived at https://perma.cc/4JR7-DZF6 (listing the commissioners, with a blank listing for Commissioner Stertz); https://blogforarizona.net/more-about-airc-commissioner-richard-stertz/, archived at https://perma.cc/9A8G-U77Y (offering a highly partisan description of Commissioner Stertz).

[32] At one point in the process of selecting members for the 2010 commission, it appeared that Paul Bender would be considered an independent eligible to serve as chair. Bender had been dean of the Arizona State University law school (and probably registered as an independent to be able to deal with legislators from both parties as administrators at public universities must). He had served as the "political" deputy in the office of the Solicitor General of the United States during the presidency of Bill Clinton. Republicans in Arizona were skeptical about his independence from partisan commitments.

[33] I have located two U.S. university programs that offer certificates in election administration (at Auburn University and the University of Minnesota).

Nicholas Stephanopoulos surveyed commissioners on several boundary commissions that are widely regarded as successful, asking them about the considerations that they thought contributed to success.[34] They identified several. First, a selection mechanism that screens out obvious partisan influence. Ex officio membership is an example, because the official designated to serve will not have been chosen for his or her principal job on the basis of partisan leanings regarding districting. Stephanopoulos also refers to mechanisms "that aim for bipartisan consensus," which for him appear to include consultations across party lines. Second, some expertise in election management generally, basically as technocratic administrators "whose professional backgrounds incline them toward the proficient and dispassionate drawing of district lines."[35] Third, a requirement that decisions be made by consensus rather than majority vote. This requirement is sometimes specified by law, but sometimes is a normative commitment by the commission's members. Next, expressly excluding partisan concerns, including incumbent protection and electoral competitiveness, from the criteria the commission can take into account, even in a subsidiary role as in Arizona. And finally, "strong norms of institutional independence" that have roots in a general political culture rather than specifics of constitutional design.

The commissioners had an obvious self-interest in painting themselves in the best light, but their observations seem plausible. Whether the considerations that mattered can be captured in constitutional design – especially the normative commitments that the commissioners described – is fairly open to question, though. As we have repeatedly seen, constitutional design as a solution to the problems of conflicts and convergences of interest in a party-political world seems to have nontrivial limitations. That might lead us to be skeptical about the fourth branch's project itself.

7.3 THE INDIAN ELECTORAL COMMISSION IN THE 1990S: THE POLITICS OF TECHNOCRACY

According to Madhav Khosla, the leaders of India's Congress Party in the 1940s and the drafters of the Indian Constitution faced a constitutional dilemma. Committed democrats, they agreed with long-standing political theories according to which a well-functioning democracy required a politically literate citizenry, but they believed that large swaths of India's population

---

[34] Nicholas Stephanopoulos, "Depoliticizing Redistricting," in COMPARATIVE ELECTION LAW (James Gardner ed., forthcoming).

[35] But see Section 7.3, discussing the politics of expertise.

were not yet politically literate. Their response was to revise the underlying social theory of democracy: ordinary people could become politically literate through the very act of self-governance (implicitly, for the Congress Party's leaders, guided with a light hand by the Congress Party itself).[36]

Their theory required, among other things, that ordinary elections be well-administered. The Indian Constitution created an independent Election Commission with a single head, though Parliament could choose to add members (as it did in the 1990s). The chief election commissioner was guaranteed tenure like that of Supreme Court judges; other commissioners could be removed only with the chief election commissioner's approval. The Constitution gave the Commission authority over "the superintendence, direction, and control of the preparation of the electoral rolls for, and the conduct of, all elections" (Constitution of India § 324). While occasionally reining in the Commission, the Supreme Court interpreted the Commission's powers to be quite broad.[37]

Initially, the Commission's primary task was election administration narrowly defined: maintaining election rolls, ensuring that voters could cast their votes freely and without intimidation (a not insubstantial requirement in a society characterized at least in part by a social hierarchy in which deference to "higher ups" was common), and ensuring that votes were honestly counted. Given India's size, both physically and more important in population, these "mere" administrative chores were quite substantial.[38]

By all accounts, the Election Commission's performance over its first decades was impressive. India's elections were indeed reasonably free and fair, with election rolls reasonably accurate given the size of India's population, although of course there were incidents of failures to register voters and of voter intimidation.[39] Political elites and the public appear not to have

---

[36] Madhav Khosla, India's Founding Moment: The Constitution of a Most Surprising Democracy (Harvard University Press, 2020).

[37] Alistair McMillan, "The Election Commission," in The Oxford Companion to Politics in India 99–101 (Niraja Gopal Jayal & Pratap Bhanu Mehta eds., Oxford University Press, 2010), provides the background for and overview of the Commission's creation. *See also* Aditya Sondhi, "Elections," in The Oxford Handbook of the Indian Constitution 200–204 (Sujit Choudhry, Madhav Khosla & Pratap Bhanu Mehta eds., Oxford University Press, 2016).

[38] Starting a bit prematurely in the 1990s, the Election Commission promoted electronic voting as a technical improvement in election administration made possible by new technologies. I deal with controversies over the introduction and expansion of electronic voting in Section 7.4, in conjunction with an examination of the relation between election commissions and constitutional courts.

[39] Manjari Katju, Institutional Initiatives towards Expanding Democracy: The Election Commission of India and Electoral Mobilisation, Contemporary South Asia (June 7, 2020),

attributed these problems to the Election Commission. The Election Commission garnered substantial popular support and respect: a report in 1999 found that the Commission had a higher level of public trust than any other institution, including the courts and the police.[40]

The Commission was able to do a good job of election administration during this period in part because of the political context. The Congress Party was dominant politically, drawing on its legacy from the independence struggle and on policy stances that were broadly supported. That context changed in the 1970s and 1980s, first with the emergence of serious challenges to Congress Party rule, then with the imposition of an emergency regime, which resulted eventually in a system of coalition government that lasted into the early twenty-first century. The new political context pulled the Election Commission in somewhat conflicting directions. A system of coalition government made Madisonian mechanisms more available to control election fraud and manipulation, with the potential for reducing the need for an independent Election Commission. Yet, the end of dominant-party rule opened space for the Election Commission to develop its own agenda for running elections, moving beyond mere administration into more substantive control of political campaigns – because *some* significant political actors would support any such initiative (whatever its content), and would be in a position to block efforts to rein the Commission in.

One effect of the end of Congress Party dominance was the addition of two election commissioners in 1993, over the objection of Chief Election Commissioner T. N. Seshan.[41] The background is significant. Prior to the 1989 national elections, the Rajiv Gandhi (Congress Party) government added two additional election commissioners. After the election, the new coalition government, believing that the Commission had been packed to favor the Congress Party, rescinded the appointments. The Supreme Court upheld the rescissions. It observed that the new appointments were made "when the work of the Commission did not warrant their appointment," and that "were it not for the restraint and sagacity shown by the Chief Election Commissioner, the work of the Commission would have come to a standstill and the Commission would have been rendered inactive." It found "instructive and interesting" the

doi.org/10.1080/09584935.2020.1775179, archived at https://perma.cc/3BVX-TN58, at 8–9, details the difficulties associated with compiling accurate electoral rolls in India.

[40] The report is cited in McMillan, "Election Commission," *supra* note 37, at 113.

[41] Seshan's reasons are unclear. He was a career civil servant, though his career had been fast-tracked under Congress Party rule. He might have seen, accurately, that the appointments were an expression of party leadership's lack of confidence in his "reliability." He might also have seen that judgment as a personal insult.

fact that the two new commissioners acceded to Gandhi's "desire" to hold the election on a specific date, over the chief election commissioner's objection.[42]

In the course of its opinion, though, the Court stated (in what clearly was dictum), "when an institution like the Election Commission is entrusted with vital functions and is armed with exclusive and uncontrolled powers to execute them, it is both necessary and desirable that the powers are not exercised by one individual, however wise he may be." Notably, the Court had expressed no such concerns during the earlier period of Congress Party dominance, but the emergence of a multiparty system raised the specter that a single election commissioner with strong guarantees of tenure might favor one party, whether consciously or unconsciously. And, in a multiparty system, Madisonian mechanisms would guard against the kind of commission-packing that Gandhi had done.

Another effect of the change in the party system was that the parties agreed upon a "Code of Conduct" for conducting election campaigns. Initially adopted through multiparty negotiations in the state of Kerala in 1960 – importantly, a state with vigorous party competition even then – the Code gained national prominence within a decade, and became part of the Election Commission's public-facing communications.[43] Some features of the Code suggest its origins in Madisonian mechanisms – a sort of mutual disarmament pact. A telling example is a provision stating, "Organizing demonstrations or picketing before the houses of individuals by way of protesting against their opinions or activities shall not be resorted to under any circumstances." Other provisions mirrored constitutional and statutory limits on the kinds of "appeals" permitted during campaigns: no activities "which may aggravate existing differences or create mutual hatred or cause tension between different castes and communities," and "no appeal to caste or communal feelings for securing votes." Compliance with the Code is voluntary, at least nominally: the Election Commission cannot sanction a candidate or party merely for doing something "prohibited" by the Code.

A new chief election commissioner arrived at the same time that the new party system emerged. T. N. Seshan, whose work in the civil service culminated in the position of cabinet secretary (a policy advisory and coordinating position, not a policymaking one), took office in 1990 at a time when the

---

[42] S. S. Dhanoa v. *Union of India*, 1991 AIR 1745, 1991 SCR (3) 159. The relevant constitutional language gives the chief election commissioner tenure comparable to a Supreme Court justice but does appear to authorize removal of other commissioners basically at will (with the chief election commissioner's agreement). Having objected to the appointments, Seshan acceded to the removals.

[43] For the Code's origins, see McMillan, "Election Commission," *supra* note 37, at 109.

Congress Party was providing support in Parliament to a government headed by Chandra Shekhar without a formal coalition agreement. Seshan was a dynamic figure – one author refers to his "megalomaniac and autocratic tendencies" – who ushered in what one scholar calls "a period of activism ... engag[ing with] a fluid party system and new aspects of political mobilization." One critic attributed Seshan's "unusual power" to the fact that the Congress Party and the BJP "alternately appeas[ed] and collud[ed] with him." Arun Thiruvengadam speculates that Seshan may have "felt he had far more room to flex the institutional muscle power" of the Commission "because he took office at the start of the coalition era in Indian politics," though of course at the moment of taking office no one could know that a new era was about to start. Though initially viewed as a Congress Party partisan, Seshan "almost systematically ... antagonized every major party." Seshan's successors took roughly the same view of their role as he did.[44]

Seshan continued the Commission's election administration work, including an unsuccessful effort to create a comprehensive system of voter identification, which failed because it was technologically premature. His more important initiatives, though, involved the conduct of election campaigns.[45] As we have seen, Gandhi packed the Commission to get it to exercise its power to determine the precise dates of elections. Invoking the idea that politics should be conducted differently once votes are being cast – for example, a candidate should not be able to adjust her campaign platform after some voters had cast their votes in light of the platforms they had been presented with – Seshan used that power as a method of getting parties to comply with campaign regulations he favored.[46] As the period between the opening of a campaign and the first days of voting contracted and the length of the voting period grew – according to McMillan, from two days in 1980 to

[44] Christophe Jaffrelot, "T. N. Seshan and the Election Commission," in THE GREAT MARCH OF DEMOCRACY: SEVEN DECADES OF INDIA'S ELECTIONS 107 (S. Y. Qurashi ed. 2019); David Gilmartin, *One Day's Sultan: T. N. Seshan and Indian Democracy*, 43 CONTRIBUTIONS TO INDIAN SOC. 247, 265 (2009); McMillan, "Election Commission,"*supra* note 37, at 99, 112; ARUN THIRUVENGADAM, THE CONSTITUTION OF INDIA: A CONTEXTUAL ANALYSIS 155 (Hart Publishing, 2017). *See also* E. Sridharan & Milan Vaishnav, "Election Commission of India," in RETHINKING PUBLIC INSTITUTIONS IN INDIA 441 (Devesh Kapur, Pratap Bhanu Mehta & Milan Vaishnav eds., Oxford University Press, 2017) ("Gill [Seshan's successor] continued Seshan's practice[s]").

[45] Alistair McMillan, *The Election Commission of India and the Regulation and Administration of Electoral Politics*, 11 ELECTION L. J. 187 (2012), provides an overview of the Commission's expansion of its own jurisdiction in the 1990s.

[46] Seshan apparently rooted this distinctive morality in an expansive notion of voter coercion. *See* Gilmartin, *supra* note 44, at 253 (quoting a speech by Seshan).

about a month after 1996 – the Commission's ability to control campaign behavior increased as well.[47] Seshan suspended elections scheduled to fill vacant seats because in one case the local chief minister used a government helicopter to campaign and in another the governing party promised "to include Dalit converts to Christianity in the list of Scheduled Castes" – that is, had made a campaign "appeal to caste."[48]

Seshan had other weapons at hand. Widespread illiteracy meant that parties appeared on the ballot – and so in their campaign activities – with symbols; today Congress's symbol is the palm of a hand, that of the governing Bharatiya Janata Party a flowering lotus. The Election Commission allocates symbols to registered parties. Registration requires a party to submit its party constitution, which must "conform to the spirit of the Constitution." Seshan used the registration power to induce compliance with campaign regulations. He proposed legislation that would allow the Election Commission to withdraw registration from parties that engaged in election malpractice, meaning that they did not comply with the Model Code. This and subsequent similar initiatives never were enacted, but the possibility of converting the Model Code into law enforced through the registration process may have given the Code more force than its nominal voluntary status would indicate. Manjari Katju argues that "in most cases of Code violations, parties fall into line subsequently," fearing possible future sanctions and, probably more important, "realiz[ing] that setting a wrong precedent of non-compliance would mean disturbing the political equilibrium." This argument suggests that parties are willing to test the limits of the Code itself – or even to breach the Code in obvious ways – but are unwilling to take on the Commission, which indicates the Commission's reasonably strong role in the political system.[49]

An insightful article by historian David Gilmartin describes several of Seshan's interventions. Seshan challenged "the announcement or undertaking of any government policies during election campaigns that might be construed as government attempts to use its power to unduly influence the

---

[47] McMillan, *Regulation and Administration, supra* note 45, at 194.

[48] Rehna Ali, The Working of the Election Commission of India (Jnanada Prakashan, 2001), at 51. The Supreme Court twice overrode Seshan's refusals to set election dates, finding his concerns about election security and voter identification misplaced. McMillan, "Election Commission," *supra* note 37, at 105.

[49] Manjari Katju, *Mass Politics and Institutional Restraint: Political Parties and the Election Commission of India*, 4 Studies in Indian Politics 77, 85 (2016). For the proposals, see McMillan, "Election Commission," *supra* note 37, at 106. McMillan notes that the Commission "censured" a BJP candidate for using "seriously provocative language" regarding Muslims.

voters." A government promise to expand the list of Scheduled Castes, announcements of new development plans, even visits by government ministers to areas with by-elections – all came under Seshan's critical eye. He attempted to block the government from adopting a new cotton export program during a campaign. Seshan vigorously "enforced" – via publicity – Code policies aimed at reducing purely emotional appeals to voters, through loudspeakers, banners, and posters. According to Jaffrelot, the 1996 elections "were no longer marked by innumerable rallies, a plethora of posters, and the use of blaring mobile loudspeakers or video vans." Gilmartin notes that Seshan's initiatives took place against a background of public concern that "muscle and money power" rather than deliberation about policy were determining election outcomes. "Suspicion of politics . . . was particularly pervasive in the urban middle class," and Seshan tapped into that concern – a concern that may well have resulted from the end of Congress Party dominance. As Jaffrelot observes, "While this newly introduced discipline cut back on the festive aspect of the elections, it also reduced the funding needs of parties, which was expected to impact the degree of corruption."[50]

Gilmartin reprints a cartoon in which Seshan says, "Promise of prosperity, jobs, exports, border security . . . . He is clearly trying to influence the voter? Can't be allowed!" He also quotes a prominent politician apologizing for an evident Code violation by saying, "Election rules do not permit me to promise you anything. So I cannot do so. I shall settle all your grievances after the election."[51] Taken broadly, Seshan's project to make political campaigns the location for rational public deliberation about competing policy agendas was never realistic, as the cartoon and the politician's speech show.

We might take Seshan's project more narrowly, though. Read against a background political tradition in which politics has "a carnival-like atmosphere,"[52] the project might be understood as an effort to change the balance in campaigns to make them somewhat more deliberative. Even on this understanding, the project was probably unrealistic as well, unless we count quite small changes as indications of the project's success. Further, every party at some point would run up against Seshan's informal proscriptions, placing the project in continual peril – though sometimes parties with short time-horizons would support challenges to a rival's form of campaigning, only to turn on the project when it came to their own forms. Constraining the government-in-power's use of the levers of governance to further the party's electoral prospects

---

[50] Jaffrelot, *supra* note 44, at 109; Gilmartin, *supra* note 44, at 257, 261, 267.
[51] Gilmartin, *supra* note 44, at 268, 274–75.
[52] Gilmartin, *supra* note 44, at 277 (quoting Swapan Dasgupta).

would always be quite difficult. The apparent reemergence of dominant party government in the 2010s might undermine the Commission's independence as well. And, finally, to some extent Seshan's project was his own, as suggested by McMillan's comment on Seshan's "egotism and faculty for self-promotion," and his successors were not as committed to it as he was – though McMillan also observes that Seshan's immediate successor M. S. Gill "proved almost as susceptible to the power and profile" that Seshan gave the Commission.[53]

Manjari Katju describes several cases from 2004 to 2012 in which the Election Commission intervened to promote its vision of "proper" political campaigning.[54] Shortly before a local election in 2005, the leader of a regional party handed out cash to a group of Dalit (lowest caste) women. The Election Commission ordered the candidate's party to show cause why it should not be "derecognized" for this obvious Code violation. The party responded by cancelling a campaign rally at which the candidate was to have been a featured speaker. This satisfied the Commission, which took no further action.

In 2009, Varun Gandhi, a member of the Nehru-Gandhi political family who had abandoned the family's Congress Party tradition to become a member of the BJP, gave a widely noted speech as a candidate for a parliamentary seat. One report described the speech as filled with "rapid vitriol" against Muslims, with Gandhi playing on the Congress Party's "open hand" symbol to say that his own hand would "cut the throat" of Muslims. The Commission issued a statement censuring Gandhi and calling upon the BJP to withdraw his candidacy. It did not, and Gandhi continued to serve in Parliament and as a high official within the BJP.[55]

Katju's final example comes from 2012. During the campaign period for elections in Uttar Pradesh, a Congress Party leader and government minister spoke at an election rally. The minister promised that if elected the Congress Party would increase the reservation of positions for a specific subgroup of "other backward classes" so that it would come to one-third of the reservations. The Commission found this to violate the Code and, after the minister failed to respond adequately, complained to the nation's president. At that point, the minister apologized for making the statement.

---

[53] McMillan, *supra* note 37, at 112.

[54] Katju, *supra* note 49, at 85–86.

[55] "EC Notice for Varun Gandhi Hate Speech," *Outlook*, Mar. 16, 2009, https://www.outlookindia .com/newswire/story/ec-notice-for-varun-gandhi-hate-speech/655997, archived at https://perma .cc/26QJ-SHWP. Gandhi was indicted for making this speech but was acquitted.

As Katju notes, these cases suggest that the Commission's practices survived Seshan's tenure and responded to "the growing intensity of political competition." Gilmartin argues that Seshan's rationalistic view of political campaigns "was associated with a significant sense of popular empowerment."[56]

The discussion to this point has focused on the Commission's role in the period before the reemergence of dominant party rule.[57] The preceding case study, then, should be understood as examining the Election Commission during a specific and perhaps limited period, not an account of its enduring functioning. But the case study might give us some insights into Election Commissions as IPDs nonetheless. Seshan's vision of political campaigns is regularly characterized as bureaucratic and middle-class; a recent discussion refers to "a kind of technocratic efficiency by the ECI that appeals to the Indian middle class." Thiruvengadam includes his discussion of the Election Commission in a chapter headed, "Technocratic Constitutional Institutions."[58]

The word "technocratic" is appropriate in a comparative study. The vision Seshan offered, whatever its specific roots in Indian history and society, derived in part from the largely technical work associated with election administration, a task performed by election commissions around the world. Seeing compiling voter rolls and accurately identifying voters as largely technical tasks, election commissioners may come to see the *other* matters in their jurisdiction, including the regulation of political campaigns, as similarly subject to technical constraint. And the source of the constraint is obvious: counting votes is an objective activity; so (on the technocratic view) should political campaigns be objective.[59]

---

[56] Katju, *supra* note 44, at 65; Gilmartin, *supra* note 44, at 276.

[57] Sridhavan & Vaishnav, *supra* note 44, at 444–46, describe a controversy over a recommendation by the outgoing chief election commissioner that one of the election commissioners be removed because he was a Congress Party partisan, a view put forward publicly by the BJP. Such a controversy probably would not arise in a BJP-dominant world because commissioners would likely be BJP sympathizers. In unpublished work, Michael Pal describes several actions by the Election Commission after the reemergence of dominant party rule where the Commission "appears to have exercised its authority to the aid of the BJP." (Michael Pal, "The South Asian Fourth Branch: Designing Election Commissions for Constitutional Resilience").

[58] Sridharan & Vaishnav, *supra* note 44, at 442; THIRUVENGADAM, *supra* note 44, at 139. Gilmartin, *supra* note 44, at 281, also connects Seshan's approach to "long-standing assumptions among literate Indian elites that they had a special duty ... to tame the unruliness of India's everyday life" through advancing "transcendent principles of law."

[59] I believe that Katju's argument that the Commission pursued a "logic of appropriateness" is, at least in broad outline, similar to mine. *See* Katju, *supra* note 49, at 83. According to that argument, the Commission defines permissible and impermissible campaign activities by

But, as Seshan's failed attempt to distinguish between political promises and voter bribery indicates, the technocratic vision of political campaigns is itself a political one. In unpublished work, Michael Pal suggests that the technocratic vision is part of a political program of nation-building. And the politics of expertise can be political in a narrower sense, as the use of the term "middle-class" to describe Seshan's vision suggests. Though that term might not be entirely accurate, it does suggest that just as economic classes support political agendas depending upon their class position, so to do technocrats. Seshan's project thus appears to provide a good example of what I described in Chapter 4 as the politics of expertise.[60]

7.4 SOUTH KOREA (AND INDIA): THE ELECTION COMMISSION, THE CONSTITUTIONAL COURT, AND THE IMAGE OF POLITICAL LIFE

Analyzing the relation between the Indian Election Commission and the Indian Supreme Court, M. Mohsin Alam Bhat begins by describing the Court's commitment to an ideal of what he calls "discursive democracy."[61] According to the Court, that ideal requires that voters have available a wide range of information about candidates' life histories, including their criminal records, educational qualifications, and wealth. Politics should be pure, not polluted, as Bhat puts the ideal. And, Bhat argues, the Supreme Court recruited the Election Commission as an ally – or, perhaps more accurately, the Court and the Election Commission collaborated in developing the image of the politics of discursive democracy. So, for example, the Court used the Election Commission as the vehicle for elaborating and then enforcing disclosure requirements. And, as we have seen, the Election Commission itself expanded its authority in pursuit of its vision of a deliberative politics.

Bhat locates this collaboration in part in the Court's doctrine of deferential review of Election Commission decisions. As noted in Chapter 3, one feature

asking whether they are appropriate to the nature of political campaigns as the Commission understands that nature.

[60] Pal, *supra* note 57, argues that Seshan's work shows that an election commission can become "too" independent. In one sense that is true: Seshan operated with a great deal of independence from political parties and the government. In another sense, though, Seshan was accountable to the norms of political fairness associated with a technocratic view of politics.

[61] M. Mohsin Alam Bhat, "Between Trust and Democracy: The Election Commission of India and the Question of Constitutional Accountability" (manuscript in author's possession). *See also* Manoj Mate, *High Courts and Election Law Reform in the United States and India*, 32 BU L. Rev. 267 (2014).

of IPD design is the relation between an IPD and the constitutional court. Probably as a matter of constitutional theory, in which the constitution must be supreme law regulating all institutions, and certainly as a matter of constitutional practice, constitutional courts will supervise the work of IPDs. The central question then is, What standard of review will the constitutional court use when conducting that supervision?

Chapter 4 argued that the distinctive forms of expertise associated with IPDs counseled in favor of deferential review. Bhat's argument suggests another basis for such review: the constitutional court and an IPD might converge upon a single vision of the political system within which they both operate. The convergence need not be complete; occasionally, for example, the court will find that an election commission acted arbitrarily or that it did not take relevant considerations adequately into account.[62] All that's required is that the court and the IPD find themselves in roughly the same location in the ideological space defining democracy.

The relation between the Korean Constitutional Court and the National Election Commission offers another illustration of the phenomenon of convergence and deferential review, though with a bit more complexity because of the Constitutional Court's use of a proportionality test in cases where it rejects the NEC's position.[63] Created in 1963, the NEC has nine members, three chosen by each of the president, the National Assembly, and the Supreme Court. Members serve six-year terms. The Commission has a full-time staff, but most of the commissioners serve only part-time, holding other positions as well. One commissioner, though, works full-time as a commissioner. The Commission chair is, by custom, a Supreme Court justice. The NEC is a typical election management agency charged with administering elections and enforcing the nation's election laws (including its system of campaign finance).

---

[62] Bhat argues as well that sometimes the Court and the Commission have converged on an inadequate vision of democracy, and that the Court should ramp up its standard of review when that occurs. I take no position on this normative question. I observe, though, that Bhat's primary example is drawn from the Indian Supreme Court's approval of electronic voting systems without strong "paper trails," systems that opposition parties believe are invitations to fraud. Those decisions were made after the reemergence of dominant-party government in India, which might account for the inadequacies Bhat identifies. (A secondary example Bhat offers involves sanctions the Election Commission imposed on some BJP candidates for speeches essentially identical to unsanctioned speeches made by Prime Minister Modi. This too seems readily explicable by reference to party-system factors.).

[63] I have benefited from comments on the South Korean cases by Jonghyun Park of the College of Law, Kookmin University.

Following the end of the Japanese occupation in 1945, South Korea was first administered by the U.S. Army. Accepting the post-1945 division of the peninsula, the Republic of Korea adopted its first constitution in 1948. From that time until 1987, South Korea had an authoritarian government, sometimes civilian, sometimes military.[64] Widespread protests in the 1980s ultimately led to the creation of a new democratic government. Since then, Korean politics has been dominated by what one scholar calls a "two plus two" system: "[T]wo major parties (the conservative and the center-left) and two minor parties (another conservative and the progressive)," with the conservative party holding a majority in the National Assembly for most of the time since 1987.[65] The major parties, though, regularly split and recombine into new ones, primarily when factional leaders find themselves frustrated at developments within the parties with which they have temporarily affiliated themselves. Parallel to electoral politics, and important to the story that follows, there have been recurrent upsurges in politics "in the streets," organized by social movements without formal affiliations to the existing parties.

Several Constitutional Court decisions reflect the view that politics should be relatively orderly. The Constitutional Court of South Korea has nine justices, three nominated by each of the Supreme Court, the parliament, and the president. Justices serve six-year terms, which are technically renewable but in practice aren't; no justice since 1994 has served two terms. By convention, the main minority party in the parliament nominates the candidate for one of the seats allocated to parliamentary choice; the effect is that a president supported by a majority in the parliament can nominate five candidates, and a president whose party is in the minority can nominate four. Po Jen Yap and Chien-Chih Lin summarize the Court's relation to the political order: "[P]olitical fragmentation ... strengthens judicial independence as every major political party knows it has allies on the bench," and "judges are freed from ruling with an eye to reappointment."[66]

For example, the Court required the legislature to modify legislation requiring presidential candidates to deposit relatively large sums before qualifying for the ballot, with candidates who receive less than 10 percent of the vote forfeiting the entire amount and candidates receiving more than 15 percent getting a full refund. The Court acknowledged the legislature's "policy

---

[64] A brief period between April 1960 and May 1961 was an exception.

[65] Yoonkyung Lee, "Political Parties," in ROUTLEDGE HANDBOOK OF KOREAN POLITICS AND PUBLIC ADMINISTRATION 83 (Chung-In Moon & M. Jae Moon eds., Routledge, 2020).

[66] Po Jen Yap & Chien-Chih Lin, Constitutional Convergence in East Asia, ms. p. 35 (forthcoming).

discretion" to design a system that would "prevent[] many insincere and indecent candidates" from running, and accepted the view that some monetary deposit before being allowed on the ballot was acceptable. A dissenting judge made the same point in these terms: "[I]n presidential elections, there is a desperate need to prevent too many candidates from running for office."[67] The problem, in the Court's eyes, was that the amount required to be deposited was too large. Its decision took the form of a "modified decision" that gave the legislature the opportunity "to consider diverse circumstances" and adjust the statute, perhaps by lowering the amount required to be deposited.

In discussing a statute limiting people from publishing advertisements supporting or opposing political candidates – basically, spending on campaigns independent of the parties – three justices observed that independent expenditures could result in "personal attacks or slandering the opposing candidates by spreading false information," particularly when done anonymously online. This would, they said, disturb "the tranquility and fairness of the election."[68]

The Constitutional Court has decided only a handful cases challenging the NEC's regulatory decisions, but two of them are quite dramatic.[69] Both involved President Roh Moo-Hyun. Roh, the candidate of the liberal Millennium Democratic Party (MDP), won the presidency in December 2002.[70] Though reasonably popular himself, Roh faced large political problems. The conservative Grand National Party (GNP) had a majority in the National Assembly, and the MDP itself was internally divided with Roh representing a younger insurgency within the party. Roh's supporters left the

---

[67] Deposit Money in Presidential Elections Case, 20-2(b) KCCR 477, 2007Hun-Ma1024, Nov. 27, 2008).

[68] Prohibition of Distribution of UCC (User-Created Content) in Prior-Electioneering, 21-2(a) KCCR 311, 2007Hun-Ma718, July 30, 2009. Five justices out of nine would have held the prohibition unconstitutional, but the Korean Constitution requires a six-judge majority to invalidate the statute. The Court later held that the statute would be unconstitutional were it interpreted to prohibit political expression and election campaigning on the internet, arguing that the possibility that defamation and false information might be disseminated could not justify a complete ban of online campaigning even during a limited period. Prohibition of Internet Use for Political Expression and Election Campaign 23-2(B) KCCR 739, 2007Hun-Ma1001, 2010Hun-Ba88, 2010Hun-Ma173·191(consolidated), December 29, 2011.

[69] In addition to the cases discussed in detail, see also Case on Restoration of Returned Electoral Deposit and Campaign Expenses by Candidate Whose Election is Invalidated, 23-1(b) KCCR 62, 2010Hun-Ba232, April 28, 2001) (upholding the regulation described in the case's title; the relevant statute deals expressly only with return of deposits by unsuccessful candidates).

[70] For full details, see Youngjae Lee, *Law, Politics, and Impeachment: The Impeachment of Roh Moo-Hyun from a Comparative Constitutional Perspective*, 53 Am. J. Comp. L. 403 (2005).

party in September 2003 to form the Uri Party, and the old guard formed an informal anti-Roh coalition with the GNP. On the policy level, Roh faced a weak economy and suspicion from the United States that he was likely to be an unreliable ally.

Elections for the National Assembly were scheduled for April 2004, and Roh hoped that its outcome would strengthen his political position by installing a substantial number of his supporters in the new Uri Party in the Assembly. Following up on an earlier speech urging people to support his party, in February 2004, Roh gave a speech in which he urged voters to support the Uri Party, saying that he "would like to do anything that is legal if it may lead to votes for the Uri Party." Four days later, the MDP filed a complaint with the NEC alleging that Roh's speech violated a statute requiring that the president be impartial in elections. Within a week, the NEC sent a letter to Roh "requesting" that he remain neutral. A week after that, Roh held a press conference in which he refused to apologize for making the speech and said that he disagreed with the NEC's substantive conclusion about his duties as president: "I would like to make it clear that the decision of the National Election Commission at this time is not convincing," and was a continuation of pre-1987 practices in which the government "mobilized ... the state institutions" to produce election results it favored.

His opponents then impeached Roh, citing his defiance of the NEC as one of many grounds; the precise formulation was that in refusing to do what the NEC asked, Roh had failed to protect the constitutional order. Roh sought review in the Constitutional Court, which had the power, express in the Constitution, to review impeachments. Roh was suspended from office while the case was pending, but the April elections went forward. The Uri Party won a massive victory, gaining 105 seats, far more than the 47 it had held in the prior Assembly, amounting to an absolute majority; the MDP, Roh's former party, went from 63 to 9 seats.

The Constitutional Court held that Roh had indeed violated his constitutional obligations, but that the violations were not serious enough to warrant his removal from office.[71] The opinion discussed all the grounds the National Assembly had cited in impeaching Roh, but here I focus only on the charge related to the NEC's letter. The Court's analysis began with a discussion of the duty of public officials to be neutral in elections, which, it said, followed from the "principle of free election ... that the voters should be able to make their own judgment and decisions in a free and open process." The president was a

---

[71] Impeachment of the President (Roh Moo-Hyun) Case, 16-1 KCCR 609, 2004Hun-Na1, May 14, 2004).

public official covered by this principle because he was "in a position to threaten" the free-election principle; in this he was different from legislators, "from whom political neutrality concerning elections cannot be requested" because they are "active figures at the electoral campaign." Note that this suggests that Roh's mistake was to express an opinion about who should win the upcoming election for the National Assembly (and note as well that no president would ever be in a position to "influence" his or her own election campaign because Korean presidents serve a single nonrenewable six-year term).

The Court acknowledged the president was a member – indeed, the leading member – of a political party. And, the Court agreed, the president could continue to act within the party, for example, by participating in a party's convention. But, though elected as a party member, once in office, the president doesn't "implement[] the policies of the ruling party," but "is obligated to serve and realize the public interest," which presumably must be defined as distinct from the party platform on which the president ran. "The President is obligated to unify the social community by serving the entire population beyond that segment of the population supporting him or her." Turning to the "feverous competition" among parties in legislative campaigns, the Court held that a presidential statement "unilaterally supporting a particular political party" necessarily "distorts the process of the independent formation of the public's opinions based on a just evaluation of the political parties and the candidates." That competition "is significantly perverted by one-sided intervention of the President supporting a particular party."

The Court agreed with the National Assembly that Roh's response to the NEC request violated his duty to protect and defend the Constitution. Of course, Roh could criticize the underlying law on which the NEC relied, and could seek its repeal or amendment. But "questioning the constitutionality of [the] statute itself in front of the national public constitutes a violation of the President's obligation to protect the Constitution." Such statements "might have [a] significantly negative influence on the realization of a government by the rule of law ... by lowering the public's awareness to abide by the law." Note here that this is an extremely strong rejection of the view that each branch of government is entitled to decide for itself on a statute's constitutionality, subject only to an ultimate duty to comply with judicial holdings. And this anti-departmentalist stance implicitly assimilates the NEC to the judicial branch, because the NEC's request plainly rested upon a contestable judgment about the constitutionality of the "political neutrality" statute's applicability to the presidency.

But, after all this, the Court allowed Roh to remain in office because his constitutional violations were not "grave" enough to justify removal. His statements were "unaggressive, passive, and incidental, during the course of expressing the president's political belief or policy design in the form of a response to the question posed by the reporters at a press conference." And, returning to a theme it had briefly addressed, the Court noted the "blurred" boundary between permissible presidential actions within his party-political role and impermissible statements violating the duty of political neutrality.

Returned to office, Roh was not done with conflicts with the NEC. Roughly six months before his term ended in 2008, he again got into trouble with the NEC. This time a presidential election was in prospect (held in December 2007). Roh made a largely ceremonial speech to a public forum, in the course of which he said that "it will be a problem if foreign newspapers comment that the Korean leader is the daughter of a dictator [referring to Park Geun-hye, who narrowly lost the GNP primary election in several weeks later]." He also said that the GNP "is an irresponsible party." A few days later, Roh received an honorary degree from a Korean university and delivered an address nominally on democracy. In the speech, he criticized proposals put forth by the GNP's presidential candidate. Two days later, he offered "congratulatory remarks" at a celebration of the anniversary of one of the 1987 protests that led to the establishment of a democratic government in Korea. Among his comments were criticisms of his opponents, "those who were in power in the past allied with conservative press." Within days of each speech, the NEC met and reviewed Roh's statements, finding in each case that he had violated the duty of political neutrality. It sent him "notifications" of its conclusion that he had "defamed the opposition party and its potential presidential candidate," and "advised" him "to abstain from making any speech which may influence elections." Roh sought review in the Constitutional Court, arguing that the NEC's notices violated his right to free expression.

Again, the Court found against Roh.[72] After disposing of the objection that, as mere "notices," the NEC's letters were not exercises of public power that could be unconstitutional, the Court turned to the merits. In a section headed, "President as a politician," the five-justice majority opinion devoted somewhat more space here than the Court had in 2004 to the real problem

---

[72] Petition to Invalidate the Notice of Compliance Request for President's Duty of Impartiality toward Election, 20-2(a) KCCR 139, 2007Hun-Ma700, Jan. 17, 2008).

posed by the NEC's position. The discussion opened with the sensible observation, "Modern democracy has changed from representative democracy to party politics democracy." Parties "shape political ideas and influence state policies."[73] And, having been nominated by a party and winning as a party candidate, the president could continue to participate in party affairs. All this simply restated the analysis from 2004. But now the majority acknowledged openly that the president "is likely to be closely related to the policy and interests of a certain political group," which created the possibility of a conflict between the president's "freedom of political activity" and his duty of impartiality in elections. The president "not only executes his political party's policy but also owes the duty to promote public goods" and must "serve all the people." But, when a conflict arose, the duty of impartiality prevails.

The difficulty with this analysis of course is that, from the viewpoint of the president considered as party leader, the party's policies *are* the "public goods" that he or she must promote in his or her capacity as president. The opinion hints at a solution by suggesting that officials charged with the on-the-ground administration of elections might be influenced by, for example, Roh's statements criticizing the GNP: The statements might matter "because public officials tend to consider the political orientation of the President who supervises the personnel management although their employment is guaranteed under the law." Exactly what this means is obscure, although it might be hinting at the possibility that civil servants will exercise their discretion to tilt their services in favor of the President's position and against the opposition's. Yet, when we combine civil service protections with the fact that a president can serve only one term and the fact that presidential statements directed at elections have to be made in some temporal proximity to an election, this risk seems quite small.[74]

Taken on its face, the Constitutional Court's image of politics blends two ideas. One is express: that voters should choose their representatives based upon an unbiased evaluation of the candidates' position – phrases like "free and open process" and "truly free decisions" recur in the opinions. The other is implicit but clearly present: that voters will be "unduly" deferential to statements made by the president, who – again implicitly but clearly – they

---

[73] The official translation of the opinion into English is more stilted than others I have quoted, and I have freely adapted the language to make it more readable.

[74] The majority ended by finding that Roh's statements violated the duty of impartiality: they were made within six months of the scheduled presidential election, at a time when the potential candidates and "their general policies were already known to the public," they were made at relatively large public gatherings (rather than in small private settings), and they occurred during the ordinary hours of work.

believe represents the nation as a whole. And the latter is true even though voters of course know that the president was elected in a competitive party-based election. The decisions discussed here seem to be seeking to impose a degree of orderliness on the messiness of politics in such a world.

Of course, the two decisions on which I have focused dealt with a single political figure, who perhaps fell outside the boundaries of what the legal and electoral specialists on the two institutions believed to be permissible (roughly centrist) politics. Notably, the membership of the NEC when it acted against Roh consisted almost entirely of appointees of officials in place before Roh became president (appointees of the prior president and the chief justice). And Roh's governing style of appealing directly the people was in tension with the dominant elitist style of governance that seeks to make politics "orderly." It is not that the NEC membership was unfamiliar with politics, but rather that most of its members had a specific view of how politics should be conducted, a view that conflicted with Roh's governing style.[75]

That said, neither the NEC nor the Constitutional Court seem to have a sensible account of a president's duties (or, more generally, of the idea of electoral fairness) in a party-political world. Recall the conceptual and functional cases for IPDs (Chapters 2 and 3): they are needed because Madisonian mechanisms are inadequate to ensure the stability of democratic institutions in a party-political world, and they do so by deploying relatively less political forms of expertise. The institutions' difficulties in coming up with a plausible account of the president's duty of electoral fairness suggests that IPDs might not be an adequate supplement to Madisonian mechanisms.

7.5 THE IMAGE OF POLITICS IN U.S. CONSTITUTIONAL LAW

U.S. constitutional law offers a dramatic contrast to what's found in South Korea and India. Essentially all of the regulations found permissible in South Korea and India would be clearly unconstitutional in the United States, largely because the U.S. Supreme Court has a dramatically different vision of what election campaigns can be: raucous, non-deliberative, something like a free-for-all. For present purposes, the U.S. Constitution's guarantee of freedom of expression is the main source of rules about how candidates can campaign.

The canonical statement about the bounds of political discourse in the United States comes from *New York Times* v. *Sullivan*, a major case dealing

---

[75] Here, too, we see the constitutive role of the Election Commission and the Constitutional Court, as described by Stacey and Miyandazi. See Chapter 3.

with allegedly libelous statements about a public official. According to the Court, the First Amendment requires that states allow "debate upon public issues … [to be] uninhibited, robust, and wide-open."[76] In India and South Korea, as we have seen, political discourse is envisioned as properly inhibited.

In the context of regulating election campaigns, the relevant materials deal with statutes purporting to prohibit candidates from making objectively false factual statements. Several states have statutes prohibiting such statements.[77] The U.S. Supreme Court has not considered the constitutionality of these statutes.[78] It has held unconstitutional a statute making it a criminal offense to lie about the fact that one has received a military honor. Among the reasons offered by the Court's plurality was that the nation's "constitutional tradition stands against the idea that we need Oceania's Ministry of Truth." The government could punish false statements only when they are used to gain "material advantage."[79]

We might think that making a false statement to enhance a candidate's chance of election would count as material advantage. The leading commentator and the most important lower court decisions contend otherwise, though. Dealing with one such statute, a court wrote, "we do not want the Government … deciding what is political truth – for fear that the Government might persecute those who criticize it. Instead, in a democracy, the voters should decide."[80] Note, though, that the phrase "political truth" might be thought an overstatement when what is punished are objectively false factual statements: saying that a candidate voted for a bill when she in fact voted against it, for example, or that a candidate's net worth tripled during her period of public service when it had actually stayed stable. The problem is this: factual statements sometimes come dressed up in figurative language. Is the statement, "Candidate Smith bought a mansion while working in city government" true or false in a case where Smith bought a five-bedroom house?

The challenged statement in the case in which the judge made the observation about political truth was, "[The candidate] voted FOR taxpayer-funded abortion!" The statute to which the statement referred actually did not provide for taxpayer-funded abortion in the usual sense, but it did allow for taxpayer funding for certain forms of contraception that some anti-abortion

[76] *New York Times* v. *Sullivan*, 376 U.S. 254, 270 (1964).

[77] For a review of the cases, see Richard L. Hasen, *A Constitutional Right to Lie in Campaigns and Elections?*, 74 MONTANA L. REV. 53 (2013).

[78] It once addressed a preliminary procedural question that arose in a challenge to one such statute, and remanded the case to the lower court, which then held the statute unconstitutional. *Susan B. Anthony List* v. *Driehaus*, 573 U.S. 149 (2014).

[79] *United States* v. *Alvarez*, 567 U.S. 709, 723 (2012) (opinion of Kennedy, J.).

[80] *Susan B. Anthony List* v. *Ohio Elections Comm'n*, 45 F. Supp. 3d 765 (2014).

activists regard as equivalent to abortion. The litigation should almost certainly end with the conclusion that the statement was not objectively false, but the prospect of defending against a criminal charge might well make people careful about the figurative language in which they clothe factual statements.

And that is inconsistent with the idea that political discourse should be uninhibited. As another judge observed, "We . . . leave room for the rough and tumble of political discourse."[81] Applied to political campaigns, these rules and the impulse underlying them constitute U.S. political campaigns as raucous events, focused on what some might think trivialities, full of overstatements and heightened rhetoric – the opposite of the image of politics offered by the South Korean and Indian courts and election commissions.[82]

Perhaps the different images emerge from different political histories: much more turbulent overall in South Korea and India than in the United States until recently. If so, recent developments in the United States might induce some rethinking in the United States. One such development is rising concern, centered in the Democratic Party, about the prevalence of "fake news" promulgated by non-U.S. sources and intended to undermine confidence in U.S. elections. Another is a concern, centered in the Republican Party, that election administration has not prevented widespread fraud in the actual process of voting. The first concern might generate novel legislation aimed at policing political discourse to ensure something like "accuracy" in political assertions. The second concern might generate legislation restoring a much older system in which all ballots were to be cast on a single day of civic participation. Were the U.S. Supreme Court to uphold these or similar laws it might in turn generate an image of desirable politics more like that conveyed in South Korean and Indian law.

The recently inaugurated Facebook Oversight Board provides an alternative model: a public body that monitors political campaigns and issues reports lacking the force of law assessing the compatibility of campaign statements with "good practices," along the lines of the Indian code before Seshan ramped up the pressure on parties to comply with it.[83]

---

[81] 281 *Care Committee* v. *Arneson*, 766 F.3d. 774, 795 (8th Cir. 2014).

[82] Again, I use the term "constitute" to evoke Stacey and Miyandazi's analysis of IPDs' role, described in Chapter 3.

[83] The Facebook Oversight Board is of course a private body, and its jurisdiction is transnational (within the Facebook "space"). A full analysis of that body if well beyond the scope of this book (it would implicate questions about transnational governance, for example), and I invoke it as an institution without public enforcement power. I note as well that an old U.S. Supreme Court case might place some limits upon what such a "finger-wagging" public entity might do (if the Court concluded that the finger-wagging was in practice close to coercive). *Bantam Books* v. *Sullivan*, 372 U.S. 58 (1963).

7.6 CONCLUSION

Election commissions are supposed to reduce the risk that elections will be conducted unfairly when political parties alone control how elections are run and votes counted. Even on these terms the record of fourth-branch election commissions is mixed at best. They have proven to be subject to the same kinds of partisan manipulation that can affect statutory commissions, for example. Antonio Ugues's study of four Central American countries suggests the difficulties. In all four, expertise is expressly taken into account in appointing members. Only in Guatemala does the election commission operate without strong partisan bias.[84] In El Salvador, the presence of members chosen on the basis of party seems to have infected the body's operation. In Nicaragua, members of the Supreme Election Council are nominated by the executive and legislature after consulting civil society members, and confirmed only after receiving a 60 percent vote in the legislature; according to Ugues, "the Council . . . has become highly politicized through various formal and informal measures."[85] Using the example of the addition of two commissioners to India's NEC as his example, Michael Pal points out that drafting "gaps" – what I earlier called underspecification – can provide opportunities for partisan manipulation.[86]

Yet, even complete "success" in reducing, even eliminating, the role that party politics plays in election administration doesn't mean eliminating politics. A different sort of politics replaces party politics. We can use the descriptions offered of Indian and South Korean politics to develop an idea of the non-party politics of election administration. Elections there were raucous, festive, loud, engaging ordinary people in ways they are comfortable with – messy and undisciplined. The politics that election commissions produce is a restrained, deliberative, calm one. As we have seen, some observers call that sort of politics "middle class"; I have described it as technocratic and orderly.

---

[84] The Supreme Electoral Commission there is nominated by "a special nominating commission and confirmed by the national legislature with a two-thirds vote." Antonio Ugues, "Electoral Management Bodies in Central America," in ADVANCING ELECTORAL INTEGRITY (Pippa Norris, Richard W. Frank & Ferran Martinez i Coma eds., Oxford University Press, 2014), at 129.

[85] *Id.* at 128. Pal identifies one subtle problem: Often the election commission's charge is parasitic upon legislation. It might be charged with compiling an accurate electoral roll of eligible voters, but the legislature can sometimes define eligibility criteria. Or it might be charged with making sure that the person casting a ballot is in fact a registered voter, but the legislature might have the power to define documents needed to ascertain the person's identity. Pal, *supra* note 15, at 106–7.

[86] Pal, *supra* note 15, at 107–8. Pal provides additional examples from Kenya and South Africa showing how dominant political parties can exploit design gaps.

Seen in its best light, that sort of politics engages ordinary people in ways that might incline them to become "better" democratic citizens – more informed about the issues, more deliberative, more attentive to "the merits" of parties' policy proposals. Seen in a less glowing light, this politics might suppress citizen engagement – and, as the "middle class" description suggests, perhaps in ways that have differential effects on the policies politics generates.

As IPDs, then, electoral commissions do protect constitutional democracy – but a specific form of constitutional democracy. Whether that form is preferable to the messy contestations of party politics, with their attendant risk of biased election administration, will of course depend upon how effective Madisonian mechanisms are in the context of specific party configurations. The snapshots of Malaysia and the United States with which this chapter began suggest that the question might be a close one both in dominant-party systems where Madisonian mechanisms would be expected to work badly, and in well-organized two-party systems where they would be expected to work well.

7.7 CODA

After Joseph Biden defeated Donald Trump in 2020's presidential election, Trump alleged that his margins of defeat in several states resulted from widespread fraud. Among the claims were two that came before state election administrators. In both states, the party-affiliated voting officials resisted pressures from Trump and other Republicans and certified Biden's victories.

In Georgia, the elected secretary of state, a Republican, certified Biden's relatively narrow victory in the state recount that matched the votes tabulated by electronic voting machines with the votes recorded on paper that accompanied the machine tallies.

In Detroit, Michigan, the canvassing board that certifies vote counts is composed of four people, two appointed by each major party. Initially, the board divided along party lines on certifying the result. Within hours, the Republican members changed their votes and certified the results, which confirmed Biden's victory in the state, on the condition that there be a later audit to find out why there had been persistent discrepancies, not affecting vote outcomes, between the number of votes recorded as having been cast by mail and the total recorded absentee votes recorded as Republican and Democratic.

These were of course quite high-stakes controversies. The results suggest that something akin to professionalism in election administration was at work. We can't be sure what the limits to professionalism are, or, to use an earlier formulation, how much professionalism constrains partisanship. Trump's challenges, generously described, bordered on the frivolous. Even a weak sense of professionalism – a professionalism strongly constrained by partisanship – might well have been sufficient to produce these results. That professionalism apparently had some effect in a highly partisan setting is something, of course. But, I believe, we should be cautious about drawing too strong conclusions from this quite extreme case. Had the Trump challenges had a bit more foundation in reality, we have to entertain the possibility that partisanship might have prevailed over professionalism.

8

Audit Agencies

Audit agencies are among the oldest fourth-branch institutions. Their primary mission has always been to track the use of public money. Sometimes the payments are "merely" wasteful: the official making them paid too much because he did not take the time to look for cheaper sources of the goods or services. Here auditors detect government inefficiency. At other times, auditors detect some important forms of fraud: payments to cronies and payments for work not done, for example.[1]

Auditing activities blend technocratic expertise with concern for ensuring public trust in government in the way that anti-corruption efforts do. This chapter focuses on the rhetoric associated with audit agencies seen as IPDs. It distinguishes between an *internal* discourse – how auditors and their supporters talk about the methods and goals of auditing – and an *external* discourse that tries to explain how auditing bodies have come to take on the roles they currently have, and how they operate within their political contexts. The examples drawn from Canada and India are much less than full-scale case studies of auditing activities. They should be understood as merely suggestive about rhetoric rather than about on-the-ground performance.

8.1 THE INTERNAL PERSPECTIVE

Vinod Rai transformed the role of India's comptroller and auditor general (CAG) in much the same way that T. N. Seshan transformed the Election Commission. Rai gave his memoir the title *Not Just an Accountant*, which

---

[1]   This differs from bribery, which involves money flowing from someone outside the government rather than government money flowing out (although sometimes the out-flow is to a government official, as for example a payment to a family member – including the person making the payment – who does not do any public work).

accurately captures the way in which many of today's chief auditors see their job, though they sometimes hedge their bets by also describing their work as highly technical.[2]

Auditing of government spending is inevitably a tool for discovering corruption and waste.[3] Typically, and mostly still today, auditing agencies do not have direct enforcement authority. They investigate how executive agencies spend the money they have been given. These investigations result in reports. Ordinarily the reports' formal recipient is the legislature (because the agency is looking into how executive officials carried out their instructions), but today the reports can receive wide public distribution and attention.[4]

Initially, auditing consisted of matching paper records: the government check sent to a supplier for an office chair or an office cleaning coupled with a document showing that the chair arrived or that the office was cleaned. Paper is not enough, of course, and classical auditing also involved spot checks – actually looking to see where the chair was or how clean the office was. If the chair cannot be found the auditor reports that fact, and other authorities decide what to do.

Auditing gradually evolved.[5] Suppose the auditor discovered that the same chair was available from a different supplier at lower cost. That might signal classical corruption, with the purchasing agent helping out a crony. It might signal mere laziness or inefficiency, though. The purchasing agent might have looked into one brochure (or, today, went to a single website), saw a suitable chair, and bought it without looking around for other suppliers. Or the purchasing agent did not realize that putting the chair order out for competitive bids would be a better way of identifying suppliers.[6] Auditors began to make recommendations about processes government agencies could employ to make the best use of the funds under their control.

---

[2] This chapter focuses on audit agencies headed by a single person. Other models are in wide use. They include court-like bodies and multimember agencies. For an overview of the types, see Paul L. Posner & Asif Shahan, "Audit Institutions," in THE OXFORD HANDBOOK OF PUBLIC ACCOUNTABILITY (Mark Bovens, Robert E. Goodin & Thomas Schillemans eds., Oxford University Press, 2014), at 493–96.

[3] This description is quite general and attempts to capture the principal features of most auditing agencies. Almost every specific agency diverges from the general description in one or more ways.

[4] Executive agencies can and do also conduct internal audits of their own performance, sometimes through a general auditing body within and for the executive branch, but by definition these audits are not part of a fourth-branch activity.

[5] The following account draws on the discussion of the "evolution of audit" in Posner & Shahan, *supra* note 2, at 490–92.

[6] The first is an example of laziness, the second of inefficiency.

The next step was natural – the so-called performance audit. Performance auditing assesses how well the agency is doing its job. Roughly speaking, auditing for efficiency asked whether the agency was getting as much as it could for what it was spending. Performance auditing or auditing for effectiveness asks how well the agency is doing its ultimate task.

To see how the evolution of auditing works, consider an audit of an environmental regulatory agency. At first, auditing looked into whether the agency actually got the tests on contaminated water that it paid for, then at whether someone might have supplied those same tests at lower cost, then at whether the agency used "best practices" in locating providers of the tests, then at whether there might be better tests available at the same or lower cost. Performance auditing asks whether the agency is actually reducing water contamination as much as it can given the budget it has.

Speeches by Sheila Fraser, Canada's auditor general from 2001 to 2011, and Vinod Rai, India's from 2008 to 2013, illustrate their understandings of the role of the audit office as a fourth-branch institution. First, some background on the offices, the two figures on whom the discussion focuses, and the contexts in which they spoke.

During their tenures, both Fraser and Rai investigated "scandals" about public expenditures that received a great deal of public attention, enhanced the public standing of their offices, and had significant political effects. Canada's auditor general is appointed by the prime minister (formally, by the governor general upon the advice of the cabinet) for a nonrenewable ten-year term. Fraser was a career auditor, though her father had been a member of the Quebec provincial legislature when she was in secondary school and college. She worked as a private sector accountant, sometimes seconded to government agencies, before entering public service.

India's CAG is appointed by the president and may be removed "in like manner" as judges of the Supreme Court, and is disqualified from any public office after completing his or her service. B. R. Ambedkar, the principal drafter of India's constitution, said, in a statement that regularly appears in discussions of the office, that the CAG was "probably the most important officer in the Constitution," whose duties were "far more important than even the duties of the Judiciary."[7] Rai was a career civil servant who worked in the finance departments of numerous government agencies.

---

[7] Ambedkar quoted in Arun K. Thiruvengadam, The Constitution of India: A Contextual Analysis 143 (Hart Publishing, 2017).

8.1.1 *Canada*

In October 2005, Fraser gave a speech to a joint meeting of the Canadian and American Evaluation Associations. Three years earlier, she had issued a preliminary report on what was known as the "sponsorship scandal." The scandal involved payments by the Liberal Party government, headed by Jean Chrétien, to advertising agencies in Quebec, to develop and place advertisements within the province touting the contributions the national government made to Quebec's prosperity – a public relations campaign rather clearly designed with the political goal of countering the Quebec nationalist Parti Québécoise. Some of the advertising agencies, with links to the Liberal Party, simply pocketed the money, hired Liberal Party activists, or turned some of the government payments into contributions to the Liberal Party. Fraser's final report, issued in 2004, said that up to $100 million had been misspent.[8]

The Liberal government, still in power but at the time headed by Paul Martin, created a Commission of Inquiry headed by John Gomery, a well-known Montreal judge. The Gomery Commission's investigation received some criticism for political bias, and ultimately a court determined that some comments in the commission report were inappropriate. Fueled by the scandal, pressure on the Liberal government mounted through 2005. It lost a no-confidence vote in November 2005, then lost the general election in 2006, with Conservative Stephen Harper ultimately becoming prime minister. Through all this Fraser's reputation for integrity was unaffected and she became a well-known and respected public figure.

Fraser's speech began by defining her task as conducting performance audits, which "examine the practices, controls, and reporting systems" of public agencies, and "are carried out by independent practitioners in accordance with professional standards."[9] The goal was to secure *"well-managed* and accountable government." The work was "evidence-based," required "professional judgment," and was performed by "trained professionals" who were "immune from the undue influence of the organizations being examined." At the outset, then, Fraser stressed professionalism, expertise, and independence, to an audience of co-professionals who were surely aware of the political impact of her report on the sponsorship scandal.

---

[8]   Over the next several years, two heads of advertising agencies and one public employee were convicted of various forms of fraud.

[9]   Sheila Fraser, *The Role of the Office of the Auditor General in Canada and the Concept of Independence*, 21 CANAD. J. PROGRAM EVALUATION 1 (2006). All quotations from the speech are drawn from this article.

She then described herself as in the first instance a servant of her "fellow Canadians" and then as "a servant of the Parliament." After describing the types of audit activities her office performed, Fraser turned to "dispelling misconceptions." She was not, she said, "a government watchdog." Rather, the Parliament was the watchdog, taking "the information we provide ... to question or challenge the government on behalf of Canadians." Her job was "to help parliamentarians to do *their* job well." Further, performance audits "look[] at how the government *implements* its policies," but do not "question the actual *merits* of those policies." Nor was her job "to put organizations under a magnifying glass in order to expose waste and boondoggles and discredit government." Rather, she was "to bring to light information that will improve the management and accountability." Here Fraser implicitly invokes distinctions among intent, remote and proximate causes, and effects. She is looking for information to improve management, not "in order to" find waste. Disclosing the information, including information about waste and boondoggles, might have the effect of discrediting government, but she understands those effects to be independent of her job definition.

Still, she emphasized that her "work does make a difference for Canadians." The government responds to the audit reports she provides. A parliamentary Standing Committee on Public Accounts holds hearings at which she answers questions and generates questions to which the government is required to respond.

The final section of Fraser's speech dealt with her office's independence, "vital to our credibility and our effectiveness." Structurally, independence was guaranteed by the fixed term and her ability to hire her own staff. But, she continued, "There's another set of safeguards ... our ultimate allegiance to a professional discipline" as embodied in the standards of the Canadian Institute of Chartered Accountants. Her "staff is made up of multidisciplinary professionals who are trained in audit. They range from accountants to engineers and statisticians to people trained in the social, environmental, and management sciences." "Our meticulous adherence to methodology and professional standards stood us in very good stead" in the investigation of the sponsorship scandal. During the parliamentary hearings on the program, she recounted, some witnesses "challenged" her office's findings, but the Public Accounts Committee's report noted "our rigorous and painstaking methodology" and explicitly stated that the evidence "consistently confirmed and supported" her office's conclusions.

At the end of her remarks, Fraser said, "Professional standards provide an anchor when the professional is buffeted by storms of controversy." How does that anchor work? In part, because the vast bulk of the office's work is quite routine – classical auditing showing that almost every transaction is on the up and up, or revealing ordinary and easily rectifiable management missteps. Within the audit agency, this creates an atmosphere in which auditing is indeed a largely apolitical activity. Professionalism is sustained by routine. Then, almost at random, the audit agency is drawn into a political controversy. Fraser's observation shows that he knows that audit offices operate in a political context and that their activities can become intertwined with major political issues. The professional anchor, though, lets her ignore her office's role in politics – leaving that, as we will see in Section 8.2, to external observers. The professional anchor is the form that the politics of expertise takes in this setting.

8.1.2 *India*

Several of auditor Rai's reports were designedly eye-catching: the government lost $40 billion by botching the auction of telecommunications spectrum; private coal companies gained $33 billion more than they should have when government coal "blocks" (basically, mines) were auctioned. Numbers like those seemed to vindicate Ambedkar's prediction about the office's importance.

The spectrum scandal was a case of seemingly straightforward corruption. With the expansion of cell phone service in India came a huge increase in demand for spectrum, which was licensed by the telecommunications ministry. At the time, the minister for telecommunications was Andimuthu Raju. Raju, a Dalit, was a leading member of one of the parties in Prime Minister Manmohan Singh's Congress Party-led coalition government. Singh directed Raja to conduct an auction for a large swathe of the spectrum. The rules Raja adopted were generally consistent with prior practices.

A ministry press release on September 25, 2007, included the provisions that led to the scandal. The press release said that a week later, on October 1, 2007, spectrum would be allocated on a first-come, first-served basis for a fee that had been set in 2001; understandably, some applicants interpreted the release to mean that the ministry would consider all bids received by October 1. In January 2008, though, the ministry retrospectively "changed" the cutoff date to September 25, the date of the ministry's initial press release. Some companies had filed their bids in the afternoon of September 25.

The scandal centered on the claim that the telecommunications minister had been bribed to move the date forward by the companies that had been able to file applications on September 25 (and that other public officials had conspired to support the favored companies). Raja's only "explanation" for the retrospective date change appears to be that he had acted with the prime minister's concurrence. It is conceivable that what happened in January 2008 was that the ministry clarified its initial press release, explaining that it had intended that the clock on listing applicants pursuant to the "first come, first served" policy would start on September 25 and would stop on October 1. If that explanation were accepted, the companies that filed applications on September 25 might not have had inside information but simply had better legal advice than their competitors.

Investigating the scandal fell mostly to ordinary criminal investigators, but Rai became involved because of the auction's financial dimension. Market conditions had changed so much since 2001 that a new fee should have been set. The argument that the government lost $40 billion dollars was based on a calculation of what a fair price would have been and on evidence that two of the companies that bought spectrum allocations almost immediately resold them for substantially higher prices.[10] The spectrum allocations were eventually all canceled. A special court acquitted everyone involved of corruption charges in 2017; appeals to the Supreme Court are pending at the time of writing.

The coal block issue was more complex. The government owned the nation's coal resources. Prior to the late 1990s, it issued licenses to operate coal mines. The licensing process identified about a dozen qualifications needed to operate the mines under license and set the license fee. Many of the qualifications were general enough that the committee set up to assess applications had a fair amount of discretion to determine whether or to what degree an applicant actually was qualified.

The coal ministry then selected a licensee from among the qualified applicants. In the 1990s, India's governments moved toward privatizing many previously government-owned entities, including the coal mines, and independently decided that economic development required a substantial expansion of coal mining to produce energy for the domestic market. It used the traditional licensing system.

Rai investigated the licensing process used from 2005 to 2009. He reached two central conclusions: the coal ministry had the legal authority to shift from licensing to an auction system for the coal mines; and had it done so, the government would have realized a much larger amount (in a preliminary

---

[10] In calculating the fair price, Rai apparently used 2010 prices rather than the more appropriate 2007 prices, but the difference might not have been material.

report, Rai estimated the lost revenue at around $150 billion, reduced in the final report to $33 billion).[11]

The legal conclusion was the trigger for Rai's criticism of the process. He acknowledged that existing administrative guidance required licensing rather than auctions, but argued that the ministry could have freely changed the guidance. Singh's coalition government challenged both the legal predicate and the financial inferences, arguing that the ministry was legally required to license rather than auction and that Rai had used inflated estimates of a number of variables to generate his final numbers. Both Rai and the government pointed to legal advice the coal ministry had received from the justice ministry, which said that the coal ministry probably could shift from licensing to auctions on its own but that the change would be put on a better legal basis if the relevant statutes were amended first.

Probably to no one's surprise, the controversy morphed into a corruption scandal when the press and civil society organizations, shocked by the "revenue foregone" numbers, began to wonder why the ministry had stuck with licensing. One answer was bureaucratic caution; a more attractive one, at least for the press, was corruption and crony capitalism: the discretionary component of licensing allowed the decision-makers to allocate the licenses to their friends and political allies, whereas auctions would not. A small handful of politicians did have relations – as family members or friends – with executives of some of the coal companies that received licenses, giving the corruption charges some credibility, though no one ultimately was found guilty of a corruption offense. The BJP, then in opposition, built the scandal into its political strategy to win elections. Eventually, the Supreme Court ordered that most of the licenses be canceled.

As his time in office was coming to an end, Rai spoke at Harvard University's public policy school. Describing himself as "a bureaucrat all [his] life," Rai denied that bureaucracy was opposed to innovation, rigid, and unresponsive.[12] Strikingly, and quite unlike Fraser, Rai framed his discussion with the observation that governance was "exercising power and taking decisions on behalf of people." It was, he asserted, "too important to be left only to the government," and modern governance had produced a "vociferous

---

[11] Different sources report these figures differently, primarily because they use different conversions from Indian rupees to U.S. dollars. The magnitudes rather than the precise amounts are what matter for present purposes.

[12] NDTV, "Govt Auditor (CAG) Vinod Rai's Speech at Harvard Kennedy School," Feb. 8, 2013, https://www.ndtv.com/india-news/govt-auditor-cag-vinod-rais-speech-at-harvard-kennedy-school-512634, archived at https://perma.cc/Q6GW-VYSM. All quotations from the speech are drawn from this article.

and demanding" set of new stakeholders in civil society. It is probably worth mentioning here that, as described in the electoral context in Chapter 7, political rhetoric in India is often flowery and heated, and some of Rai's phrasing may come out of that rhetorical tradition.

During his tenure, Rai said, he had "introspect[ed]" his office's duties, in the face of advice "by the highest in the land" that the office "should not exceed our mandate, which they believe to be mere accountants ... [doing a] mechanical audit of government's expenditures." For Rai, the fact that the auditor general was a constitutional office demonstrated that it had to be more than a "mere accountant[] ... do[ing] arithmetic over government expenditure." Rai argued that then-current anti-corruption movements in civil society showed that political parties had not taken demands for dialogue and transparency seriously because the demands came from "people who merely engaged in living room debates and never came out to vote." Rai argued that the "paradigm shift in civil society" on good governance should elicit "a paradigm shift in the objective and approach of public auditing."

For Rai, contemporary auditors should "seek to sensitize public opinion on our audit observations." He did so by premising his audit activities "on the firm belief that we are as much engaged in the business of upgrading governance as any other agency." He now engaged in "positive reporting," not merely fault finding but reporting on "good practices." In addition, he instituted a proactive program of public distribution of his reports through "small booklets" distributed widely, because of his "firm belief that an awakened citizenry, once sensitized about the inadequacy of government departments, would exert pressure ... thereby ensuring better delivery of government services." Accompanying this was a program of "social audit," by which Rai meant not performance audits but outreach to "credible citizen's groups" to assess how programs "are being implemented on the ground" – a mechanism for performance audits, though Rai did not use that term.

After reviewing audit activities in several other nations, Rai returned to this theme, posing rhetorical questions: "Do not public auditors have obligations that go beyond those achieved by conventional methods? If the outcome of good governance is improvement in the quality of life of its citizenry, should the same not be the outcome of effective public audit?" Answering Yes, Rai said that he had "push[ed] the envelope" and encountered "very sharp resistance" from the executive, which charged him with "interference in policy formulation." To meet such charges, the agency had to "practice objectivity and transparency" in conducting audits. Wrapping up his description of his work, Rai said, "We may not be able to wipe out corruption, but endeavour to uncover instances of crony capitalism." Then, addressing his audience of public policy students, Rai challenged them to become "change agents" – implicitly, like him.

Whether or not Rai's diagnosis of the causes of his office's more expansive political role, or his description of what he did, is accurate, the mere fact that he offered a diagnosis referring expressly to political parties distinguishes his discourse from Fraser's. She saw her office as fundamentally apolitical; he saw his as thoroughly political. For her, objectivity and professionalism defined the job; for him, objectivity and professionalism were instrumental to being a successful change agent.

8.1.3 *An Academic Internal Perspective*

Fraser and Rai were chief audit officials. As with all fourth-branch institutions, there is an academic literature placing audit agencies in their best light – basically, providing academic support for the insiders' perspective.

One such presentation is a chapter on "Public Audit Accountability" in *The Oxford Handbook of Comparative Administrative Law*, a work in a prominent series for academic overviews.[13] Auditors, the authors write, "can offer relevant input to Parliament in controlling the executive power" and "can report on whether the administration offers value for money." They "investigate whether the government did what it was reasonably expected to do."

Auditing agencies contribute to good governance, the account continues, by ensuring accountability, which "is a fundamental basis of trust and administrative legitimacy in a democratic society." Auditing "facilitates the accountability of administrations to Parliament by increasing the availability of information about the actions of the former to the latter." The information is trustworthy because of the audit agency's independence. And the agency's work is transparent because it uses "a predetermined set of audit standards" that are themselves objective, drawn from laws, regulations, and "sound principles or best practices."

Notably, the reference to best practices, repeated in several forms, is the only statement that approaches a reference to professionalism as the source of objectivity. And nowhere in the account do the authors situate audit agencies in a larger political system. This particular academic idealization of audit

---

[13] Alex Brenninkmeijer, Laura Frederika Lalikova & Dylan Siry, "Public Audit Accountability," in THE OXFORD HANDBOOK OF COMPARATIVE ADMINISTRATIVE LAW (Peter Cane, Herwig C. H. Hofmann, Eric C. Ip & Peter L. Lindseth eds., Oxford University Press, 2020). Unless otherwise indicated, all quotations in the following paragraphs come from this article. (I note that have coedited two books in the Oxford Handbook series.)

agencies refers to the democratic values of accountability and transparency but not to the daily practice of democracy – how and why parliaments respond to auditors' reports, for example. As we have seen, Fraser and Rai too offered somewhat idealized accounts, but they also acknowledged the role their agencies played in a larger political system as a somewhat more granular level.

8.2 THE EXTERNAL PERSPECTIVE

The internal perspective on audit agencies emphasizes professionalism and objectivity. One kind of external perspective sees these agencies as integrated into an ongoing political system. So, for example, Arun Thiruvengadam observes that Rai's reports on the 2G spectrum and coal blocks affairs "burnished the image of the Comptroller and Auditor General" in the public's eyes, and notes that "[p]olitical commentators speculated" that the coalition government's defeat in the 2014 general elections "could be attributed, at least in part, to the severe damage" Rai's reports inflicted on the coalition's image. And he observes that, "somewhat predictably," Rai's successor Bhanu Pratap Sharma, another career civil servant, "opted for a much lower profile."[14] Thiruvengadam rests his analysis on a structural feature: that the position is filled by executive appointment without participation by opposition parties or civil society.

Another structural feature, though, might operate on a somewhat higher level. To function effectively, the CAG has to find political support from somewhere. Rai drew upon support from civil society and the political opposition. Sharma lacked Rai's personal record, which reduced the support he could find from those sources, at least in his early years on the job. To them, he could only tout the office's general reputation. He might have calculated that he could replace the reduction in support from those sources by support from the government itself – which means maintaining a lower profile, just as Thiruvengadam describes.

---

[14] THIRUVENGADAM, *supra* note 7, at 147. *See also* Ronojoy Sen, *Going Beyond Mere Accounting: The Changing Role of India's Auditor General*, 72 J. ASIAN STUD. 802, 810 (2013) (reporting "misgivings that the government might choose someone 'bland and ignorable'" to succeed Rai, and that those misgivings "have not been unfounded, with the agency maintaining a lower profile" under Sharma). Indian politics at the national level is a hothouse of suspicion, rumor, and gossip, and Sharma's appointment was attended by a minor controversy because he had previously been involved in the contracting process at the Defense Ministry, whose accounts the CAG would be auditing. A court ultimately held that any potential conflicts of interest would be resolved by Sharma's recusal from audits involving his prior work.

Academic articles on the Canadian and Indian offices illustrate the external discourse about audit agencies.[15]

8.2.1 *Canada*

An article published in 2016 directly incorporates politics into its description of the Canadian auditor general as "a mature, self-aware political institution."[16] Looking at the auditor general from the outside, Jordan Taft put politics rather than professionalism at the center of his analysis. For example, he explained a drop in the number of parliamentary hearings and briefings by the auditor general by pointing out that the drop occurred when the government "move[d] from minority to majority status, which allowed it to fully control Parliamentary committees" and "limit the OAG from discussing sensitive matters in the public forum ... and block the opposition from gaining political ammunition." Taft suggested that this exemplified a typical pattern because "in a minority [coalition government] setting, opposition members outnumber government members on standing committees." With a majority government, one interviewee pointed out, the government "can make the committee process much slower, they can send it in different directions." Similarly, incoming governments give the office "a honeymoon" because the agency is investigating the *prior* government's activities, which benefits the new government politically.

Writing in 2016, Taft thought that the agency had "entered an era where it is largely beyond reproach," because it had "cultivat[ed]" its own credibility. Taft does not offer a deep political account but he adverts to politics in a way that does suggest one: the Canadian auditor general is able to stand above politics because it operates within a relatively stable two (or so) party system, with regular rotations in office. A Madisonian system, that is, might have been a precondition for the Canadian auditor general's success as a fourth-branch body. More important than any such conclusion, though, is the fact that the external perspective brings politics into the story far more directly than internal ones that focus on professionalism and expertise.

---

[15] I did not choose the articles because they were typical of a larger group, or because they are especially insightful. I located them in a general search of the literature and found that they offered useful examples of the external perspective.

[16] Jordan Taft, *From Change to Stability: Investigating Canada's Office of the Auditor General*, 59 CANAD. J. PUBLIC ADMIN. 467 (2016).

8.2.2 *India*

A 2013 article by Ronojoy Sen begins by quoting Rai's Harvard speech, then outlines Rai's investigations.[17] He explains "the fuss now" by referring to "the scale of the graft" and the place anti-corruption efforts had in Indian politics, pointing to a widely publicized hunger strike by an anti-corruption activist. He also refers to the development of audits as a tool for "policy advice," though that is less an explanation for the fuss than a description of Rai's approach. Finally, he notes that "the reputation of India's elected representatives and Parliament has reached an all-time low." Here too we see the external perspective focusing on politics.

The focus continues in Sen's discussion of the reports' "spectacular" effects – not on government procurement policies or the like, the meat and potatoes of auditing before the rise of performance audits, but on politics. The first item Sen mentions was Raja's resignation as telecommunications minister. He then describes the opposition BJP's parliamentary maneuvers to keep the scandal in the public eye. Sen downplays the CAG's expertise, noting for example that "the last seven incumbents ... including Rai ... [had] no particular expertise in auditing." And he argues that the agency had "not played as significant a role as one would have expected." In part, that was because the CAG could only report, not enforce, and the parliamentary committees receiving the reports "have rarely looked at [them] in any detail." Sen found, for example, that in one year the committees had discussed twenty-nine paragraphs from the forty-two reports they received.

Sen concludes by expressly grouping the CAG with the Election Commission and the Supreme Court in its constitutional-review capacity as fourth-branch institutions.[18] According to Sen, "The Indian media has portrayed Rai as doing a 'Seshan' by not only giving more teeth to a moribund organization, but also having grown bigger than the outfit he headed." Professionalism and expertise as characteristics of an audit agency are basically absent from Sen's thoroughly political analysis.

8.2.3 *An Academic External Perspective*

Finally, another "handbook" article. Paul Posner and Asif Shahan conclude their presentation of the institutional characteristics associated with audit

---

[17] Sen, *supra* note 14. All further quotations in the following paragraphs are from the cited article.
[18] Sen used the phrase "third force," meaning that the CAG came third after the Supreme Court and the Election Commission. He also quoted "a prominent retired bureaucrat" who described the CAG as one of "five organs of state."

institutions and their evolution with the observation, "While ... formal organizational models are important, informal organizational factors, such as capacity limitations and the underlying political environment ... also shape the actual roles" these institutions play.[19]

They offer a typology focusing on the degree to which the agency is able to control expectations about its performance. For present purposes, the two most relevant categories are "political SAIs" (Supreme Audit Institutions) and "professional SAIs." Political SAIs "function in a unique environment," where politicians control the agency's budget and can define its functions. Yet, "the audit staffs are generally highly skilled and enjoy a degree of discretion in performing their designated role of auditing." The staffs rely on "professional norms" to sustain their credibility, which in turn makes the agency "of value to political officials in advanced democratic systems." Posner and Shahan do not explain why this is so, but perhaps their reference to "advanced democratic systems" is meant to evoke the two categories of stable party systems (multiparty or with a small number of parties) discussed in Chapter 4.

In contrast, political actors have little control over professional SAIs. These sustain themselves through various strategies. Performance auditing in particular allows the agency "to define performance" and hold governments accountable to the agency's understandings. Sometimes, though, professional SAIs preserve professional autonomy by insulating themselves from political controversy; here "the price of autonomy is limited influence over policymaking."

Posner and Shahan conclude by asking about audit agencies' effect on policymaking and implementation. They emphasize that audit agencies today are part of a thick network of accountability institutions, including "budget and financial management offices" but also the traditional political branches and civil society organizations and interest groups. Within this network, audit agencies' "influence stems from their expertise and legitimacy." "The independence of audit institutions is fortified through career nonpolitical staffs and the appointment of agency leaders with exceptionally long tenure. But even with such institutional protections, these agencies can become a magnet for criticisms when their studies affect deeply held partisan or pluralist influences."

This external analysis combines attention to politics with attention to professionalism, which is itself understood to be at least in part a political

---

[19] Posner & Shahan, *supra* note 2, at 498.

activity. Audit agencies rely upon professionalism to defend themselves from political attacks and, as already noted, sometimes trade off policy influence for continued independence. More broadly, though, Posner and Shahan describe a politics of expertise of the sort discussed in Chapter 7: "The influence of audit institutions in government agencies can be best described as a process of internalization and socialization of the norms of epistemic communities comprised of financial managers, evaluation specialists, and other related groups."

8.3 CONCLUSION

Chapters 6 and 7 concluded with assessments of the conditions under which fourth-branch institutions achieve the goal of protecting democracy, based upon case studies of significant events. This chapter cannot do the same. Its "case studies" are examinations of the forms of discourse surrounding audit agencies as IPDs. The events they refer to are part of the background that allows us to see what the discourse is about.

The internal and external perspectives show that considerations of politics, professionalism, and expertise interact in shaping the discourse of both insiders like Fraser and Rai and outsiders like some scholars who take audit agencies as an object of study. Note, of course, that this entire book is also a discursive exercise about the fourth branch. This chapter, then, might be taken as presenting a micro-example of a form of meta-discourse that characterizes the book as a whole.

9

Conclusion

Contemporary constitutional design probably includes IPDs on the list of best practices. In a party-political world, which is to say, in today's constitutional world, the case for creating IPDs to complement the traditional Montesquiean branches rests on seemingly cogent theoretical and functional arguments. Examining IPDs in design and operation, though, might lead to some troubling conclusions: that they don't systematically improve the quality of constitutional democracy beyond the level generated by the traditional branches; that their functioning is so dependent upon local circumstances and contingencies that there are few lessons to be learned from them; that their performance may depend upon the overall party system within which they operate; and, troublingly, that they might work best in systems where they are least needed (those with stable competitive parties or dominant parties with stable programmatic factions) and even in those systems might actually weaken the Madisonian mechanisms of constitutional guardianship.

I begin with the observation that what follows are descriptions of general tendencies, not guaranteed regularities. They are empirical in a loose sense, founded upon my reading of relevant literatures but not the result of systematic inquiries about how each form of IPD actually works around the world. As I emphasized in Chapter 1, we are in the early days of the study of IPDs as such. One consequence of this state of affairs has some implications for the quality of empirical information generated by individual studies. Much of the literature is written by scholars who are enthusiastic about the possibility that IPDs will improve the quality of governance. While sometimes acknowledging imperfections, which they treat as fairly easily remedied, these scholars tend to use examples and generate longer case studies of successful IPDs. The examples and case studies are of course typically accurate, but we don't know enough to know how representative they are. Well-grounded empirical studies are of course to be welcomed; but even at this stage, it seems sensible to make some informed guesses about the ways IPDs actually work.

My summary and perhaps inaccurate descriptions yield skepticism about the ability of IPDs to do much systematically to protect constitutional democracy. As we have seen, sometimes IPDs do work as designed, but almost randomly and driven by specific (and transient) circumstances. One can expect these occasional successes to be followed by a reversion to the mean – that is, to general ineffectiveness.

South Africa's public protector offers a cautionary example. Public Protector Thuli Madonsela's actions contributed to – perhaps we can even say were the cause of – Jacob Zuma's removal from office. Her successor, Busisiwe Mkhwebane, was a long-time civil servant promoted from within the public protector's office by then President Zuma, a promotion that generated controversy because of her closeness to Zuma and his faction within the ANC.[1] Since her appointment, she has been embroiled in controversies over investigations that, some observers believe, have been targeted at other factions within the ANC. Her investigation of campaign contributions to Cyril Ramaphosa, for example, was set aside by the courts, and she was found to have lied (and ordered personally to pay a damage award) in connection with an investigation of a decades-old bailout of Barclays Bank's South African affiliate.

Now to the general tendencies. Consider the theoretical argument that in a party-political world constitutional guardianship must be located in an institution that is above party politics. Observation shows, though, that in such a world no institution can be completely above party politics, and observation suggests that IPDs merely hover above party politics, so to speak, rather than operating at a sufficient height to transcend party politics systematically. Appointment and removal mechanisms, for example, inevitably incorporate some degree of accountability to party-political institutions, for good functional reasons. Requiring that members of IPDs have what I have called professionalist commitments – to the law as such, to electoral fairness, and the like – can do something to insulate IPDs from party politics, but again, experience suggests that the insulation is thin, in part because professionalism has its own politics that is correlated with party politics (differently in different nations, but correlated nonetheless).

---

[1] See Siyabonga Mkhwanazi, "How PP Busisiwe Mkhwebane Went from 'Nowhere' to Centre of Political Storm," https://www.iol.co.za/news/politics/how-pp-busisiwe-mkhwebane-went-from-nowhere-to-centre-of-political-storm-29983638, archived at https://perma.cc/W8ZK-4LCD (describing her appointment).

Further, in a party-political world, strong partisans will be suspicious of claims by IPDs and their defenders that the institutions are indeed sufficiently above politics. And, as the case studies presented in Chapters 6 and 7 show, sometimes those suspicions may be well-founded – or at least, may have enough evidentiary support to give them political heft. For example, Public Protector Mkhwebane has been the target of political challenges from the Democratic Alliance, an important party opposed to the ANC, and COSATU (the peak South African labor organization, affiliated with the ANC and generally opposed to Zuma's faction). Suspicions about an IPD's political independence will weaken the support the IPDs have in the political system as a whole, thereby limiting the extent to which they can be effective.

A second tendency is that IPDs may function well systematically only in systems with specific forms of party politics, in which the Madisonian mechanisms of constitutional guardianship can do a decent job. Yet, the good that IPDs do in such systems might be offset to some degree by harms to the party-political system itself. This concern has been articulated best in connection with constitutional courts, which some argue contribute to the weakening of constitutional fidelity in the political branches.[2] It can arise, though, in connection with other IPDS. A well-functioning electoral boundary commission might lead partisans who might otherwise find themselves negotiating and compromising over boundaries to harden their partisan stances across the board. A well-functioning anti-corruption agency might lead a party to foist off on to the agency internal policing that the party would otherwise use as a mode of anticipatory defense to Madisonian challenges from other parties.

These skeptical observations suggest that we might want to return to the (theoretical) starting point. We saw there that Madisonian mechanisms for protecting constitutional democracy rely upon *institutions* as an alternative to civic virtue, which Madison argued could not be generated widely enough in a sustained way to be a generally effective mode of constitutional protection. He and his generation knew that civic virtue itself arose from institutions, but – for them – not primarily from public ones. So, for example, in a party-political world, we cannot expect public education to do a systematically good job of inculcating civic virtue in the young, which they will carry with them throughout their lives. Rather, the institutions that generate and sustain civic virtue would have to be outside of politics.

We know what those institutions are: religion, the market, the family, and civil society. Today, I believe, we cannot rely upon religion as such to support

---

[2] This is one theme, for example, in James Bradley Thayer's classic critique of judicial review in the United States.

civic virtue. Religious pluralism serves in that domain as the analogue to party politics in public institutions. Some religious commitments support civic virtue; others focus on personal virtue to the exclusion of civic virtue. Religious diversity means that many people will be committed to faith traditions in which civic virtue plays a small role, or even none at all (as with traditional Mennonism).

The "doux commerce" theory linked the market to civic virtue.[3] Greatly oversimplifying a complex account: That theory held that the face-to-face interactions of commercial traders, who had to negotiate and compromise over market transactions, would inculcate habits of moderation and balance that translated into the public sphere. The transformation of small-scale commercial capitalism into the modern capitalism of large industrial and other enterprises – including service industries in which face-to-face interactions are structured around routines rather than negotiation – undermined the doux commerce theory. The same transformation placed great pressure on the family as a venue for fostering civic virtue.

The agrarian tradition in U.S. social thought, coupled with a vision of small towns as venues for face-to-face interactions, offers a civic parallel to the doux commerce theory of markets.[4] Transformations in agriculture and urbanization occasioned by economic and social changes including widespread cross-border migration have made these accounts obsolete.

We can of course imagine forms of market and family interactions – and even some forms of organizing public institutions – that might foster civic virtue, and in so doing protect constitutional democracy. The most promising candidates, I believe, involve radical decentralization of decision-making – basically, mechanisms that restore the face-to-face interactions that the doux commerce and similar theories said would generate civic virtue. In conclusion, I sketch a highly idealized, even utopian account of how radical decentralization can foster civic virtue.[5] My primary aim is to draw the outlines of the institutions of radical decentralization in a way that highlights its possible

[3] For an influential account of the doux commerce theory, see ALBERT O. HIRSCHMAN, THE PASSIONS AND THE INTERESTS: POLITICAL ARGUMENTS FOR CAPITALISM BEFORE ITS TRIUMPH (Princeton University Press, 1977).

[4] For two accounts of the second of these traditions, see STEVEN ELKIN, RECONSTRUCTING THE AMERICAN REPUBLIC: CONSTITUTIONAL DESIGN AFTER MADISON (University of Chicago Press, 2006); JANE MANSBRIDGE, BEYOND ADVERSARY DEMOCRACY (Basic Books, 1980).

[5] In Chapter 6, I concluded that Fuller-ian observation about judges fitting polycentric problems into a legalistic framework could be recharacterized as creative adaptation, but that the adaptations might not be creative enough. The discussion here might be understood as pursuing that thought.

benefits for civic virtue – and that highlights as well the complexities of radically decentralizing policy-making power.

Some accounts of federalism as a mode of allocating public policy-making power include among its benefits decentralization's effects on individual character. Radical decentralization means that people will be working regularly with their co-citizens on projects whose effects on them will be immediately visible; in this way, it attempts to reproduce in modern settings the lost forms of social interactions in small towns. They will have to negotiate, bargain, compromise, and persuade – all of which will encourage them to see things as others see them, not merely as they personally do. And, the argument goes, that way of thinking is an important component of civic virtue. Further, modern technology enables the relevant kinds of interactions on a larger scale – "face to face" now can mean "real-time conversations with a large number of people."

Gandhi's advocacy of the panchayat system of governance offers one vision of radical decentralization in the service of civic virtue. The Indian Constitution was amended in 1992 to require a version of panchayat governance. This study is not the place to evaluate how that system has actually performed, though it is probably important to note that it does not seem to have been a runaway success.[6] Still, one formal feature of the system deserves note here: the Indian system requires that at least one-third of all seats in the governing bodies be reserved for women, as a way of drawing into the domain of governance a historically marginalized population.

A second form of decentralization has been created by constitutional courts and international human rights bodies in so-called engagement remedies for violations of constitutional rights.[7] Such remedies require that policy-makers from the center engage with – that is, have meaningful interactions with – people claiming that a proposed course of action would violate their constitutional rights. Engagement remedies are justified primarily because of their substantive benefits; they are thought to lead to better policy outcomes because the affected communities can provide the central decision-makers with information ("local knowledge") that, when taken into account, opens up new policy possibilities. Proponents of engagement remedies argue that

---

[6] Ajit Kumar, *Effective Local Self-Governance through Gram Panchayats: A Case Study from Rural India*, 1 INT'L J. LOCAL & COMMUNITY DEVELOPMENT 106 (2019), provides a summary of research on the ineffectiveness of panchayat governance in much of India and a case study of one effective panchayat.

[7] For a study of engagement remedies in South Africa, see BRIAN RAY, ENGAGING WITH SOCIAL RIGHTS: PROCEDURE, PARTICIPATION, AND DEMOCRACY IN SOUTH AFRICA'S SECOND WAVE (Cambridge University Press, 2016).

engagement is a form of self-governance by the affected communities as well – a case- or problem-specific form of radical decentralization, with the accompanying fostering of civic virtue. And, considered in this setting the fact that one of the engagement cases in South Africa involved a single apartment building,[8] indicating precisely how deep the decentralization can go.

As suggested in Chapter 1, we should not romanticize either the panchayats or engagement remedies. In practice, they are at best seriously imperfect institutions of governance. I refer to them here solely to identify one component of their underlying *theory*, that radical decentralization can produce the kind of civic virtue that helps support constitutional democracy.

For market institutions, radical decentralization leads to ideas about workplace governance by those in the workplace themselves. For public governance, it leads to a strong principle of subsidiarity – locating policy-making in the smallest unit able to make a category of policy effectively. We know two things relevant here about subsidiarity. First, devolved power can be abused. A majority of skilled workers at a plant can develop safety programs that benefit them but provide nothing for unskilled workers. And the petty local tyrant is a recurrent figure in accounts of federalism. Second, "the smallest unit able to make a category of policy effectively" is not an objective fact that can be read off from features of the category itself. Somebody has to decide what that unit is, and that decision can be mistaken in both directions (allocating to a larger unit a policy where a smaller one could come up with better policies, and allocating to a small unit policies that cannot be effectively made except on a larger scale).

As a legal principle, then, subsidiarity requires that ultimate power over determining the relevant unit be lodged at the center – in the national government – because only the center has the power to identify and remedy abuses at every lower level and because only the center has the power to ensure that power is allocated to the center when the nation as a whole is the smallest unit for effective policy-making. The national legislature is the institution that in the first instance implements subsidiarity. But, when subsidiarity is treated as a constitutional principle, legislative implementation entails review by a constitutional court to guard against errors, again in both directions, by the national legislature. And, at this point all the ordinary questions about the standard of review arise, and need not be addressed for purposes of the present project.

---

[8] *Occupiers of 51 Olivia Road v. City of Johannesburg*, [2008] ZACC 1; 2008 (3) SA 208 (CC).

The preceding discussion is both in and outside the Madisonian tradition: inside in seeking to identify institutional mechanisms, but outside in seeking institutions to support civic virtue under contemporary conditions. Some observers of contemporary constitutionalism seem to look elsewhere, that is, to look away from institutions to a culture of constitutionalism that, they say, develops and is sustained organically. I find such accounts either gauzy and, to use a term already introduced, romantic or, more important, incomplete. A pro-constitutional culture may be more important than any specific institutional mechanisms for sustaining democracy, but for me sustaining such a culture requires *institutions* too.

Put another way, skepticism about the efficacy of IPDs as institutions is one thing; skepticism about institutions as such is another, and may well amount to a denial of the possibility of organizing societies in any coherent way. More narrowly, patriotic rituals and national days of celebration may contribute to sustaining the pro-constitutional culture, but institutions have to organize those rituals and celebrations. And almost certainly some of those institutions will have to be public ones so that the patriotic observances and the like support the national constitution as such rather than some one-sided account of what the constitution means.

The foregoing elaboration on the idea of radical decentralization in the private and public domains shows that it is an institutional choice rather than something that emerges organically from human interactions. And, as such, the choice has to be made, in the end, by the same public institutions that are not now populated by civically virtuous members. So, it is no small task to figure out how to get from here to there.

Yet, if institutions cannot serve systematically to preserve constitutional democracy, and if – as we should – we want to preserve it, we have to strengthen the institutions that generate civic virtue. Perhaps the conclusion to draw from my investigation of IPDs is that to preserve democracy we have to get from institutions to civic virtue – and that the growth of IPDs might have been a distraction in our theorizing about constitutional design. Perhaps we should devote attention to getting from here – a world with political institutions staffed by people not committed enough to civic virtue, and a citizenry with similarly weak commitments to civic virtue – to there, the radically decentralized world in which civic virtue would indeed emerge organically from everyday life.

Index

9 781009 048491